The Fre
and Inte

M000014376

The French Revolution and Intellectual History

Edited by

Jack R. Censer

George Mason University

The Dorsey Press
Chicago, Illinois 60604

© RICHARD D. IRWIN, INC., 1989

All rights reserved. No part of this publication may be
reproduced, stored in a retrieval system, or transmitted,
in any form or by any means, electronic, mechanical,
photocopying, recording, or otherwise, without the prior
written permission of the publisher.

Sponsoring editor: Casimir Psujek
Project editor: Jean Roberts
Production manager: Ann Cassady
Design: Diana Yost
Compositor: Editing, Design & Production, Inc.
Typeface: 10/12 Times Roman
Printer: R. R. Donnelley & Sons Company

LIBRARY OF CONGRESS
Library of Congress Cataloging-in-Publication Data

The French Revolution and intellectual history / edited by Jack R.
    Censer.
        p. cm.
    Bibliography: p.
    ISBN 0-256-06856-9 (pbk.)
    1. France—History—Revolution, 1789–1799—Causes. 2. France-
-History—Revolution, 1789–1799—Historiography.   3. France-
-Intellectual life—18th century.   I. Censer, Jack Richard.
DC138.F7 1989   88-22898
944′.04—dc19   CIP

Printed in the United States of America
1 2 3 4 5 6 7 8 9 0 DO 5 4 3 2 1 0 9 8

Preface

The intellectual history of the French Revolution is currently flourishing, as scholars venture into many different areas. Expanding rapidly is the study of the book trade, the pamphlet, and the periodical. Scholars working on these materials mainly want to discover the conditions of production and the ideas disseminated. Interest in political theory has also increased tremendously as historians are now busily unraveling the political history of the Old Regime. The efforts of absolutist monarchs to stifle political involvement as much as possible has made this subject very complicated. Indeed, in order to act politically, men and women of the eighteenth century often had to express themselves carefully in a nonpolitical language. Often, they spoke and wrote about literature or religion when they wanted to discuss power. Even those permitted to broach the subject of politics or those daring enough to try anyway usually were forced to resort to circumlocutions. Another subject gaining much attention is revolutionary ceremony. And the list of research areas in intellectual history might be extended still much further.

These subjects represent a revival of and an addition to more traditional pursuits in intellectual history. Although significant numbers of researchers still focus, as in the past, on the beliefs of intellectual and political elites, these must now share the spotlight with an increased concern about what the middle and lower classes thought. Furthermore, new methods have also been added. Some scholars still read materials from all sources to understand, in a commonsense way, what the writer or creator intended. However, increasingly historians wish to document, or at least speculate, about how contemporaries understood what was said. Furthermore, past scholars—working mainly on the ideas of the highly educated—customarily interpreted words and images as part of a flow of thought. Understanding a thinker meant placing that person between his intellectual antecedents and heirs. Influenced by literary critics and cultural anthropologists, though, many historians have of late ignored the past and future, to focus on the situation facing their subject. Some of these researchers have elected to understand such beliefs as a manifestation of more profound social, political, or economic circumstances. Others, in contrary fashion, believe that language itself represents the deeper reality, and its message provides the best understanding of the entire range of goals. For example, both groups would evaluate revolutionary ceremonies as narrations. However, the first would seek the social reality underlying and reinforced by these events, while the second would treat the language itself as the accurate indicator, possibly even the governor, of all ideas including beliefs about social conditions. This short list does not exhaust the variety of approaches currently in use, some of which are hybrids created from several, sometimes potentially contradictory tendencies.

In addition, this explosion of work holds potential impact for the study of the French Revolution. Examining the theories and beliefs that various social groups maintained can help explain why revolutionary elites and crowds acted as they did. Investigating these same materials may also lead to a reevaluation of the effect of the Revolution on the world. Always considered an epic event, the French Revolution, through intellectual history, may be more closely linked to the modern world of democratic and authoritarian politics.

Yet these new directions, genuine as they are, have not achieved their proper impact, for these studies are disparate and require their readers to put them together. The practitioners in this field, currently enjoying their various pursuits, have neglected synthesizing what they have uncovered. Not only are general synopses lacking, but the monographic work that has appeared is often published in obscure places. Collecting some of these materials, suggesting some areas of agreement, and indicating certain omissions constitute the purposes of this volume.

Understanding this innovation in the intellectual history of the Revolution necessitates a brief recapitulation of the context for this increased interest. Indeed, this growth, which became evident in the early 1970s, came only after a fairly long period of quiescence. Although not completely silent in the 1940s, 1950s, and 1960s, intellectual historians had steadily withdrawn from studying the causes of the Revolution and revolutionary decade itself. Peter Gay's magisterial two-volume work on the Enlightenment provides a conspicuous example of this tendency, for his work scarcely mentions the Revolution.

No simple explanation can illuminate the virtual withdrawal of intellectual historians from the study of the French Revolution. Certainly a discipline-wide commitment to sociological explanation of revolutions was significant in this regard. Scholars tended increasingly to explain political change as a function of social discontents. Perhaps more directly relevant for the decline in intellectual history was the preeminence of a Marxist explanation for the occurrence of the French Revolution. Marx and his successors had always found the upheaval of 1789 significant, but, until the 1930s, for most historians the Marxist viewpoint had been only one of several competing interpretations. Only in the supple hands of Georges Lefebvre (1874–1959), perhaps the greatest scholar ever to examine the Revolution, did a Marxist analysis that captivated the historical profession emerge.

In a great volley of works, mainly published in the 1930s and absorbed rather rapidly, Lefebvre constructed a massive empirical and theoretical base, whose outlines can be presented here. Retaining Marx's interest in class struggle, Lefebvre described the French Revolution essentially in those terms. He argued that over time the aristocracy, composed of nobles and clergy, came increasingly to resent the rise of the absolutist monarchs. When King Louis XVI required the assistance of the nobles to raise taxes during the late 1780s, they resisted and benefited from the tacit support of the inferior classes. No sooner had the aristocrats successfully challenged the king than the middle class, or the bourgeoisie, used this breach at the top to mount a challenge that they had desired for decades. Although possessing no political authority, the bourgeoisie had amassed in the eighteenth century overwhelming economic power. Moreover, through the Enlightenment's emphasis on talent over birth, the members of the middle class possessed an ideology critical of the aristocracy. They thus turned their animosity on their long-term enemy. But the manpower for their revolt would come from the lower classes both rural and urban. Eventually, these working people would turn on the bourgeoisie, but at first they directed their frustrations against the aristocrats. Together the middle and lower classes overwhelmed the nobility and clergy in a series of uprisings in 1789 and set up a revolutionary society that guaranteed legal equality and left unclear the economic settlement. Although Lefebvre called this achievement admirable and liberating, he posited that, once the bourgeoisie came to understand that this union with the lower classes might entail sharing power and restricting private property, the middle class endeavored to withdraw. In its major outlines, his argument held that the remainder of the revolutionary conflict may be seen as different social groups jockeying for predominance.

Although this short description cannot do justice to the subtle construction of Lefebvre's work, perhaps it explains enough to make clear why this scholar's books captivated others. Even in the precis presented here, one sees a comprehensive explanation that includes all the social elements and that can explain why the Revolution held promise yet often disappointed its participants. To comprehend fully the success of Lefebvre's interpretation, one should also consider that his grasp of the sources was sure and his arguments buttressed by powerful description. Reinforcing all this was the centralized French university system, whose teaching of history, dominated by Lefebvre and his disciples, made possible the broadest spread of his explanation.

As Lefebvre's work proved compelling to the postwar generation, it discouraged intellectual historians by stressing the preeminence of class characteristics and by undermining the study of ideas as a major variable. This theory evaluated the Enlightenment largely as a manifestation of class interests.

Although in the late 1950s an assault on Lefebvre's vision began in England and America, these revisionists were uninterested in intellectual history. They did not emphasize the role of ideas that Lefebvre had omitted; rather, they challenged his findings about the place of social classes and asserted that many contentions could not be empirically sustained. They mainly concentrated upon the fissure between the aristocracy and the bourgeoisie and maintained that Lefebvre had overstated this divide. Baldly put, they found that the middle class and the aristocracy greatly resembled one another, and were, despite the difference in legal status, actually quite unified. Sharing social aspirations, they often intermarried. And class proved a very imperfect predictor of revolutionary allegiances, as revolutionaries sometimes trained their fire on bourgeois oligarchies and at other times embraced sympathetic nobles. By the end of the 1960s, these Anglo-American investigators had challenged Lefebvre and his successors on a wide front but had not suggested that intellectual history deserved closer study.

Nonetheless, by undermining an unquestioned interpretation, this dispute among social historians surely did leave open the possibility for scholars interested in ideas to expand their interpretations into the Revolution. Also encouraging them was a growth in interest in anthropology, which tended to emphasize systems of belief. Yet another source stimulating this trend was the rise to eminence of François Furet. Interested in the role of ideas and for a long time holding a very important position in France's School for Advanced Studies in the Social Sciences, he developed a base outside the Marxist-dominated universities to promote the study of beliefs. So beginning as a trickle in the early 1970s, intellectual histories about the Revolution grew rapidly in number.

In order to present these new excursions into intellectual history, this book of readings divides its offerings into three sections. Part One provides selections from two famous interpretations of the French Revolution published early in the 1970s. The first of these permits an appreciation of the historiographical state of the field at the time that intellectual history began its resurgence. The other article is an important effort to reestablish ideas as critical to explain the French Revolution. Part Two consists of four articles that provide excellent examples of the current work on the intellectual origins of the French Revolution. Each article examines different aspects of the Old Regime as linked to the political upheaval at the end of the century. The four essays of Part Three all illustrate historians' attempts to analyze the ideas of the revolutionary period. For those whose interest goes beyond these selections, a very brief listing of suggested readings in English is appended.

The focus of this book on intellectual history and its new dynamism is no attempt to suggest that social historians—both Marxist and revisionist— have retired from the field. Indeed, they have continued their work in many profitable ways. Such efforts have, of course, influenced intellectual historians, whose explanations have often been cognizant of the investigations of social historians. As the history of ideas has re-emerged, those scholars. studying society have become far more aware of such matters. Perhaps, the ultimate and most desirable end for this extraordinary flourishing of the study of beliefs would be an understanding of the Revolution where words and things share the spotlight.

Acknowledgments

This project owes many debts to friends and colleagues. Most helpful to me in preparing this volume has been my wife, Jane Turner Censer, who has taken away time from her busy career to serve as a sounding board for my ideas and to edit my prose. In addition, I would like to thank all the contributors, not only for writing such interesting essays for me to work on, but, in several cases, for readily responding to my inquiries. I also owe a great debt to the National Endowment for the Humanities. I put much of this book together in the evenings, on the weekends, and in the subway during a year when I was on loan from my university to the Research Division of the Endowment. In that special environment, I had an opportunity to consider in detail how best to present the broad significance of specialized scholarship. That thinking has, no doubt, helped and, one hopes, improved my efforts to introduce these materials. My employment at NEH has had one other very happy result. Because of constraints on my time, I had to locate some assistance, and I was very fortunate to ask Tina Raheem. Her good sense, dedication, and skill are all greatly appreciated. Finally, editors at Dorsey Press, Casimir Psujek and David Follmer, have helped through their generous support and gentle prodding.

France before 1789 (Map by Harold K. Faye is reproduced from THE AGE OF REVOLUTION AND REACTION, 1789–1850, by Charles Breunig, by permission of W. W. Norton & Company, Inc. Copyright © 1970 by W. W. Norton & Company, Inc.)

France in 1791 (From **FRANCE 1789–1815: REVOLUTION AND COUNTERREVOLU-TION** *by D. M. G. Sutherland. Copyright © 1985 by D. M. G. Sutherland. Reprinted by permission of Oxford University Press, Inc.)*

Contents

PART ONE

The Revisionists

Two brilliant efforts to go beyond the classic interpretation, framed by Georges Lefebvre and enhanced by several followers, including Albert Soboul, constitute this section. Both excerpts published here rest upon the assumption that the earlier approach, which emphasized the battle between the middle and upper classes, had been seriously undermined. Yet, after that beginning, Colin Lucas and François Furet's writings quickly diverged. In the first article, Lucas, although abandoning Lefebvre and Soboul's version of class conflict, continues to assert that other, very specific social antagonisms between the middle class and the nobility lay at the root of the Revolution. Lucas also prominently features politics. Furet focuses on intellectual, and to a lesser extent political, factors. These two scholars also disagree about the meaning of the Revolution. To Lucas, it represents the triumph of the middle class and a society in which wealth and power were interlocked. Furet, however, equates the Revolution with a radical equality for all.

Comparing the accounts of these two revisionists casts light upon the beginnings of a revitalized intellectual history of the Revolution. As Lucas's readers quickly discover, he bases his article on an extraordinary mastery of the information provided by secondary studies. His essay thus extends directions already taken or strongly implied in other books and articles, mainly written by English and American scholars. In contrast, Furet is indifferent to current scholarship and provides a far more speculative and original essay. By ignoring the vast weight of social history, Furet could highlight a new, far more important, role for the study of ideas. If scholars in intellectual history have not always followed his specific approach, they are nevertheless greatly indebted to his boldness, which was perhaps at first necessary to point out the significance of ideas.

Nobles, Bourgeois, and the Origins of the French Revolution*

Colin Lucas

This essay seeks to resolve an apparent problem. If scholars can no longer use the middle class's unseating of the nobility as a primary cause of the Revolution, then what explains the Revolution's drive to reward middle class hopes and deny aristocratic aspirations? In other words, if social conflict did not cause the political upheaval, why were there social results?

Social cleavages provide part of Lucas's answer to this question. To be sure, he accepts and even promotes the notion that the upper-middle class and the nobility of the eighteenth century were in the process of fusing. Nonetheless, internal social struggles, or as Lucas terms them, "stress zones," still existed. These tensions, born of contracting opportunities for an expanding population, affected the lesser nobles and the bourgeois office holders more heavily. In the revolutionary conflict, such small irritations grew to be major inflammations. In particular the decision to separate politically the middle classes from the rest of the elite in the elections of 1789 angered the former and made them unwilling to brook opposition.

This initial step led the bourgeoisie to alliances with the working class. In such circumstances, the middle classes ended up attacking legal inequalities. However, they asserted their own import by relegating power to wealth. Consequently, Lucas explains the revolutionary change in values favoring money over birth as a result of societal fissures that were exacerbated by politics rather than the predictable impact of a long-term social struggle.

*World Copyright: The Past and Present Society, 175 Banbury Road, Oxford, England. This article is here reprinted in abridged form, with the permission of the Society and the author, from *Past and Present: a journal of historical studies,* no. 60 (August 1973) pp. 84–126.

3

O nce upon a time, the historians of the French Revolution laboured fraternally in the vineyards of the past. They were united in simple yet satisfying beliefs. In the eighteenth century, the French bourgeoisie had become aware of the increasing disparity between its wealth and social usefulness, on the one hand, and its social prestige and opportunities, on the other. Its way was blocked and recognition of its worth denied by a decaying class of parasitic, hereditarily privileged, noble landowners. Its vitality was further jeopardized by a monarchy not only committed to antiquated aristocratic values, but also incapable of giving the country that firm yet benignly restrained direction under which the initiative of men of business might flourish. The conflict of these elements produced the French Revolution. It was, furthermore, a deeper conflict between the progressive capitalist-orientated classes and the retrograde aristocratic classes. The French Revolution was won by the bourgeoisie, despite some interference from below, thus establishing the framework for the emergence of the capitalist economy and a class society and—*eureka*—the modern world. This, in capsule form, was the interpretation of the revolutionary crisis of the late eighteenth century favoured by the great authorities of the first half of this century from Jaurès to Soboul, each one giving to it a more or less explicitly Marxist tone according to his personal convictions. But Marxist or non-Marxist, we were all united in the belief that we could not escape this groundswell of history.

This interpretation has been the subject of increasing debate among Anglo-Saxon historians ever since the publication in 1964 of the attack launched upon it by the late Professor Cobban in his Wiles Lectures of 1962. A parallel, though apparently unrelated, debate has also been developing in France, where Monsieur Furet and Monsieur Richet in particular have been attempting to elaborate a more theoretical schema than Cobban's yet on basically the same lines. Cobban's essential contribution to the historiography of the French Revolution was to question the notion of the bourgeoisie as a capitalist or even proto-capitalist class. He thereby questioned the whole nature of the Revolution. Cobban was a brilliant polemicist and his book displays both the qualities and the defects of this type of writing. He had an unerring eye for the weaknesses in the arguments of others; but they tended to capture his attention to the exclusion of all other considerations. His book, therefore, remained a very piecemeal affair, concerned primarily with destroying what he took, rightly or wrongly, to be a number of commonly accepted fallacies with only a relatively loose thread connecting them. Cobban made no attempt to produce any systematic construction to replace the whole edifice of interpretation, which he was very conscious of having undermined. At most, he carved a few stones for a new façade.

Thus, for example, he proposed a new definition of the revolutionary bourgeoisie, which he saw as a declining class of venal office-holders, yet he did not attempt to work out the structure of social conflict implied in such a view. He presumably believed this group to be but one element of the Ancien Régime bourgeoisie and he also suggested that the nature of the bourgeoisie was altered during the Revolution, yet he did not try to examine what the bourgeoisie was before the Revolution nor what the relationship was between the various component parts that he perceived. Above all, Cobban does not seem to have questioned the notion that a noble-bourgeois class conflict was the fundamental element in the genesis of the Revolution. He merely sought to alter one part of that proposition. In this sense, therefore, he retained a class interpretation of the French Revolution which did not stray too far from the classic mould.

Nevertheless, Cobban's remarks on the nature of the revolutionary bourgeoisie together with Professor Taylor's fundamental work on French capitalism in the eighteenth century have in fact brought into question the whole schema of the Revolution as the product of a conflict between nobles and bourgeois, as Taylor himself has pointed out. For such an interpretation is necessarily based on the premise that there existed in eighteenth-century France two distinct and antagonistic classes of bourgeois and nobles. If, however, in our attempt to define the eighteenth-century bourgeoisie we can discover no such clear division, then it becomes extremely difficult to define a class conflict. But, in that case, we have to decide why, in 1788-9, groups which can be identified as non-noble combatted and defeated groups which can be identified as noble, thereby laying the foundations of the political system of the nineteenth-century bourgeoisie; and why they attacked and destroyed privilege in 1789, thereby destroying the formal organization of eighteenth-century French society and preparing a structure within which the socio-economic developments of the nineteenth century might blossom. It is the aim of this essay to examine these questions in the light of recent research. It sets out to provide a constructed synthesis of the directions in which it seems to the author that French and Anglo-Saxon scholars have been moving in research and debate. It remains one man's point of view and its ultimate purpose is simply to suggest some hypotheses which may help to clarify, whether by assent or dissent, a few of the major problems of interpretation which currently beset the period of the revolutionary crisis of the late eighteenth century.

*   *   *   *

The orthodox approach to the upper strata of eighteenth-century French society has always been to stress exclusively the elements of disparity and division within them and to split them into two clearly defined and clearly antagonistic classes of nobles and bourgeois. Such an approach ignores all the elements that conferred on these strata a degree of homogeneity in some important respects. We may understand this without difficulty if, instead of peering so closely at the top of society, we stand back and attempt to view it as a whole. Whatever the distinctions and whatever the striking differences in wealth levels inside these strata, they achieved a certain common identity as a minority with disproportionate wealth in relation to the mass of poor Frenchmen. The primary articulation in Ancien Régime society was not the distinction between the privileged and the Third Estate,[1] rather, it was between those for whom manual labour provided their livelihood and those for whom it did not. Clearly this division, in common with all those in this society, was neither rigid nor absolute. It did not have the character of a boundary, but more that of a frontier with its attendant no-man's-land formed by transitional categories. The inhabitants of this zone were the artisans—the *sans-culottes* in Paris— the degree of whose penetration into the ranks of the lesser bourgeoisie can be determined by the extent to which trading activity had become preponderant in the combination of trade and manual production which characterized their state. Moreover, some trades were more prestigious than others, either inherently so or because of local factors, and allowed those who exercised them to reconcile status with manual labour more easily than in the majority of cases. For example, those engaged on luxury articles, such as the goldsmiths (*orfèvres*) or the wig-makers (*perruquiers*), derived status either from the value of their raw material or from the nature of their clientele. This was a highly permeable frontier: the passport was basically the acquisition of a modest capital.

There was, then, an important and real sense in which all levels of the bourgeoisie and nobility attained in very general terms a community of interest in face of the vulgar mechanic classes and of the vile and abject poor. At the other end of the scale, the apparent simplicity of the distinction between privileged and unprivileged is misleading. In reality no such absolute, horizontal division existed. Certainly trade was definitely inferior; certainly the hereditary noble was evidently superior. But between the two the permutations, the nuances, the ambiguities were infinite. The pursuit of ennoblement remained a realistic enterprise for the bourgeoisie of the eighteenth century. The king continued to concede Letters of Nobility to honourable, successful and well-connected men. Venal offices which carried nobility—particularly the office of *secrétaire du roi*,[2] certain judicial posts, and municipal office in nineteen towns—could be purchased throughout the century. Privilege, which, in its origin, was the most tangible

---

[1]The commoners.
[2]Secretary of the king, a royal office that, by the eighteenth century, often had no function but conferred many privileges.

expression of noble social superiority, had long since been infiltrated by non-nobles. Fiscal exemption, the commonest form of privilege, could be acquired without particular difficulty by men of substance and even, in a partial way, by men of very little substance. On the other hand, the eighteenth-century noble always paid some taxes—more indeed than the wealthy bourgeois of certain towns favoured by a history of bargains with the Crown—while, in practice, rich commoners benefited as much as nobles from the complaisance, deference or laxity of administrators and collectors of taxes. Similarly, seigneurial rights were certainly not restricted to the nobility. They had become a merchandise possibly more readily obtainable than venal office. Fiefs and rights had been divided, subdivided, and shared out to such an extent that in some places it was impossible to know their origin. In 1781 22 per cent of the lay seigneurs in the *Élection*[3] of Le Mans were non-nobles. Just before the Revolution, the Duc de Chaulnes sold his seigneury and viscounty of Amiens to a certain Colmar, a Jew and therefore definitely not noble, while the Polignacs' alienation of their seigneuries in the Velay around the beginning of the century was a veritable godsend for the socially ambitious wealthy of that region. In sum, between the privileged noble and the unprivileged commoner stood an important transitional category of indeterminate social mutants. They were neither nobles nor commoners. Indeed, almost everywhere except in Normandy, the appellation "noble" really meant a superior sort of non-noble; hence the birth certificate of the future Director Larevellière-Lépeaux stated that he was the son of "nobleman Jean-Baptiste de la Revellière, bourgeois of the town of Angers". How noble was a man whose office conferred on him personal nobility but who had not yet served the twenty years necessary to obtain the *lettres d'honneur* which declared that nobility now hereditary in the family? Was a man privileged or not when he possessed a fief, where he paid no taxes and levied seigneurial dues, and also non-noble land, where he paid both taxes and dues? Of course, it had been stated as early as the Ordinance of Blois (1579) that possession of a fief in no way made a man noble. But, when taken with a certain life style and other similar attributes, it was an important element in helping to make a man appear noble. And in social promotion in this period, appearances were the first step towards reality. In the 1780s an authority on jurisprudence complained that the usurpation of rank had got quite out of hand with men ennobled (*anoblis*) styling themselves in a manner reserved to lords of early fifteenth-century extraction, and commoners of good standing having themselves addressed as *marquis, comte, vicomte or baron,* and even passing themselves off as such in legal documents. More modest, but more commonplace, were the eighteenth-century families which had added

[3]A tax jurisdiction.

the particle[4] to their name, and had acquired over a number of generations a surreptitious accumulation of partial recognitions of privileged status which allowed them to establish as a fact exemptions and privileges to which they had no real documented right. Provided that such a family was of some wealth, conformed to the standards of noble behaviour and married advantageously, it was sufficient for its members to claim indefatigably enough and for long enough a customary privileged position in order to obtain ultimately the Intendant's[5] tacit acquiescence to their inclusion in some list of privileged persons, thus achieving irrefutable evidence of privileged status. A sustained effort of this kind by succeeding generations could finally be crowned either by the grant of Letters of Nobility or by an official decision ratifying explicitly or implicitly a claim to nobility.

Jaurès sought to explain these anomalies as "a hybrid social force at the junction of the Ancien Régime and the new capitalism". Obviously, such an interpretation alone was capable of safeguarding the concept of two distinct and antagonistic classes. In fact, however, it does not seem possible to discern a fundamental cleavage at this time between the bourgeoisie and the nobility. The middle class of the late Ancien Régime displayed no significant functional differences from the nobility, no significant difference in accepted values and above all no consciousness of belonging to a class whose economic and social characteristics were antithetical to those of the nobility. The commercial middle class of France at this time was not capitalist in one vital respect. The business of making money was subordinated to a non-capitalist social ideal, and social classifications and values did not depend upon a notion of productive force. The middle class accepted really without debate aristocratic values and sought to gain social approval by adhering to these standards. Social promotion required the abandonment of trade as soon as was financially possible. The consistent pattern of the eighteenth century, as of the seventeenth, was that commercial families placed their capital in land, in government and private annuities (*rentes*), and in venal office, all of which gave returns on investment in the order of 2 to 4 per cent, instead of seeking the higher returns on commercial investment. These men were dominated by the social motive, not by the capitalist profit motive. They accepted that trade was by definition ignoble and dishonourable. If the corn merchant speculated on the misery of the times or if the cloth merchant risked his all in the chance of large profits from army contracts, it was in order that their progeny

---

[4]By adding a particle (usually "de," which means "of"), individuals could suggest they possessed noble origins.

[5]Beginning in the seventeenth century, royal officials sent out by the monarch in order to improve the king's control of the provinces.

might the more quickly retreat into the social respectability of professional status and that, hopefully, they might themselves retire to live the life of noble idleness on revenues from land, government stock and private loans. Thus, in economic terms, nobles and bourgeois resembled each other to the extent that both sought to secure the greater part of their fortune in non-capitalist forms; at the same time, nobles indulged quite as much as wealthy commoners in proto-capitalist industrial and financial activities. It seems difficult to perceive here the representatives of significantly different stages "in a complex set of socio-economic relationships, the one feudal, the other capitalist". Such fundamental divisions and their ensuing antagonisms did not properly begin to appear in France until the nineteenth century, possibly during the reign of Louis-Philippe, and even then the socio-economic pattern described in this paragraph remained predominant among the entrepreneurial group.

Hence, in the upper reaches of French society the great articulation was not between noble and commoner which, as I have tried to show, is an almost impossible division to demonstrate. It was between those who traded and those who did not. Of course, this dividing line, like all the others in this society, was neither absolute nor drawn horizontally across society. Each family made its own calculation of the amount of fortune necessary before severing its connection with the generating source of wealth in trade. In the few great cities and seaports, with their opportunities for massive accumulation of wealth, oligarchies of trading families appeared, of such great wealth that social respect and even noble status could not be denied them. Clearly, such men may be adduced as evidence of a capitalist *haute-bourgeoisie* in the classic sense; but the extent to which their careers are typical of the middle class as a whole is highly debatable. Moreover, in most cases, despite having been able to rise so high socially while in trade, even they quickly sought to take root among the landed nobility and retreated behind the discretion of intermediaries if they continued their business interests.

In general it would appear true to say that above this frontier of trade—and always provided the possession of a level of wealth sufficient not to live meanly—there stood an élite whose internal distinctions could not destroy a common identity between its component elements. It was united, in the first place, by its control of landed property, both directly as the landowning class and indirectly through the exercise of seigneurial rights. In the second place, the tangible manifestations of social superiority—essentially fiscal and seigneurial privilege—were becoming increasingly accessible during the century to the majority of its members without regard to their nobility or lack of it. This is very clearly the message of the difficulties which one encounters in trying to distinguish between noble and rich commoner. The third major element of unity is that *in origin* the nobility of the late eighteenth century was no different from those members of the élite who had not yet achieved noble rank. Already in 1660 an observer estimated that hardly 5 per cent of noble families could trace their lineage back to the medieval feudal age. The great majority of the nobility of France dated from the sixteenth, seventeenth and eighteenth centuries. They were the product of that very same patient acquisition of social pre-eminence upon which the non-noble élite of the later eighteenth century was so ardently engaged. Most of the élite shared a common origin in that, in the first instance, it was some measure of wealth which had given them access to land and office. From that base, there began the slow ascension through the devious channels of a careful accumulation and permutation of a succession of progressively prestigious offices, of advantageous marriage alliances, of inheritances and so on.

One may suggest that the confusion of the Ancien Régime social scene is largely due to the fact that the mechanisms of social ascension were extremely delicate. They demanded constant vigilance and a fine judgement. Although history records more prominently the success stories, the reality of a society can usually be seen much more clearly in its failures. The common story of failure in the Ancien Régime is that of a family which had miscalculated, had made an ill-timed exit from trade towards an insufficient capital and property basis, had failed to gain access to a proper professional clientele, and had compounded these errors by unfortunate marriages, unwise procreation, lack of cunning, and so forth. Indeed, a close reading of even the standard success story suggests that the actual passage from commoner to noble status was almost incidental to the attainment of pre-eminence, for it guaranteed nothing. With the exception of the great aristocracy, whose position was unassailable, those noble families which did not continually strive to nourish their position stagnated or declined. The nobility contained individuals of widely different wealth, prestige and power, ranging from those living more or less overtly on charity to men of great influence and vast estates. At the end of the Ancien Régime, rank in the upper reaches of society was far too subtle a notion to be confined within the ungainly corsetry of nobles versus commoners. It depended above all upon a shrewd dosage of wealth, profession, family background, patrons and connections, title, privilege and office. Even the sort of people to whom one loaned and from whom one borrowed money counted, since in respectable circles these transactions seem to have taken place very much between people of similar status. To take but one example, Bertrand Barère's father was a commoner and his mother a noble; his father acquired the seigneury of Vieuzac and enjoyed seigneurial rights, but could never aspire to nobility. Barère himself did have pretensions to nobility, but still jumped at the opportunity of marrying into an old-established noble family of the vicinity despite its impecuniosity. Even within a body of men with common privileges, such as the Parlement of

Paris,[6] sharp contrasts existed between personal fortunes, between the scions of illustrious houses and those of no less ancient but undistinguished lineage, and so on. The wealth of a financier was less ignominious than that of a merchant; the *avocat*[7] tended to carry more weight socially in a small town than a *notaire*[8] of greater fortune. Indeed, the bitter quarrels of precedence that enlivened provincial life throughout the eighteenth century were evidence less of friction over a strict social hierarchy than of ambiguity about social rank.

What I have said does not necessarily deny the existence of a "middle class" that was within the élite and that did not merely consist of the trading elements—these latter both stood outside the élite and played little direct part in the genesis of the Revolution. But until considerably more detailed research which does not postulate a "bourgeoisie" separate from and in contradiction with the élite has been accomplished, it is difficult to define it exactly. Above all, one may debate whether such a definition would be of major significance when there is little evidence that it possessed either a "class consciousness" or an alternative social structure. This argument does, however, deny the notion of two clearly defined and clearly antagonistic classes of nobles and bourgeois in eighteenth-century France and therefore denies the existence of a class conflict in the classic sense. It does not deny—and is not intended to deny—the existence of very real distinctions, divisions and antagonisms within this élite. Nor does it deny the existence of a social crisis, for, as H. R. Trevor-Roper remarked in quite a different context, "social crises are caused not by the clear-cut opposition of mutually exclusive interests but by the tug-of-war of opposite interests *within one body*". It is quite wrong to consider that the upper reaches of late Ancien Régime society were static and decaying. Any analysis confined to only a few decades will inevitably project a static image unless that period be one of actual crisis or revolution. A wider context of a couple of centuries suggests that, on the contrary, this élite was the product of a process of evolution and that it was still evolving.

It is evident from the preceding pages that the nature of the nobility had been undergoing tremendous change since the end of the fifteenth century. Indeed, the historian of the later Valois[9] would not find unfamiliar our description of the ambiguity of the frontier between nobles and commoners, with its references to the escape from trade, venal office, usurpation, the adoption of the particle, ennoblement, and the purchase of

---

[6]See the glossary entry *parlements.*

[7]Barristers.

[8]Notaries provided the basic legal services, including the drawing of wills, marriage contracts, and the like.

[9]French royal family, 1328–1589.

fiefs, of elements of privilege and of nobility itself. Noble complaints about the debasement of their estate sound very much the same whether written in the 1780s or the 1580s. The combined action of three major factors seems to have been responsible for this development: first, the financial difficulties of the late medieval and Renaissance nobility; secondly, the attempts of the emergent absolute monarchs to secure their power upon a service nobility; thirdly, the financial difficulties of these monarchs which prompted them to abandon ennobling offices into the possession of their incumbents and subsequently to resort to the downright sale of privileges and offices. The great period of the transformation of the élite was unquestionably the seventeenth century. It was in this period that the monarchy expanded its power and the business of its government enormously, and thus multiplied its officials and the machinery for the enforcement of its will; it was also the period when a great series of wars, undertaken on an unprecedented scale and in a time of economic instability, obliged the monarch to exploit office and privilege for revenue purposes. This double process, reaching its apogee under Louis XIV, accelerated the infiltration of the nobility by wealthy commoners which had been taking place during the sixteenth century. More important perhaps, by encouraging its generalization, it finally rendered irrevocable the sixteenth-century encroachment on characteristically noble attributes by wealthy non-nobles. Louis XIV in particular exploited every financial opportunity provided by office and privilege. He even resorted several times to the direct sale of nobility, whereas neither of the eighteenth-century kings did more than sell the confirmation of nobility acquired in the normal ways. His extensive warfaring allowed commoners to enter the officer corps in relatively large numbers. A man with wits enough to discover profit in the ruins of the economy and intelligence enough to further the extension of royal power could rise rapidly. In this sense, we may restore a dimension to Saint-Simon's much abused description of the Sun King's rule as the "reign of the vile bourgeoisie". Early in the seventeenth century, the famous jurist and political theorist Loyseau still based his work on the concept of a society divided into three separate estates. In the last decade of that same century the theorist Domat, whose writings influenced jurists for the next ninety years, was dividing society on a functional basis; the first rank, with honour, dignity and authority, he accorded to the prelates, high magistrates and military commanders, and in the second rank, endowed with honour but not dignity, he placed without differentiation—and this is significant in the context of this essay—the *avocats,* the doctors, the members of the liberal and scientific professions generally and also the "gentlemen" (*gentilhommes*).[10]

---

[10]The *gentilhommes* were legally nobles.

This, then, had been the hey-day of social promotion and, as a result, not merely was the composition of the nobility altered but also its traditional attributes diffused and its traditional functions adulterated. The situation in the later eighteenth century was simply the development of conditions already apparent in the second half of the seventeenth. By the end of the Ancien Régime the distinction between the Robe nobility and the Sword nobility,[11] which had appeared so vital during the preceding two centuries, had become largely meaningless. Similar life styles, intermarriage, the parallel pursuit of military, judicial and administrative careers by the different sons of the same Sword or Robe family had abolished the distinction. Some old provincial nobles still attached a significance of prestige to the profession of arms, but found rich commoners among their brother officers for most of the century. After 1750 the most important distinction inside the nobility was that between the men of noble descent (*noblesse de race*) and those ennobled (*anoblis*). But since, as we have seen, the vast majority of noble families had originally been ennobled, noble "purity" was essentially a biological question of survival while successive generations of nobles left the family origins behind. With all other things being equal, the *anobli* family of the sixteenth century was, in 1780, more prestigious than that of the seventeenth century, which was in turn more prestigious than that of the eighteenth century.

But all these distinctions, by whose shifting complexities Frenchmen sought to keep abreast of social evolution, mask from us as they did from contemporaries the fact that the fundamental effect of these changes was to alter nobility over a long period of time from being the expression of certain hereditary virtues to being the crude expression of great wealth and powerful connections. At the end of the Ancien Régime this evolution was not complete, it was only implied.

*   *   *   *   *   *

The social crisis of the later eighteenth century is often ascribed to a phenomenon referred to as the "aristocratic reaction", whereby the nobility is said to have sought increasingly during the last thirty or forty years of the Ancien Régime to close its ranks to commoners and to restrict access to high office and to certain occupational preserves deemed noble. As far as the social aspects of this phenomenon are concerned, three major features are usually cited as characteristic—first, that whereas the bishops, ministers and great civil servants of Louis XIV had numbered a good proportion of men of common origin, the overwhelming majority of those

---

[11]Robe families were those whose nobility stemmed from members who had held particular judicial offices, while those of the sword claimed their nobility from military position.

of Louis XVI were of noble origin; secondly, that the great Parlements restricted the right of entry to nobles; and thirdly, that by the Ségur Ordinance of 1781 the king ordered army commissions to be reserved to men who could display at least four quarterings of nobility. William Doyle has recently exposed the weaknesses of the whole concept of an aristocratic reaction. We may add to his criticisms the argument that such an analysis is vulnerable above all because it begs the question of the nature of nobility. It emphasizes the simple possession of nobility to the detriment of such essential problems as lineage, date of acquisition and so on. Louis XVI's Intendants were nobles, certainly, but they came from families of relatively recent ennoblement and could barely claim to belong to the *noblesse de race*. A number of these men went on to hold ministerial office. Only Louis XVI's bishops were almost exclusively aristocrats of ancient lineage. One cannot equate socially these bishops and these Intendants within an aristocratic reaction; nor can one really cite either as direct evidence of noble exclusiveness. Both patterns were the product of royal policy. The trend towards the appointment of Intendants from newly rising families increased distinctly during the century; aristocrats were chosen as bishops essentially because, as a group, they appeared less contaminated by Jansenism,[12] to whose extirpation the monarchy was committed, than either the Parlementarian families or respectable non-nobles. Moreover, the ministers of the eighteenth-century kings were no more of predominantly ancient noble extraction than Louis XIV's ministers had been—their origins were mostly among the judicial and ennobled families. The other elements of the aristocratic reaction also require a certain amount of adjustment in detail. As far as the Parlements are concerned, it is certainly true that as early as 1732 the Parlement of Rennes did explicitly limit its recruitment to those already possessing nobility, although this was not ratified by the Crown until 1775; the Parlements of Nancy, Grenoble, Aix and Toulouse eventually followed suit. But these bodies only constituted one-third of the total number, and it is important to remember also that of the five which alone conferred hereditary nobility as from the first generation on their members, only Grenoble figured on this list. Indeed, in three of the others of this type, the prejudice in favour of noble candidates was notably absent. It is true that such statements may reflect a state of mind; it is also true that most Parlements in practice admitted a majority of new members who were already noble. On the other hand, the only detailed study of the rejection of a candidate on these grounds—the Dupaty case at Bordeaux—reveals that the motives for the rejection were quite different from those expressed. Moreover, in the most prestigious of all these courts, the Parlement of Paris, about ten per cent of the new members at the end of the Ancien

---

[12]See the glossary entry *Jansenism*.

Régime were non-nobles, just as they had been at the beginning of the century. Indeed, as Doyle emphasizes, the nobility of many of the noble entrants to the Parlements during the fifteen years before the outbreak of the Revolution was of relatively recent acquisition. Finally, as for the Ségur Ordinance, a simple reading of the text reveals that it did not apply to commissions in the more specialized arms such as the engineers or the artillery, while the extent to which it was ever properly enforced in practice is not altogether clear. It was just one of a series of such measures which had been promulgated over several decades with a notable lack of success.

Notwithstanding these considerations, the thesis of an "aristocratic reaction" may well reflect a truth in the sense that it postulates a contraction of social promotion leading to social conflict. It is evident that the conclusions that we have drawn about the configuration of the élite imply a rejection of the notion of an across-the-board conflict between an upper section, the nobility, and a lower section, the bourgeoisie. But to deduce that consequently no conflict existed would be to deny the evidence of mounting tensions between elements that can be identified in one way as nobles and commoners, and ultimately the evidence of the Revolution itself. Rather it seems that we must introduce a notion of what we may call "stress zones", that is to say various areas within this complex social structure where friction developed during the century, eventually sparking off a revolutionary conflagration. It is difficult in the present state of research to identify with clarity all the stress zones and to establish their parameters. But possibly the most significant in terms of the genesis of the Revolution was the one which seems to have developed in the established channels of social promotion.

So little detailed research has been done so far in the domain of office-holding that it is impossible to answer accurately the vital question of how widespread and how real these possibilities for promotion were in the eighteenth century when compared with the fluidity of the situation as it appears in the seventeenth century. In general terms, however, one can argue plausibly that as the eighteenth century progressed the capacity of these traditional channels (largely established in the seventeenth century) for providing social fulfilment diminished. Many, though not all, of these high offices and their access routes were colonized by an oligarchy for much of the century. This phenomenon was already visible in some places, such as the Parlements of Rennes and Toulouse, well before the end of the seventeenth century. It was indeed a natural consequence of the expansion of opportunity during the central and later seventeenth century with its great multiplication of offices, privileges and ennoblements, with its fortunes made in the wars of Louis XIV and, more recently, in Law's System, and with its increase in the numbers of ordinary judicial and administrative positions. For the first half of the eighteenth century, at least, an atmosphere of pause descended on these groups while families digested, as it were, the seventeenth century, some waiting out their time in a necessary social purgatory, others repairing fortunes, yet others seeking to augment them.

Of course, although access to office and wealth were the most important elements in social status, they were not the only ones as I emphasized earlier in this essay. The other, less calculable elements of prestige really resided in the nature of a family's relations and connections, for a man was what he was accepted to be by those who counted. But, although this question is still far from clear, it does seem that even in this sense the eighteenth century may have seen a contraction of opportunity through the development of dynasties and closed groups of wealthy, respectable families contracting marriages among each other or else outside the locality, whether for fear of inferior alliances or for need of mutual reassurance through alliance with their own kind.

Such a situation would not necessarily have produced a social crisis, if it had not been for the incidence upon it of the demographic and economic developments of the century. Of course, the poor multiplied more than anyone else largely because there were more poor to multiply. But the effects of the demographic explosion (an increase of the order of thirty per cent or more between 1715 and 1789) were also felt in the area under discussion. It was naturally an added stimulus to this phenomenon of colonization as worried fathers found themselves with an extra boy to establish without loss of honour and/or an extra girl to marry off advantageously but economically. At the same time, of course, demographic factors contributed to increase the pressure for social promotion from the lower end of the élite. The economic prosperity of the eighteenth century was, however, far more potent as an aggravating factor. In the seventeenth century, economic uncertainty had operated in a sense as a social filter, for those who had managed both to get and to stay rich had done so in a fairly decisive fashion. But in the eighteenth century, not merely were spectacular fortunes being made but also almost anyone with a modicum of business sense was acceding, at least between 1730 and 1770, to modest wealth in small town provincial France. In effect, this meant that an increasing number of families were able at this time to make the break from trade. The bottom end of the élite and consequently the lower reaches of the promotional channels probably began to swell. At the same time, the greater noble families with large estates could benefit from the rise in land rents and in agricultural prices.

Conversely, however, the economic prosperity of the century did not really affect the majority of established members of the élite to anything like the same degree. It was above all a commercial prosperity and they had, by definition, cut themselves off from it. They were faced by an average price rise of 48 per cent between 1730 and 1788 without any equivalent increase in income. One effect of this was to stimulate the energy with which some noble and commoner holders of seigneurial rights indulged in the so-called "feudal reaction".[13] More important, it would have added a remunerative element to the phenomenon of colonization and would also have helped to attract men already noble to lower offices. Those professional families, which with patient dexterity were rising through the channels of promotion, would thus be likely to encounter more competition for positions to which seventeenth-century precedent taught them to aspire. Of course, commoner families still continued to rise to ennobling high office through the traditional channels. But it can also be plausibly argued that conditions generally may well have become more precarious for those provincial families which had long since abandoned trade and settled comfortably into the middle-rank judicial and administrative positions. For one can doubt whether a great many of them had land and wealth enough to do more than hold their own from traditionally acceptable sources of income, while the increase in numbers from below would have meant more competition for business. In the smaller provincial towns, the *avocats,* the *notaires,* the judges of the lesser courts, only achieved an adequate income by garnering together every available form of revenue. Naturally, there always existed a huge gap in terms of wealth and prestige between the mass of middle-rank lawyers and the great officers of the Parlements, the *Chambres des Comptes,* the *Cours des Aides,*[14] and so on; but it does appear that, in these ways, the established channels of social promotion within the law courts and the administration which led from the one to the other became progressively clogged. Even an *avocat* pamphleteering in favour of the Parlements in 1789 thought that the high Robe positions should be accessible to all citizens with a degree in law, a respectable income and good morals. The monarchy contributed materially to this situation by failing to increase the number of venal ennobling offices and to multiply the number of its acts of direct ennoblement. Indeed, on the contrary, the Crown seems to have tried actively to limit the amount of ennoblement by office.

The problems which thus faced the professional men and the office-holders were not unlike those that faced another section of the élite, the lesser provincial nobility. Certainly, the poverty-stricken *hobereaux*[15] were only a minority and most nobles managed their affairs with attention, but these families had few opportunities to do more than hold their own financially, and the economic and demographic trends of the century made

---

[13]Some historians have labelled the effort to reclaim seigneurial rights the "feudal reaction," because these holders of seigneuries argued that they were merely re-establishing rights held in the feudal past.

[14]The *Chambres des Comptes* and the *Cours des Aides* were tax courts.

[15]Poor nobles.

it even more difficult to do that. Whether from lack of initiative or from a scrupulous regard for the stricter conventions of noble behaviour, many such families had in the past confined themselves to landed property and the exploitation of seigneurial rights, not contending for office and at most putting their sons into the army, although this could be a costly business despite the existence of ten free military colleges and the *École Militaire*[16] in the later years of the Ancien Régime. These men were the anachronistic paradox of the élite in its eighteenth-century form, belonging to its central and lower sections by fortune, prestige and life style, yet laying claim to the whole panoply of attributes which distinguished its highest echelons. Their opportunities for social promotion, in so far as it involved access to prestigious office and the establishment of alliances, connections and protections, were just as limited as those of the non-noble elements of the central and lower élite. Yet, their possession of nobility rendered them far more susceptible to a precise fear of social demotion than non-nobles of similar situation. Naturally, these men were resentful and suspicious of the great Court aristocracy and Parlementarian nobility, who had better access to prestige and profit and yet needed them less. Even the wealthier provincial nobles shared in this prejudice. But more directly, the lesser nobles came into competition with those men whose station in life in all respects other than the possession of nobility was identical to theirs. In the small provincial towns where they spent the winter, they were confronted with the sons and grandsons of tradesmen able to buy the same sort of houses and land, the same sort of clothes and food, the same sort of seigneurial rights and fiscal exemptions. With most of the tangible expressions of their superiority slipping into the common domain, such men were brought to emphasize their more intangible qualities, to insist upon those honours upon which no monarch had ever bothered to set a price and to recall his low birth to the commoner. One seigneur in Burgundy even had his honorific privileges written into his rent roll (*terrier*). It was among the provincial nobility that the notion of derogation[17] had always received the warmest support. These were the tensions that found expression in the increasing numbers of quarrels between nobles and commoners during the eighteenth century. Moreover, often unable to compete in the arena of office-holding as much for lack of inclination as of training and capital, these men resented competition in areas which they considered to be their natural preserve, especially the medium-rank positions in the church and the army where impecunious younger sons could be honourably employed. It is in this context that the Ségur Ordinance of 1781 must be understood, for it was

---

[16]Military School.

[17]Derogation is the loss of the legal status of nobility from engaging in certain occupations such as trade.

forced on the government by a provincial noble lobby against the advice of the great aristocracy and of the War Office. In 1789, the provincial nobility were not only unwilling to lose the revenue and status of the material privileges which the great aristocracy, socially and financially secure, were prepared to abandon; they were also intent on reorganizing access to prestigious and remunerative positions in their favour.

In this sense, therefore, one may discern a form of "noble reaction" during the eighteenth century. It was, however, peripheral to the major social problems of the period and, moreover, mild—almost timid—in comparison with the great inquests into nobility that could be used as evidence of such reactions in the sixteenth and seventeenth centuries. Its importance was that it tended to affect most directly precisely those groups which were having difficulty in the traditional channels of promotion; it was an irritant expressed in the traditional terms most likely to impinge upon them, and it helped to prepare them to identify in a time of crisis the lack of social opportunity as the result of specifically noble exclusiveness. Yet, despite all these developments, it is doubtful whether one can talk of an open social crisis within the élite before 1788-9. The expressed grievances of its central and lower elements during the last thirty years of the Ancien Régime were predominantly political and were directed against the system of absolute monarchy. The eighteenth-century Bourbons were reforming monarchs, albeit spasmodically. Yet their reforms usually involved increasing royal authority and appeared for that reason to be acts of arrant despotism, while even their attempts to ensure more equitable justice could be seen as interfering with the independence of the judiciary. Even the future reforming minister Turgot thought that Maupeou's[18] reform of the Parlements was an act leading towards "legal despotism", while in 1788 a wealthy lawyer from Bordeaux was writing of "the need to repress the absolute power of the ministry which would have the monarchy degenerate into despotism". Indeed, such political attitudes were another element of unity for the élite. In the main, the great nobles at Court and in the Parlements yearned for participatory politics, the lesser provincial nobles desired a system in which they could protect their interests, and the professional groups dreamed of a rational, utilitarian government which they thought they saw in classical Rome and which their studies of Roman jurisprudence in law school had taught them to admire. All disliked the steady extension of central control over local affairs since 1660. It was this attitude which produced the acquiescence of the "bourgeoisie" in the "aristocratic revolt" of 1787-8. The National Assembly inherited this struggle against absolutism. The great growth of political comment after 1770 may indeed have been a prime factor in rendering many elements of the

---

[18]Chancellor of France who in 1771 was able to abolish temporarily the Parlement of Paris.

élite aware of a common identity. This might be revealed by a closer study of the pre-revolutionary use of such terms as "nation" and "citizen", which may refer essentially to a political nation, socially definable, and possibly somewhat analogous to the English seventeenth-century notion of "freeman".

Above all, however, there seems to be very little evidence to suggest that the non-noble elements of the élite were contesting the validity of nobility as a social notion and questioning the system of privilege in a way that would indicate that they were developing a "class consciousness". Indeed, it would appear that right up to 1788 the overwhelming majority believed implicitly in the intrinsic value of a nobility, of noble standards, and hardly debated a system of privilege in which they largely participated or could reasonably aspire to participate.

Should one see, therefore, in the economic crisis of 1788–9 the mobilizing factor which produced a "revolutionary bourgeoisie" in the same way that it produced a revolutionary peasantry? Obviously, the trading classes were badly hurt. But most historians agree that these groups were noticeably absent from the revolutionary process. Even though we may well believe that the professional groups expressed some of their grievances, it does not seem that the nature of these grievances would be essentially social in this context. More relevant is the fact that since wealth was an indispensable element of social status, any threat to it was a social threat as much as an economic one. Clearly, a bankruptcy would jeopardize the government annuities (*rentes*) and, significantly enough, the Constituent Assembly took great care to protect this form of investment. Similarly, the economic crisis threatened the payment of annuities served by private persons. But these were really ancillary elements in the composition of the fortune of any member of the élite. The crisis did not affect his land; it may have endangered his revenue in the short term but it did not necessarily endanger his capital base. At all events, such considerations hardly provided an adequate stimulus to political activity in such a radical form.

Should one, therefore, agree with one recent historian in seeing the outbreak of revolution in France as essentially a political event? In this context, the importance of the decision by the Parlement of Paris in September 1788 (largely endorsed by the second Assembly of Notables) that the Estates-General[19] should meet in its form of 1614 has never been ignored. But the nature of its significance has not perhaps always been exactly recognized. This decision polarized the component elements of the élite and crystallized their latent tensions by reintroducing from the early seventeenth century concepts of French society which, already obsolescent at that time, were by now totally erroneous. The conditions demanded for entry into the noble electoral assemblies were far more rigorous than any

---

[19]See the glossary entry *Estates General.*

that had been imposed for noble gatherings and lists during the preceding century. The electoral procedure thus took on the aspect of a seventeenth-century type inquiry into nobility. The frontier between noble and non-noble, which had been of diminishing importance, was suddenly and artificially reimposed. The decision to separate the nobility from the Third Estate pushed the central and lower echelons of the élite down into the Third Estate. It rent asunder what was essentially by now a homogeneous social unit, and identified quite gratuitously a section of that unit as irremediably inferior and to be confused not merely with the trading classes but also with the manual labourers and the vile and abject poor. It is in this context that one must understand the apparent paradox of the fact that the leading voices at the national level against this decision in late 1788 were those of "liberal" nobles. As far as those who were directly affected by these measures are concerned, it needs no temerity to suggest that the *anobli* Le Chapelier, for instance, discovered his revolutionary vocation when he was excluded, despite his bitter protests, from the electoral assembly of the Breton nobility. But, in general, the position of the *anobli* was naturally somewhat ambivalent. It was men further down in the channels of promotion who reacted most categorically to the situation. At Rennes, to use examples from Brittany again, it was the *procureurs*[20] of the *Présidial*[21] who led the attack on the oligarchy of *anoblis* in the Municipality for refusing to endorse a demand for vote by head, and it was the *avocats* who organized the electoral campaign there, while at Saint-Malo and in most of the other Breton towns except Nantes the professional groups again took the initiative in the agitation. This was the situation in most of France. In Provence, however, although the same direct effects of the decisions relating to the calling of the Estates-General are visible, the situation was somewhat different in that the polarization was already well under way by this time. But, at root, a similar catalyst had operated, for the conflict took shape in the debate during the later months of 1787 over whether the provincial Estates of Provence should be re-established in the form of their last meeting in 1639, a debate which the Third Estate lost. Once again, the lawyers had taken a leading part and continued to do so in 1788.

It was their experience of problems in social promotion which rendered many of the people thus implicitly demoted by the Parlement's decision so sensitive to such distinctions. This helps to explain why the traditional liberal professions provided so many of the leaders of the Third Estate movement at the local level during the winter of 1788–9. This decision was all the more critical because it seemed to arbitrate definitively between two

[20]Solicitors.
[21]Law courts.

contradictory trends in recent comparable situations: it was all the more of a shock because the Estates-General were supremely more important than any of those situations and because this decision ran counter to the conceptions which the government had apparently been favouring. In 1787, following an earlier experiment by Necker in the Berry and a plan submitted to the Assembly of Notables by Calonne, Loménie de Brienne had established a three-tier structure of municipal, intermediary and provincial assemblies to handle some aspects of local government. Although a proportion of seats in all these bodies was reserved to the privileged orders, the system called for elections to the lowest assembly among the men of property on a tax franchise and for each assembly to designate to the one above it. Above all, there was to be no distinction by Order, voting was to be by head, and the Third Estate had double representation. Moreover, the events at Vizille in the Dauphiné in July 1788 seemed to confirm this trend towards the unity of an élite of comfortable men of property. On the other hand, the decision of September 1788 echoed the most exclusive and antiquated formulas of representation which the government had conceded, by omission at least, to the renewed Estates of Provence. Together these two events, reinforced in December 1788 by the widely-read and extremely reactionary *Mémoire des Princes présenté au roi,*[22] could appear as the final implementation of a threat long expressed. We do not yet possess a close study of the disputes between nobles and commoners during the years preceding the Revolution. But it is possible to argue that they usually arose because the nobleman acted in such a way as to suggest not merely that the respectable commoner was inferior socially, which in relative terms within the élite he obviously was, but that he was on a par with the vulgar mass. The nobleman who insisted on his precedence in church would certainly mortify the pride of the well-to-do commoner; but the nobleman who thrashed the son of a bourgeois was treating him as he would treat a domestic servant or a street porter—it was even worse when he had the job done for him by his lackeys. This is of course an extreme example. The propagandists of the Third Estate in Brittany still remembered the reception of the demand formulated ten years previously that the provincial Estates authorize commoners to be admitted to the charitable institution for poor gentlemen, which they indeed had helped to subsidize. "What, do they not have the poorhouses (*hôpitaux*), the workhouses (*maisons de force*), and the prisons?" a nobleman had inquired, thereby implicitly excluding all commoners from the élite and consigning them without distinction to those institutions which catered not merely for the honest though humble poor, but also for the vagabonds and beggars who stood outside society altogether. Of course, all this was very tame when com-

---

[22]*Memoir of the Princes, Presented to the King.*

pared with noble behaviour during the previous two centuries. It is significant of the changing situation of the commoner elements of the élite that their sensitivity to this kind of attitude should have been such as to make them often the aggressors in violent quarrels.

This, then, was what Mallet du Pan was expressing in his oft-quoted observation—"The nature of the debate has completely changed. King, despotism, and constitution are now very secondary questions; the war is between the Third Estate and the other two Orders". In this sense, the doubling of the representation of the *Tiers* was a wholly irrelevant concession. The revolt of the Third Estate was a revolt against a loss of status by the central and lower sections of the élite with the approval of those elements of the trading groups which were on the threshold of the élite. It was this social group which became the "revolutionary bourgeoisie". The *abbé* Sieyès became such an influential personality because he expressed precisely their aspirations. Under the rhetoric of his most celebrated pamphlet, *Qu'est-ce que le Tiers-état?*[23] he was not in fact pressing the social and political claims of all those he defined as the Third Estate in the first chapter, but only those of the group which he called "the available classes of the Third Estate". In all his political writings, Sieyès conceived of society as composed essentially of two peoples, the property owners and the "work machines", and demanded the union of the property owners in defence of property against the poor. He militated against the privileged orders because their existence prevented that union; from the beginning to the end of the Revolution he extolled the notables as a homogeneous social and political élite. In 1789, the system of elections served this revolt for, whereas the direct election procedure for the First and Second Estates produced a faithful reflection of the stress zones within them, the indirect elections of the Third Estate not only eliminated the non-élite groups (and therefore the stress zones that their relations with the élite constituted), but also brought in a solid and unified group of professional men, that is to say precisely those who were the most directly affected by the contraction of the traditional channels of promotion. Once the Third Estate had taken control in July 1789, the National Assembly abandoned the Ancien Régime structure of privilege with reluctance and considerable reservations in August. It was hardly the act of an assembly of bourgeois liberating themselves from the restricting fetters of feudalism. Indeed, the *abbé* Sieyès did all he could to reverse it. These men became the champions of an attack on privilege in part by the force of the logic of revolutionary politics in the context of the popular revolt of 1789. But they also did so as a consequence of a number of confusions. Obliged to become the leaders of the Third Estate, they presented their own grievances as those of the whole of the Third Estate.

---

[23]*What Is the Third Estate?*

Certainly, they expressed hostility to the nobility, but their grievance was one of political and social definition in the precise context of 1788–9. However, the mere fact that they did express this hostility encouraged the peasantry, initially at least, to identify privilege predominantly with the nobility rather than with the élite as a whole and to confuse the grievances of the "revolutionary bourgeoisie" with its own. It was this which enabled the revolutionary behaviour of the representatives of the Third Estate to find support among the protest movements of the vile and abject sections of the community, which were not their natural allies. Furthermore, in 1788–9 the circumstances and background which have been elaborated in this essay allowed the "revolutionary bourgeoisie" to identify, erroneously and in general terms, the Ancien Régime nobility as an exclusive group threatening its social position, while the political developments of the early days of the Estates-General incited it to confuse this conception of the nobility with the system of absolute monarchy, and to see the two as interdependent and as allies. But such a thought-process necessarily imposed the identification of the nobility as a distinct social group, which, as we have seen, was an unrealistic enterprise; the easiest solution to this paradox was to indulge in another confusion and to identify the nobility by the traditional system of privileges which had originally been specifically noble attributes. Thus, spokesmen of the Third Estate could quite happily refer to the first two Estates as the "privileged Orders", forgetting that they themselves were in many cases at least partially privileged. It was for this reason that the attachment of the "revolutionary bourgeoisie" to that system of privilege, in which they themselves participated, was weakened. In mid-1789 the combination of the counter-offensive of the Ancien Régime and anti-privilege pressure from below brought the revolutionary leaders to jettison privilege.

However, the true sense of the rejection of the Ancien Régime system of privilege by the "revolutionary bourgeoisie" was revealed by the Constitution of 1791. In this document, this assembly of men from the Ancien Régime élite redefined that same élite in such a way that it could never be divided again by artificial distinctions within it. The characteristic of élite status was recognized to be the control of landed property. The tangible attribute of élite status was defined as access to public office and the political control of the country. This is the sense of a Constitution which made every public position elective and largely confined eligibility to men of some substance expressed in property. The Thermidorians and the Directorials reasserted these same conceptions of politics and society far more explicitly and successfully, as the surviving Jacobins, not to mention Babeuf,[24] clearly understood. The Constitution of 1791 in no way implied

---

[24]The first advocate of communism.

a rejection of the Ancien Régime nobility, for it was comprised within this definition as much as were wealthy non-nobles. It was merely because some noble elements chose rather vociferously not to participate that the Revolution was made to appear as a revolt against the nobility as a social class. In the same way, the technical detail of the ordering of the Estates-General, while crystallizing the tensions of the Ancien Régime, also forced them to be expressed in terms which can easily be taken as those of a conflict between nobles and bourgeois, a conflict which did not exist in any very meaningful sense in the eighteenth century. Nevertheless, the redefinition of the élite by the Revolution was indubitably of fundamental importance. Although nobility as an institution was only momentarily abolished and Napoleon was indeed to reinforce it in a certain sense, the revolutionary crisis did result in the emergence of an élite defined in terms of landholding and function, with the hereditary element confined to the simple passage of wealth and its advantages from one generation to another in a family. The Revolution did therefore provide a social framework within which the acquisition of nobility was to be increasingly irrelevant and which allowed élite status to develop into the attribute of men of wealth however acquired and however expressed. In this sense, we may say that the Revolution made the bourgeoisie even if it was not made by the bourgeoisie.

The French Revolution Is Over*

François Furet

In a series of books and essays, François Furet has endeavored to replace the Marxist interpretation with a radically different reading of the Revolution. The selection included in this collection illustrates the heart of his argument. His analysis begins with the claim that by the eighteenth century the centralizing monarch had deprived society of any political role. Far too dynamic to accept this state of affairs, the French had set up a counterculture that mirrored the image created by the monarchy. The king claimed to possess all authority, but his opposition demanded equal access for all. In the process of the Revolution, this innovative rhetoric rapidly triumphed. Furet tries to explain why this occurred. Arguing that the king had very early in the Revolution virtually abdicated his authority, Furet contends that this led to a situation that allowed the language of equality—the only available contender—to fill the vacuum. Once this transpired, politicians were captive, competing among themselves to represent the broadest section of public opinion. Of course, they wanted to escape from this pattern because their personal goal was often to exercise power, not simply to interpret popular demands. However, the language of equality provided a compelling morality that no politician could challenge. The end result of this process was the installation of the Terror of 1793–94, when public opinion and government became thoroughly intertwined. Only the excesses of the Terror broke the spell of the appeal to absolute equality and led to the return of competition between social groups for power.

Considerations of space forced omission here of an important part of Furet's argument. Elsewhere he adds that a belief in absolute equality presumes the likelihood of a terrorist repression. If all are truly equal, the choice lies between anarchy and repression. And the French selected repression.

Thus for Furet, the history of the Revolution is the rise of a particu-

*Excerpts from an article in *Interpreting the French Revolution* (Cambridge, 1981), translated by Elborg Forster, pp. 36–50, 70–71. Reprinted with the permission of Cambridge University Press.

larly odious language of equality. This interpretation holds many consequences. First, it raises an issue antithetical to the Marxist approach, in
which ideology is far less important than social conflict. Even the Anglo-
American revisionists, represented here by Lucas, do not leave a great deal
of room for ideas to function as an independent factor. And for intellectual
historians, Furet's hypotheses provide both possibilities and problems. Of
course, his emphasis greatly highlights the study of ideas. Numerous
historians, though, do not share his confidence in the ability of beliefs to
dominate society as completely as he suggests. Furthermore, many scholars
find other powerful ideas besides equality in the Revolution, and some
others do not accept the notion that terror must necessarily result from a
commitment to equality. However, all the reservations taken together
cannot deny Furet's ideas an extraordinarily prominent place in present
day historiography.

French society in the eighteenth century was desperately searching
for responsible spokesmen. It was too highly 'developed', as we
would say today, to be kept, as in the preceding century, in silent and
obedient submission to the State. But in its search for political representation it was hampered by the legacy of Louis XIV, who had systematically closed off the channels of communication between society
and the State (such as the Estates General,[1] the remonstrances of the
parlements,[2] the municipalities and the town councils) yet also maintained and even consolidated the structure of the society of orders. It was
only natural that after the death of Louis XIV, society should attempt to
revive the traditional circuits of representation, especially the rôle of the
parlements. But since these same *parlements,* throughout the century,
gave repeated proof of their conservatism, since they condemned the
Encyclopédie,[3] and *Émile,*[4] and the unfortunate Calas,[5] they hardly
constituted the best spokesmen for an 'enlightened' society. They could
perpetuate the illusion of their representative character only so long as the

---

[1]See the glossary entry *Estates General.*

[2]See the glossary entry *parlements.*

[3]The *Encyclopédie* (published from 1750 to 1772) was a massive encyclopedia that was a
compendium of knowledge of the mid-eighteenth century and that contained many challenges
to the government and the church.

[4]A book by Jean-Jacques Rousseau published in 1762. It advocated a very domestic form
of child raising and a very restricted role for women.

[5]A Protestant merchant executed in 1762. Officials accused and convicted him of
murdering his son to prevent the latter's conversion to Catholicism. No credible evidence has
appeared that the charge was true.

monarchical State—before or after it yielded to them—fought them; but the illusion was short-lived.

That is why eighteenth-century society increasingly turned to other spokesmen, namely to the *philosophes*[6] and men of letters. No one has understood and expressed that better than Tocqueville in the first chapter of Book 3 of *L'Ancien Régime*.[7] He felt that, by abolishing the ancient 'liberties' and destroying the political function of the nobility without also permitting the formation of a new ruling class on a different basis, the monarchy unwittingly set up the writers as imaginary substitutes for that ruling class. Hence literature took on a political function:

> Considering that this same French nation—so unfamiliar with the conduct of its own affairs, so deprived of experience, so hampered by its political institutions, and so powerless to improve them—was also at that time the most literate nation on earth and the one that cared most deeply about the things of the mind, one can easily understand how its writers came to be a political power and eventually became the foremost of these powers.

That confusion of rôles, in which men of letters assumed a function they could fulfill only in its imaginary aspects, that is, as opinion-makers who wielded no practical power whatsoever, was to shape political culture itself. The men of letters tended to substitute abstract right for the consideration of facts, principles for the weighing of means, values and goals for power and action. Thus the French, deprived as they were of true liberties, strove for abstract liberty; incapable of collective experience, lacking the means of testing the limits of action, they unwittingly moved toward the *illusion of politics*. Since there was no debate on how best to govern people and things, France came to discuss goals and values as the only content and the only foundation of public life.

Yet Tocqueville's brilliant analysis, which explains so much about the intellectuals' rôle in French political debate since the eighteenth century, is not sufficient to account for the sociological conditions that shaped the elements of what was to become the revolutionary consciousness. What is missing in his general intuition is an examination of the channels by which the new power of public opinion, existing side by side with power *tout court*,[8] came to act upon society. For society produced, and maintained, alongside the traditional one, a new *political sociability*, waiting in the wings to take over the entire stage: that was Augustin Cochin's[9] discovery.

---

[6] A term applied to eighteenth-century intellectuals associated with the Enlightenment.

[7] Alexis de Tocqueville, a great historian, whose book *The Old Regime and the French Revolution* (1856) is referred to here.

[8] In its essence.

[9] Historian of the French Revolution (1876–1916).

By political sociability, I mean a specific mode of organising the relations between citizens (or subjects) and power, as well as among citizens (or subjects) themselves in relation to power. An 'absolute' monarchy implies and presents a type of political sociability in which all of society is arranged concentrically and hierarchically around the monarchy, which is the central organising force of social life. It occupies the summit of a hierarchical arrangement of *corps*[10] and communities whose rights it guarantees and through which authority flows downward, while obedience (tempered by grievances, remonstrances, and negotiations) flows upward. Under the Ancien Régime, however, the circuits of the old political sociability were increasingly stripped of their traditional meaning and their symbolic content; the administrative monarchy dealt a severe blow to ranks and *corps* when it taxed them. To the very end it clung to the image of a society it had done its best to destroy; but nothing in that theoretical society allowed it to communicate any longer with real society. Everything, beginning with the court, had become a screen.

Yet real society did reconstruct, in other ways and other places, beyond the monarchy, a world of political sociability. This new world was based on individuals, and no longer on the institutional groups to which they belonged; it was founded on the confused notion called 'opinion' that came into being in cafés, salons, Masonic lodges and the so-called *sociétés de pensée,* or 'philosophical societies'. One can call it democratic sociability— even though its network did not extend to all of the people—simply to express the idea that its lines of communication were formed 'below' and ran horizontally in a disjointed society, where all individuals were equal. 'Opinion' was precisely the obscure way of expressing the idea that something new had emerged from the silence that had engulfed the pyramid of the king's traditional interlocutors. That 'something' was based on new principles, but nobody clearly understood what they were.

The reason is that while democratic sociability did indeed begin to reunify a disintegrating society—for it played, on a practical level, the same integrating rôle as ideologies of the 'nation' on the intellectual level—it remained in many respects, like its older counterpart, impenetrable. The new centres around which it took shape, such as the philosophical societies or the Masonic lodges, lay by definition outside the traditional institutions of the monarchy. They could not become 'corporate bodies' in the traditional pyramid since they were not only of a different, but indeed of an incompatible order. The elements they were made of did not exist prior to society, as so many indivisible nuclei that together might constitute a hierarchical organisation. They were, on the contrary, *products* of a society,

---

[10]An association whose members held an exclusive privilege to practice a particular profession.

albeit of a society emancipated from power and engaged in creating a new social and political fabric based on the individual. Such a principle could not be openly proclaimed and had, in fact, long been fought against by the kings of France, so that for a very long time those new centres of democratic sociability seemed suspect and were often secret or semi-secret.

The new circuit of sociability thus had no communication with the traditional one; it was totally unrelated to the network of relationships woven by the authorities. It produced opinion, not action—or, better, it produced opinion that had no effect on action. Its image of power was thus substitutive, yet patterned on the 'absolute' power of the monarch, simply inverted in favour of the people. The very fact that a philosophical society or club claimed to be speaking for the nation, or for the people, was sufficient to transform individual opinions into plain 'opinion' and opinion into imaginary absolute power, for in that kind of alchemy there was no room for either legitimate disagreement or legitimate representation. The two symmetrical and opposite images of undivided power furnished the ingredients for notions and reciprocal imputations of conspiracy: enlightened 'opinion' believed in a conspiracy of ministers or a plot to institute a ministerial despotism; the royal administration believed in a conspiracy among the grain merchants or the men of letters.

It is precisely in that sense that the eighteenth-century French monarchy was *absolute,* and not—as has been said again and again by republican historiography on the basis of what the Revolution asserted—because of the way it exercised its authority. Its power was weak, but it conceived of itself as undivided. That notion, which remained intact even after its actual content had eroded, was precisely the sufficient and necessary reason for the concealment of the political circuit. As society wrested—or reconquered —more and more power from the monarchy, the notion of absolutism proved so persuasive that it became necessary to refashion that power in an outwardly radically different manner and yet on the model of absolutism. The two circuits were incompatible precisely because they had so much in common. If they excluded any means of communicating with each other, it was because they shared the same idea of power. The French Revolution is inconceivable without that idea, or that phantasm, which was a legacy of the monarchy; but the Revolution anchored power in society instead of seeing it as a manifestation of God's will. The revolutionary consciousness took form as an attempt to recreate undivided power in a society free of contradictions. The new collectively shared image of politics was the exact reverse of that of the Ancien Régime.

It is clear that ever since the death of Louis XIV the idea of absolute monarchy had blocked all efforts at revamping the political system, in particular the attempt at establishing a representative régime. The *parlements,* being an integral part of the traditional structure, usurped rather than exercised a representative rôle. Yet when they too finally claimed to embody 'the nation', as in the famous episode of 1769–71,[11] they unwittingly based their stand on the system of fictive equivalences that was just beginning to form the democratic texture of the philosophical societies. Nothing shows more clearly the identical though opposite character of the two sets of political assumptions, and the mutual exclusiveness this implied, than that oligarchy of privileged men who started speaking of the 'nation' and the 'people', and who could break out of the absolute monarchy only by espousing pure democracy.

Yet one must resist the temptation to rebuild our entire eighteenth century, or even its second half, in the light of 1789 or 1793. While it is true that the *materials* of the revolutionary consciousness to come existed in France in the 1770s or 1780s, there is no reason to conclude that a 'crystallisation' took place, or was inevitable. The two types of political sociability still coexisted peacefully in early 1789, when the French were called upon by Louis XVI to draw up their *Cahiers de doléances,*[12] and to send their deputies to Versailles. It would be too much to say that they blended in harmony. The king juxtaposed them awkwardly in his summons when he mixed the ancient structure for expressing 'grievances', supposedly to be drawn up by an ascending sequence of unanimous assemblies, with an electoral procedure of a modern and democratic kind, at least within the Third Estate. The incoherences of the 'Regulations' of January 1789 and the absence of public debate and of any organised contest of opinions made it possible to manipulate the assemblies; yet the immense task of writing the *Cahiers* produced a set of texts in which unanimity is far more frequent than disagreement, even among the three Orders, and in which there is nothing to foreshadow a brutal rending of the social and political fabric. The revolutionary actors emerged from the elections of 1789, but the language of the Revolution was not yet used in the *Cahiers.*

For the *Cahiers* did not speak the language of democracy, but that of the jurists of the Ancien Régime. It is not that they were more 'moderate' than the revolutionary texts that appeared later or already accompanied them in a few instances. But what they expressed was altogether different from the Revolution, for they amounted to the testament of the reform movement of the Ancien Régime, written in its own language. Quite clearly the substance of these thousands of texts, and especially, for the Third

---

[11][author's note] I am referring to the series of remonstrances of the *Cour des Aides* [tax court], many of which were written by Malesherbes himself, who was First President during these years of bitter conflict with Louis XV. The most explicit text is that of 18 February 1771. Written after the most active members of the *parlement* had been exiled and their offices confiscated, it protests against the "destructive system that threatens the entire nation" and against the arbitrary royal power that "deprives the nation of the most essential rights of a free people."

[12]Literally translated, "Notebooks of Grievances."

Estate, of the summaries drawn up at the *bailliage*[13] level, was borrowed from the practices and the vocabulary of royal officials: that is what gave them their homogeneous tone, despite their having been drawn up on behalf of communities, corporate bodies or estates. Through the voice of the *robe,*[14] the old circuit of political sociability delivered its last message: *la nation, le roi, la loi.*[15]

Yet the first hypothesis that comes to mind about the *Cahiers* is the exact opposite. The historian is spontaneously inclined to expect these texts, written in March or April, to contain a premonition of things to come and to read them as a foreshadowing of the events of June and July. His inclination is all the more 'natural' as these thousands of documents were drawn up and distributed according to the divisions within the old society, so that they seem to offer an ideal vantage point from which to discern the central antagonism between the Third Estate and the nobility, which was to be of such crucial importance. However, a term-by-term comparison between the *Cahiers* at the *bailliage* level of the Third Estate and those of the nobility does not bring to light anything of the kind; in fact the two groups of texts can be analysed far better in terms of what they have in common than in terms of contradictions or even simple differences.

The *Cahiers* of the nobility are on the whole somewhat more 'enlightened' than those of the Third Estate, in that they made greater use of the vocabulary of the Enlightenment and placed greater emphasis on such demands as personal freedom or the rights of man. The *Cahiers* of the Third Estate at the *bailliage* level were more or less obliged to take over the litany of rural demands, even though they owed their inspiration and content largely to urban texts, especially—and not by coincidence—those of 'free' inhabitants (that is, independent of the trade-guilds). Those *Cahiers* go into greater detail when enumerating needed reforms; and it is not surprising that a larger number of them call for voting by head.

But those differences did not lead to antagonism among the kingdom's estates. The last consultation conducted by the monarchy, though organised upon largely new principles, still had the power to contain public opinion within traditional channels. Thus, contrary to what Tocqueville wrote about the *Cahiers,* one finds in them almost no hint of the coming revolutionary ideology, nothing to foreshadow the character of the Revolution, nor even, in particular, a trace of the battle for the symbolic monopoly over the people's will that was to be at the centre of the great events to come. Even more important, that entire corpus of texts—a monument to the spirit of the *robe*—is still imbued with a common

---

[13]Bailiwick.
[14]Judiciary.
[15]The nation, the king, the law.

reference to tradition. The very men who had for centuries made the French monarchy were determined to reform it, but according to its true principles. Of all the demands voiced by the *Cahiers* concerning power (and they are very homogeneous indeed), the most unanimous is surely for control of taxation by periodically convened Estates General. It is related to very old notions of the monarchy: the power to tax is seen as the royal prerogative *par excellence,* indeed as more crucial to the State than judicial power, yet it must be exercised within just limits and negotiated with the Estates General, which deliver the consent of the king's subjects. Many *Cahiers* demand wider powers for those Estates—provincial or general—to the detriment of the royal *intendants*[16] and in the name of a constitution that must be not so much established as 'restored', indeed 'secured'. But, with rare exceptions, those demands remain within the limits of traditional political legitimacy. There is no better proof than the frequency with which the *Cahiers* sound the theme of the good king and the bad ministers, a typical feature of the 'absolutist' notion of monarchy.

It is true that whenever the *Cahiers,* especially at *bailliage* level, show any 'learning' at all, they speak of 'the nation' in order to demand the restoration or the securing of its rights. But in so doing they by no means reject the notion of citizen representation. On the contrary, they base their demand on the old idea that there is a set of original rights predating the monarchy itself; in adapting the ingredients of a 'Germanist' historiography or notions of 'natural' equality to a modern theory of powers, they simultaneously transformed the structure of the Estates General into a representative system. That alchemy, which becomes visible in the ambiguity of the word 'constitution', did not yet involve the notions of popular will and direct democracy that were to be held by the revolutionary clubs. It laid the groundwork for the delegation of powers, but did not inaugurate the symbolic reign of the popular will as the substitute for society.

Thus, the *Cahiers* were well in the mainstream of the old power structure: the king consulted his people, and all the communities that composed it, indeed made it a people—responded. However, that consultation involved an election, which was not part of the traditional scenario. For, unlike in 1614, when the 'natural' delegates of the various communities, such as aldermen, were simply appointed, it gave rise to political competition, a clear sign that in addition to or beyond what was stated 'unanimously' in the *Cahiers,* there was power to be had and people willing to fight for it. It was precisely during that battle that revolutionary ideology came into being and assumed the function of sorting men into different categories, which the elaboration of grievances had failed to do.

Two conditions were thus necessary for the birth of revolutionary

---

[16]Officials representing the king in the provinces.

ideology. The first was the availability of power, which, having been vacated by the traditional authorities, was there for ideology to take over. That situation is denied by the *Cahiers,* which were imprisoned in what one might call their outmoded channels of communication with the monarchy, so that these thousands of texts speak with a voice that is genuine in every outward detail, yet hides the new political configuration. But for the Revolution to gain strength as an idea, it also needed the chance to appropriate for its own benefit the interpretation of what was meant by the 'people's will.' That chance came with the balloting of 1789, which provided only for a unanimous outcome, although it was set up as a true election. The future deputies therefore had no choice but to recast absolute power for their own benefit.

That is why revolutionary ideology was born not in the *Cahiers* but in the battles of the election itself: although seemingly marginal, they were in fact vitally important for excluding certain persons in relation to the people's will. Robespierre became Robespierre only when he had to win his seat as deputy for the Third Estate from Arras. It was then that the young conformist invented the discourse of equality. Similarly, what brought national attention to *Qu'est-ce que le Tiers État?*[17] and a seat in the Third Estate of Paris to the *vicaire général* of Chartres was the fact that his famous pamphlet was both a discourse on exclusion and a discourse on origins. Sieyès's theory was that the nobility was not part of the national will, and he ostracised the order as a whole, setting it up as the enemy of the common weal and announcing the dawning of an age of a science of society and happiness for all:

> In the dark ages of barbarism and feudalism it was possible to destroy true relations among men, to sow disorder in every nation, and to corrupt all justice; but now that daylight is rising, all Gothic absurdities must flee, all remnants of ancient ferocity must crumble and die. That much is certain. But will we only exchange one evil for another, or will true social order, in all its beauty, take the place of the old disorder?

After that, it mattered little that Sieyès also developed a theory of representation, since what could be represented was precisely what the citizens had in common, that is, the will to found a nation in opposition to the nobility. With that staggering tautology the new political world was invented.

I have long thought that it might be intellectually useful to date the beginning of the French Revolution to the Assembly of Notables in early 1787, for that chronological transfer has the double advantage of dating the

---

[17] *What Is the Third Estate?*

crisis of traditional authority more precisely and of integrating what has come to be called the 'aristocratic revolution' into the Revolution itself. For the absolute monarchy died, in theory and in practice, in the year when its *intendants* were made to share their responsibilities with elected assemblies in which the Third Estate was given twice as many representatives as in the past. What foundered in the void created by the rapid collapse of the monarchy's authority was not only the 'aristocracy' or the *parlements,* but indeed political society as a whole. And the break that occurred in late 1788 between the *parlements,* which favoured a traditional summoning of the Estates, and the rest of that political society—which already called itself 'the nation'—was, as Cochin already realised, the first of the many schisms that were to divide the revolutionary camp.

In fact, Tocqueville dates what he calls the 'true spirit of the Revolution' from September 1788. He wrote long passages about it, but never put them into a definitive form, and they were published together with his working notes (*L'Ancien Régime,* vol. 2, Book 1, ch. 5). He defines that 'spirit' less exclusively than I do, tracing its various manifestations, such as the abstract search for the perfect constitution to be established once the slate of the past has been wiped clean, or the will to transform 'the very foundation of society' (p. 106). Yet he comes close to the definition I am trying to develop when he characterises the evolution of ideas in late 1788 as follows:

> At first people spoke only of working for a better adjustment in the relations between classes; soon they advanced, ran, rushed toward the idea of pure democracy. In the beginning they quoted and commented Montesquieu; in the end they talked of no one but Rousseau. He became and was to remain the only tutor of the Revolution in its youth (pp. 106–7).

I am not sure that the evolution of ideas was that simple. In order to find out, one would have to be able not only to read but to date all the pamphlets of the period, which are for the most part anonymous and undated. Tocqueville made extensive use of Sieyès's pamphlet, which he considered typical, while I feel that at that date it was prophetic and therefore exceptional. It was no doubt because he wanted to keep to his timetable of radicalisation that Tocqueville saw the *Cahiers* as a corpus of revolutionary texts. But I believe that in fact the current of traditional political ideas (or what I have called the old political sociability) lived on in the *Cahiers* and also in many political pamphlets, even those written after September 1788.

Yet the chronological break of September is important, and Tocqueville's intuition was fundamentally correct. The summoning of the Estates General, the appointment of Necker,[18] the recall of the *parlements,* all in the

---

[18]A Swiss Protestant financier brought in to head the government.

summer of 1788, were so many acts of capitulation by Louis XVI that created a general power vacuum. They touched off a war among the classes who wanted that power, a war that was fought over the modes of representation in the Estates and thus opened up a vast field for the deployment of ideas and social passions. Here was the opening through which the ideology of pure democracy surged in, even though it did not gain full control until the spring of 1789.

If one defines the Revolution as the collective crystallisation of a certain number of cultural traits amounting to a new historical consciousness, the spring of 1789 is indeed the key period. For while power had been available for at least two years, the fact became fully apparent only at this point, with the victorious revolt of the 'Commons' against the king's orders. Until May, the old mode of political sociability, centred on the king of France at the summit of the social order, more or less held up—as the *Cahiers* indicate—for the area of power he had in fact relinquished had not yet been discovered. But all that changed with the events of May, June and July. The victory of the Third Estate over the king, the capitulation of the First and Second Estates, the taking of the Bastille, and the vast popular excitement that preceded and followed it clearly went beyond the framework of the old legitimacy. Thought and speech were liberated, not only from censorship and the police—as, in fact, they had been for some years—but from the internal inhibition created when voluntary consent is given to age-old institutions: the king was no longer the king, the nobility was no longer the nobility, the Church was no longer the Church. Moreover, once the masses had broken in on the stage of history, political education gained a vast new public, whose expectations called for completely new modes of social communication. Speeches, motions and newspapers ceased to be aimed at educated people, and were henceforth submitted to the judgment of the 'people'. The Revolution marks the beginning of a theatre in which language freed from all constraints seeks and finds a public characterised by its volatility. This two-fold shift in the functioning of the symbolic circuit that surrounds and protects power was the outstanding development in the spring of 1789.

That is why, in a sense, everything indeed 'began' here: 1789 opened a period when history was set *adrift,* once it was discovered that the actors in the theatre of the Ancien Régime were mere shadows. The Revolution is the gap that opened up between the language of the *Cahiers* and that of the *Ami du peuple*[19] in the space of only a few months. It must be seen as not so much a set of causes and consequences as the opening of a society to all its possibilities. It invented a type of political discourse and practice by which we have been living ever since.

---

[19]*Friend of the People,* a periodical published by the extremely radical Jean-Paul Marat.

By the spring of 1789, then, it had become clear that power no longer resided in the royal Councils and *bureaux,* from which a steady stream of decisions, regulations and laws had been sent out for so many centuries. All of a sudden power had lost its moorings; it no longer resided in any institution, for those that the Assembly tried its best to reconstruct were bound to be swept away, rebuilt, and destroyed again, like so many sandcastles assaulted by the tide. How could the Ancien-Régime king accept them when everything about them expressed distrust of him and the will to dispossess him? And how, in any event, could so recent a creation, so new a State, rebuilt or rather reconceived on such precarious ground, quickly produce a minimum of consensus? No one believed it, though everyone professed to do so, since everyone was speaking in the name of the people. Nor did anyone have the power to create that consensus, even among those who might be called the 'men of 1789', and who were in agreement about the society and the kind of political régime they wanted. There was an essential instability inherent in revolutionary politics, as a consequence of which the periodic professions of faith concerning the 'stabilisation' of the Revolution unfailingly led to renewed bursts of revolutionary activity.

Leaders and factions spent their time wanting to 'stop' the Revolution, always for their own benefit, at a time that suited them, and in opposition to others. Mounier and the *monarchiens,* spokesmen for a kind of French Whiggism, did so as early as August 1789. Mirabeau and Lafayette pursued the same aim throughout 1790, simultaneously, but each for his own ends. Finally, the Barnave-Duport-Lameth triumvirate was the last to rally, after Varennes,[20] to the moderate politics of a constitutional monarchy. But each of these successive rallyings took place only after its leaders had taken the Revolution a step further in order to keep control of the mass move-ment and to discredit rival factions. Unable to attain the first objective, the moderates succeeded so well in the second that the weapon soon turned against them and against 'moderatism' of any kind. Thus, even during the apparently 'institutional' phase of the Revolution, when France had a rather widely accepted Constitution, every leader—from Lafayette to Robespierre—and every group took the risk of extending the Revolution in order to eliminate all competitors instead of uniting with them to build new national institutions. That seemingly suicidal behaviour was due to excep-tional circumstances, which explain the blind determination of the pro-tagonists. The *Constituants* of 1789, unlike those of 1848, were not primar-ily interested in bringing the Revolution to a 'close'. But then 1848 had its eyes riveted on 1789. There was no precedent for 1789. The politicians of

---

[20]In late June of 1791 Louis XVI tried to flee the country but was discovered and arrested in the town of Varennes, very near the northeastern border of France.

that time had, as Mirabeau put it, 'far-reaching ideas'; but when it came to political action they had to improvise.

The reason is that they were caught up in a new system of action that severely constrained them. The characteristic feature of the Revolution was a situation in which power was perceived by everyone as vacant, as having become intellectually and practically available. In the old society exactly the opposite had been the case: power was occupied for all eternity by the king; it could not become available except at the price of an act that would be both heretical and criminal. Moreover, power had owned society, and decided what its goals should be. Yet now it had not only become available, it had become the property of society, which was called upon to take it over and subject it to its own laws. Since power was held responsible for all the ills of the Ancien Régime and considered the locus of arbitrariness and despotism, revolutionary society exorcised the curse that weighed upon it by reconsecrating it in a manner that was the very opposite of that of the Ancien Régime: henceforth it was the people that was power. But by the same token society forced itself to keep that equation alive through opinion alone. Language was substituted for power, for it was the sole guarantee that power would belong only to the people, that is, to nobody. Moreover, language—unlike power, which is afflicted with the disease of secrecy—is public, and hence directly subject to scrutiny by the people.

Democratic sociability, which had characterised one of the two systems of political relations coexisting in the eighteenth century, because, like two parallel lines, they could never meet, now took over the sphere of power. But it did so only with what it was able to produce, that is, the ordinarily soft and pliable thing we call opinion. In those special circumstances, however, that material suddenly became the object of the most meticulous attention, the core, indeed the stake, of the entire political struggle. Once it had become power, opinion had to be at one with the people; language must no longer serve to hide intrigues but reflect values as in a mirror. In the frenzied collective preoccupation with power that henceforth shaped the political battles of the Revolution, representation was ruled out or perpetually put under surveillance; as Rousseau had stated, the people cannot, by definition, alienate its rights to particular interests, for that would mean the instant loss of its freedom. Legitimacy (and victory) therefore belonged to those who symbolically embodied the people's will and were able to monopolise the appeal to it. It is the inevitable paradox of direct democracy that it replaces electoral representation with a system of abstract equivalences in which the people's will always coincides with power and in which political action is exactly identical with its legitimacy.

If the Revolution thus experienced, in its political practices, the theoretical contradictions of democracy, it was because it ushered in a world where mental representations of power governed all actions, and where a network of signs completely dominated political life. Politics was a matter of establishing just *who* represented the people, or equality, or the nation: victory was in the hands of those who were capable of occupying and keeping that symbolic position. The history of the Revolution between 1789 and 1794, in its period of development, can therefore be seen as the rapid drift from a compromise with the principle of representation toward the unconditional triumph of rule by opinion. It was a logical evolution, considering that the Revolution had from the outset made power out of opinion.

Most histories of the Revolution fail to assess the implications of that transformation; yet none of the leaders who successively dominated the revolutionary scene wielded power in the normal sense, by giving orders to an army of underlings and commanding a machinery set up to implement laws and regulations. Indeed, the régime set up between 1789 and 1791 made every effort to keep the members of the Assembly away from executive power, and even to protect them from any such contamination. The suspicion of ministerial ambitions under which Mirabeau had to labour until the very end and the parliamentary debate about the incompatibility between the functions of representative and minister are telling illustrations of that attitude. It was related to more than political circumstance and the Assembly's distrust of Louis XVI. It was inherent in a specific idea of power, for the Revolution held that executive power was by its very nature corrupt and corrupting, being separate from the people, out of touch with it and hence without legitimacy.

In actual fact, however, that ideological disqualification simply led to a *displacement of power.* Since the people alone had the right to govern—or at least, when it could not do so, to reassert public authority continually—power was in the hands of those who spoke for the people. Therefore, not only did that power reside in the word, for the word, being public, was the means of unmasking forces that hoped to remain hidden and were thus nefarious; but also power was always at stake in the conflict between words, for power could only be appropriated through them, and so they had to compete for the conquest of that evanescent yet primordial entity, the people's will. The Revolution replaced the conflict of interests for power with a competition of discourses for the appropriation of legitimacy. Its leaders' 'job' was not to act; they were there to interpret action. The French Revolution was the set of new practices that added a new layer of symbolic meanings to politics.

Hence the spoken word, which occupied centre stage, was constantly under suspicion, for it was by nature ambiguous. It strove for power yet denounced the corruption power inevitably entailed. It continued to obey the Machiavellian rationality of politics yet identified only with the ends to be achieved: that contradiction lay at the very root of democracy, from which it was inseparable, but the Revolution brought it to the highest degree of intensity, as if in a laboratory experiment. One only has to read Mirabeau's *Correspondance secrète* to realise the extent to which revolutionary politics, when its protagonists had failed to assimilate its tenets like a credo, were conducted in a *two-fold language*. In offering his services to the king, Mirabeau did not become a traitor to his ideas; as his friend La Marck, who acted as his confidant and go-between with the king, put it: 'He takes payment, but he believes in the advice he gives.' In his secret notes to Louis XVI Mirabeau defends the same political aims as in his public speeches in the Assembly: a popular and national monarchy rallied to the Revolution, acting on behalf of the nation against the privileged *corps* of the Ancien Régime and all the stronger as it is henceforth called upon to reign only over individuals. But while his aims are stated clearly enough in his secret notes, they can only be glimpsed between the lines of his speeches, because in the Assembly, where his adversaries were watching his every move, where the gallery was looking on, and where he addressed himself to 'opinion', an entity that was nowhere and yet already everywhere, he had to speak the language of revolutionary consensus, in which power had dissolved itself in the people. That language had its specialists and experts, those who produced it and so became the custodians of its legitimacy and its meaning: the militant revolutionaries of the *sections* and the clubs.

Revolutionary activity *par excellence* was the production of a maximalist language through the intermediary of unanimous assemblies mythically endowed with the general will. In that respect, the history of the Revolution is marked throughout by a fundamental dichotomy. The deputies made laws in the name of the people, whom they were presumed to *represent*; but the members of the *sections* and of the clubs acted as the *embodiment* of the people, as vigilant sentinels, duty-bound to track down and denounce any discrepancy between action and values and to reinstate the body politic at every moment. As regards domestic politics, the salient feature of the period between May–June 1789 and 9 Thermidor 1794[21] was not the conflict between Revolution and counter-revolution, but the struggle between the representatives of the successive Assemblies and the club militants for the dominant symbolic position, the people's will.

Thus, each successive political group pursued the same objective: to radicalise the Revolution, by making it consistent with its discourse. The pursuit of that aim was the decisive factor in every political struggle, and through it the purest form of that discourse was eventually brought to power. Robespierrist metaphysics was therefore not a parenthesis in the history of the Revolution, but a type of public authority that the revolutionary phenomenon alone made possible and logical. Starting out as the site of

---

[21]The day of the overthrow of the Jacobin government.

power struggles, a way of differentiating political groups and of integrating the masses into the new State, ideology became, for a few months, coextensive with government itself. Hence debate lost its *raison d'être,* for there was no longer any gap to be filled between the idea and power, nor any room for politics except in consensus or death.

In that sense, the victory of the Thermidorians closed off one of the directions of the Revolution, namely, the objective that had shaped France's entire political life between 1789 and 1794, and thanks to which the ideology of pure democracy, having become the real power of the Revolution, ended up as the only true government the Revolution ever had. When the men who brought down Robespierre attempted to restore the legitimacy of representative government—which they themselves were unable to respect— they rediscovered the independence and the inertia of society, the need for political trade-offs, and the compromises demanded by the interplay of means and ends. They did more than stop the Terror; they discredited it as a type of power and dissociated it from the people's will. Like reformed drinkers, they occasionally resorted to it, in particular after 18 Fructidor,[22] but they did so shamefacedly and as an expedient rather than on principle.

---

[22]A *coup d'état* when three members of the executive expelled two of their colleagues and attempted to persecute many conservative deputies. The coup was designed to quash royalist resurgence.

PART TWO

The Causes of
the French Revolution

The revival of intellectual history of the French Revolution has centered on the search for intellectual origins. The volume of writings on this subject has outpaced any effort at synthesis, leaving many specialists in French history still groping to integrate these materials.

In order to indicate some of the contours of this explosion, this volume presents four very significant articles that are also reasonably representative of the efforts in this field. The authors of these four essays, like many others in this area, have tackled diverse subjects, and little overlap occurs among the objects of their attention. Robert Darnton concentrates on the struggling, radicalized authors in Paris on the eve of the Revolution. Focusing on a single intellectual, abbé Mably, Keith Baker examines a treatise from the 1750s that explored the possibility of a revolution. In the article included in this volume, Dale Van Kley dissects the battle between church, king, and judiciary during the second half of the eighteenth century. From this clash emerged strong attacks upon and defenses of monarchy. Finally, Jeremy Popkin scrutinizes journalists and pamphleteers in the last twenty years of the Old Regime whose writings certainly undercut the absolutist understanding of ideas and events.

Despite this panoply of interests, these scholarly essays collectively advance knowledge of the eighteenth-century background of the French Revolution. Before these studies appeared, scholars investigating intellectual life usually saw it as dominated by Enlightenment thinkers, especially the most famous, such as Diderot, Voltaire, and Montesquieu. Many historians of the Revolution, though, simply ignored the subject. What Darnton, Baker, Van Kley, Popkin, and others have accomplished is to suggest forcefully that a large number of other intellectuals existed well outside the Enlightenment mainstream. Familiar with the Enlightenment, these thinkers developed other views more strongly. These eighteenth-century writers created a language of contestation, whose essential points were clearly at odds with the ideological underpinnings of the Old Regime.

However, the general agreement on the important role played by intellectuals in the prerevolutionary ferment should not obscure significant differences among the historians. Darnton concentrates on social and economic discontent that drove writers to formulate subversive ideas; the other three historians emphasize the importance of a series of political events that began in the 1750s. Darnton's emphasis on social causes may, in part, reflect the intellectual climate in which he wrote it. This article, published several years before the other pieces, when social explanations still held absolute sway, not surprisingly emphasizes those sorts of factors.

The articles also disagree about the relationship between the ideas they outline and the Revolution. To be sure, they all wish at the least to imply a connection between the concepts they find and the revolutionary climax. Nonetheless, they differ on this subject substantively and theoretically. Darnton argues that his disaffected and radicalized writers quickly joined the Revolution in 1789 and were able to inject their views directly into the debate. Seizing the available opportunity, they applied their beliefs once in power in 1793. Darnton alludes only fleetingly and tentatively as to how, or if, these beliefs garnered converts among the public and thus contributed to the rise of the radicals. What role then would such ideas have played in the French Revolution? First, the Revolution got well underway without them. Second, because Darnton explains only the significance they had for their creators, the content of these ideas may not have much to do later in the Revolution with popular thought or popular support for the radicals. These ideas certainly influenced the few, but their influence may have been felt only after the radicals captured the instruments of power and could impose these beliefs on others.

Baker and Van Kley are more expansive, although still somewhat measured, about the power of ideology in the Revolution. Their articles uncover a group of beliefs that became revolutionary. Baker asserts, however, that a full understanding of how these ideas succeeded must await both a complete reconstruction of prerevolutionary political concepts and also of the methods contemporaries used to select among these ideas. Implicit here is a conviction, it would seem, that contemporaries chose by consulting their own social, political, and economic needs. Therefore, such an approach indicates that this scholar retains a reasonably significant role for ideas and for circumstances. Although people in a particular context select among ideas, the ideologies available to them constitute the range of choice and thus possess an important part in precipitating the Revolution. In Baker's more recent investigations, he generally keeps open in theory a place for political and social factors, but, increasingly, he finds that ideological developments govern. Van Kley does not explain here the acceptance of the ideas that he charts, but his later research indicates that he shares Baker's general approach.

Popkin goes far beyond the other three, because he argues that in the press of the 1770s and 1780s the revolutionary understanding of events had already come into existence. In his account the Revolution seems to confirm only a reality earlier outlined in the periodicals. For Popkin, language is all important, because it defines a revolution even before any individual has consciously accepted it. People are trapped in a web of ideas.

These differing conceptions of the role of ideas in the Revolution loosely relate to the theoretical perspectives commonly held by historians. Darnton's concentration on the framers of ideas situates him somewhat closer to traditional intellectual historians who have been mainly concerned with the intentions of authors. Baker and Van Kley care about language and seem to link the success of a "discourse" or point of view to social and political circumstances. They would balance between those who believe that language provides a veneer over social realities and those who ascribe great power to ideas. Their interest in the impact of ideology over time also links them to traditional intellectual historians who commonly connect future ideas to past beliefs. Finally, Popkin joins many modern critics in elevating language above other means of behavior.

The diversity and shared directions in these four articles represent much—but not all—of the aspects of the study of the intellectual origins of the French Revolution. Omitted here are a growing number of studies, especially by French scholars, of the ideas of various social classes. Among the most important of these—to list just a few—are Michel Vovelle's study of popular religiosity,[1] Jean Quéniart's evaluation of the books owned by various strata of society,[2] and Roger Chartier's examination of the politics of the peasants.[3] Unfortunately, most all these studies of the general ideas throughout society make no reference to the sort of studies presented in this volume. And the reverse is equally the case with a few notable exceptions.[4] Scholars rarely examine what the populace understood of political concerns. They are only slightly more likely to comprehend how the elite adjusted to general ideas. Intellectual historians ought to place this problem on their agenda.

---

[1]Michel Vovelle, *Piété baroque et déchristianisation en Provence au XVIIIe siècle* (Paris, 1978).

[2]Jean Quéniart, *Culture et société urbaine dans la France de l'ouest au XVIIIe siècle* (Rennes, 1978), 2 vols.

[3]Roger Chartier, "Culture populaire et culture politique dans l'Ancien Régime: Quelques réflexions," in Keith Michael Baker, ed., *The Political Culture of the Old Regime* (Oxford, 1987), pp. 243-58.

[4]Dale K. Van Kley, *The Damiens Affair and the Unraveling of the Ancien Regime, 1750-1770* (Princeton, 1984), pp. 13-55; Pierre Rétat, ed., *L'Attentat de Damiens: Discours sur l'événement au XVIIIe siècle* (Lyons, 1979).

The High Enlightenment and the Low-Life of Literature in Pre-Revolutionary France*

Robert Darnton

The revitalization of the intellectual history of the French Revolution owes much to the article presented here by Robert Darnton. At the time of its initial publication early in the 1970s, it introduced an utterly new cast of characters little known even to scholars. Additionally, it revealed primary sources rarely used before. The verve and imaginativeness it showed soon made this piece a classic and rendered many of its categories standard in other historical writings.

Darnton begins with a description of how, by the late eighteenth-century, patronage had made the Enlightenment, once challenging to the Old Regime, dependent on it. This relationship tamed and domesticated thinkers, producing little excitement. Late arrivals found most benefits taken and their way to success blocked. Imbued with the enlightenment belief that merit would yield rewards, they became indignant at their indifferent reception. Frustration, reinforced by their inability to earn a living, led them to a "Grub-Street" existence and to the development of a powerful indictment of the aristocracy. In a nutshell, they came to write and believe that the top layer of French society was rotten and was destroying the society.[1] Not formulated clearly or precisely, these ideas still generated a revolutionary point of view that the writers adopted when opportunity knocked in 1789. Indeed, such beliefs served them well and remained the core of their ideology right into the heart of the Revolution. As Jacobins, they could trace the origins of their beliefs to their Grub Street existence.

*World Copyright: The Past and Present Society, 175 Banbury Road, Oxford, England. This article is here reprinted in abridged form with the permission of the Society and the author, from *Past and Present: a journal of historical studies,* no. 51 (May 1971), pp. 81-115.

[1]Robert Darnton has continued to flesh out his picture of Grub Street. An important addition gives statistical information to explain the typicality of the situation he describes. See Robert Darnton, "The Facts of Literary Life in Eighteenth-Century France," in Keith Michael Baker, ed., *The Political Culture of the Old Regime* (Oxford, 1987), pp. 261-91.

The importance of this argument has generated a number of criticisms. Although Darnton accepts that some of his subjects did not embrace Jacobinism, he basically links Grub Street to radicalism. Some scholars have found many exceptions. In addition, the next three articles suggest another revision. Written years after Darnton's article, they emphasize the role of judicial critics of the monarch, who are nowhere to be found on Grub Street. Perhaps, this newer scholarship would encourage Darnton to revise his interpretation of the radicalism of Grub Street to include political strife as well as Enlightenment ideology.

Where does so much mad agitation come from? From a crowd of minor clerks and lawyers, from unknown writers, starving scribblers, who go about rabble-rousing in clubs and cafés. These are the hotbeds that have forged the weapons with which the masses are armed today.

P. J. B. Gerbier, June 1789

The nation's rewards must be meted out to those who are worthy of them; and after having repulsed despotism's vile courtiers, we must look for merit dwelling in basements and in seventh-story garrets. . . . True genius is almost always sans-culotte.

Henri Grégoire, August 1793

The summit view of eighteenth-century intellectual history has been described so often and so well that it might be useful to strike out in a new direction, to try to get to the bottom of the Enlightenment, and even to penetrate into its underworld, where the Enlightenment may be examined as the Revolution has been studied recently—from below.

Digging downward in intellectual history calls for new methods and new materials, for grubbing in archives instead of contemplating philosophical treatises. As an example of the dirt that such digging can turn up, consider the following letter from a bookseller in Poitiers to his supplier in Switzerland: "Here is a short list of philosophical books that I want. Please send the invoice in advance: *Venus in the Cloister or the Nun in a Nightgown, Christianity unveiled, Memoirs of Mme la marquise de Pompadour, Inquiry on the Origin of Oriental Despotism, The System of Nature, Theresa the Philosopher, Margot the Campfollower.* " Here, couched in the idiom of the eighteenth-century book trade, is a notion of the philosophical that was shared by men who made it their business to know what Frenchmen wanted to read. If one measures it against the view of the philosophic movement that has been passed on piously from textbook to textbook, one cannot avoid feeling uncomfortable: most of those titles are completely unfamiliar, and they suggest that a lot of trash somehow got mixed up in the eighteenth-century idea of philosophy. Perhaps the Enlightenment was a more down-to-earth affair than the rarefied climate of opinion described by textbook writers, and we should question the overly highbrow, overly metaphysical view of intellectual life in the eighteenth century. One way to bring the Enlightenment down to earth is to see it from the viewpoint of eighteenth-century authors. After all, they were men of flesh and blood, who wanted to fill their bellies, house their families, and make their way in the world. Of course, the study of authors does not solve all the problems connected with the study of ideas, but it does suggest the nature of their social context, and it can draw enough from conventional literary history for one to hazard a few hypotheses.

A favorite hypothesis in histories of literature is the rise in the writer's status throughout the eighteenth century. By the time of the High Enlightenment, during the last twenty-five years of the Old Regime, the prestige of French authors had risen to such an extent that a visiting Englishman described them exactly as Voltaire had described English men of letters during the early Enlightenment: "Authors have a kind of nobility." Voltaire's own career testifies to the transformation of values among the upper orders of French society. The same milieux who had applauded the drubbing administered to him by Rohan's[2] toughs in 1726 cheered him like a god during his triumphal tour of Paris in 1778. Voltaire himself used his apotheosis to advance the cause of his "class"—the men of letters united by common values, interests, and enemies into a new career group or "estate." The last twenty years of his correspondence read like a continuous campaign to proselytize for his "church," as he called it, and to protect the "brothers" and the "faithful" composing it. How many youths in the late eighteenth century must have dreamt of joining the initiates, of lecturing monarchs, rescuing outraged innocence, and ruling the republic of letters from the Académie Française or a château like Ferney.[3] To become a Voltaire or d'Alembert, that was the sort of glory to tempt young men on the make. But how did one make it as a philosophe?[4]

Consider the career of Jean-Baptiste-Antoine Suard, a typical philosophe of the High Enlightenment. Others—Marmontel, Morellet, La Harpe, Thomas, Arnaud, Delille, Chamfort, Roucher, Garat, Target, Maury, Dorat, Cubières, Rulhière, Cailhava—might do just as well. The advantage of Suard's case is that it was written up by his wife. A philosophe's rise to the top is indeed revealing when seen from his wife's viewpoint, and especially when, as in the case of Mme. Suard, the wife had an eye for domestic detail and the importance of balancing the family accounts.

---

[2]After an argument, Chevalier de Rohan sent his minions to beat up Voltaire.
[3]Voltaire's home.
[4]An intellectual associated with the Enlightenment.

Suard left the provinces at the age of twenty and arrived in Paris just in time to participate in the excitement over the *Encyclopédie*[5] in the 1750s. He had three assets: good looks, good manners, and a Parisian uncle, as well as letters of introduction to friends of friends. His contacts kept him going for a few months while he learned enough English to support himself as a translator. Then he met and captivated the Abbé Raynal, who functioned as a sort of recruiting agent for the sociocultural elite known as *le monde.* Raynal got Suard jobs tutoring the well-born, encouraged him to write little essays on the heroes of the day—Voltaire, Montesquieu, Buffon—and guided him through the salons. Suard competed for the essay prizes offered by provincial academies. He published literary snippets in the *Mercure*[6]; and having passed at Mme. Geoffrin's, he began to make frequent appearances in *le monde* —a phrase that recurs with the regularity of a leitmotif in all descriptions of Suard. With doors opening for him in the salons of d'Holbach, Mme. d'Houdetot, Mlle. de Lespinasse, Mme. Necker, and Mme. Saurin, Suard walked into a job at the *Gazette de France:* lodging, heating, lighting, and 2,500 livres a year for putting polish on the materials provided every week by the ministry of foreign affairs.

At this point Suard took his first unorthodox step: he got married. Philosophes did not generally marry. The great figures of the early Enlightenment—Fontenelle, Duclos, Voltaire, d'Alembert—remained bachelors; or, if they fell into matrimony, as in the case of Diderot and Rousseau, it was with someone of their own station—shop girls and servants. But the elevated status of the philosophe in Suard's time made marriage conceivable. Suard picked a girl of good bourgeois stock like himself; overcame the objections of her brother, the publisher Panckoucke, and of Mme. Geoffrin, who held old-fashioned ideas about the incompatibility of professional writing and family life; and set up house in the apartment that went with his job on the *Gazette de France.* Mme. Suard trimmed her wardrobe to fit their tight budget. Friends like the Prince de Beauvau and the Marquis de Chastellux sent them game from the hunts every week. And princely patrons like Mme. de Marchais sent carriages to carry the couple off to dinners, where the bride marveled at "the rank and the merit of the guests." This was something new: Madame Philosophe had not accompanied her husband on his forays into *le monde* before. Mme. Suard followed her husband everywhere and even began to form a salon of her own, at first a modest supper for literary friends. The friends and patrons responded so enthusiastically that something of a cult grew up around the *petit ménage,* as it was known from a poem celebrating it by Saurin. Formerly a fringe

---

[5]A published compendium of information whose contributors are mainly associated with the Enlightenment.

[6]A literary journal.

character picked up for amusement by the salons and readily turned out into the street for drubbings, begging, and *embastillement*,[7] the philosophe was becoming respectable, domesticated, and assimilated into that most conservative of institutions, the family.

Having made it into *le monde,* Suard began to make money. By taking over the entire administration of the *Gazette de France,* he and his collaborator, the Abbé Arnaud, boosted their income from 2,500 to 10,000 livres apiece. They succeeded by appealing over the head of a bureaucrat in the ministry of foreign affairs, who was "astonished that men of letters shouldn't consider themselves rich enough with 2,500 livres of revenue," to the foreign minister, the Duc de Choiseul, whose sister, the Duchesse de Grammont, was an intimate of the Princesse de Beauvau, who was a friend of the Suards and of Mme. de Tessé, who was the protector of Arnaud. Such obliging noblesse was vulnerable to the vagaries of court politics, however, and when d'Aiguillon replaced Choiseul, the Suards were turned out of their *Gazette* apartment. Once again *le monde* rallied to the defense of its *petit ménage.* Suard received a compensatory pension of 2,500 livres from d'Aiguillon, who was persuaded by Mme. de Maurepas, who was moved by the Duc de Nivernais, who was touched by the sight of Mme. Suard weeping in the Académie Française and by the prodding of d'Alembert and La Harpe. Then a gift of 800 livres in *rentes perpétuelles* arrived from the Neckers. The Suards rented a house in the rue Louis-le-Grand. Suard managed to get the lucrative post of literary correspondent to the Margrave of Bayreuth. His friends arranged a pension for him of 1,200 livres on the income from the *Almanach Royal.* He sold his collection of English books to the Duc de Coigny for 12,000 livres and bought a country house. He became a royal censor. Election to the Académie Française came next, bringing an income of up to 900 livres in *jetons* (doubled in 1786) and far more in indirect benefits, such as a position as censor of all plays and spectacles, worth 2,400 livres and later 3,700 livres a year. When the *Journal de Paris* was suspended for printing an irreverent verse about a foreign princess, the keeper of the seals called in Suard, who agreed to purge all future copy and to share the profits: another 1,200 livres. "He took a cabriolet, which transported him after he fulfilled the duties of his posts, to the lovely house he had given to me," Mme. Suard reminisced. They had reached the top, enjoying an income of 10,000, perhaps over 20,000, livres a year and all the delights of the Old Regime in its last days. The Suards had arrived.

The most striking aspect of the Suard success story is its dependence on "protection"—not the old court variety of patronage, but a new kind, which involved knowing the right people, pulling the right strings, and

---

[7]To be consigned to prison, the Bastille.

"cultivating," as it was known in the eighteenth century. Older, established writers, wealthy bourgeois, and nobles all participated in this process of co-opting young men with the right style, the perfect pitch of bon ton, into the salons, academies, privileged journals, and honorific posts. The missing element was the market: Suard lived on sinecures and pensions, not on sales of books. In fact, he wrote little and had little to say—nothing, it need hardly be added, that would offend the regime. He toed the party line of the philosophes and collected his reward.

But how many rewards of that kind were there, and how typical was Suard's *cas typique?* Part of the answer to those questions lies in a box in the Archives Nationales containing a list of 147 "Men of Letters Who Request Pensions" and ten dossiers crammed with material on writers and their sources of support. The list reads like a "Who's Who" of the literary world drawn up by officials in the Contrôle général to guide Calonne,[8] who had decided in 1785 to increase and systematize the award of literary pensions, *gratifications,* and *traitements.* Calonne was also guided by a committee composed of Lenoir, the former lieutenant general of police, Vidaud de Latour, the director of the book trade, and two courtier-academicians, the Maréchal de Beauvau and the Duc de Nivernais. Hardly a revolutionary group. The pension list, with the recommendations of Calonne's officials and his own notes scrawled in the margins, gives a corresponding impression. It shows a strong bias in favor of established writers, especially academicians. Here Morellet appears with his 6,000 livres a year from the Caisse de Commerce; Marmontel with 3,000 livres as *historiographe de France* and 2,000 livres as perpetual secretary of the Académie Française. La Harpe complains of receiving a mere 600 livres from the *Mercure,* the Maréchal de Beauvau pushes to get him pensioned for 1,500, and the pension is granted, despite a subordinate official's observation that La Harpe also collects 3,000 livres for lecturing in the Lycée. And so the list goes, one figure of the High Enlightenment succeeding another: Chamfort (granted 2,000 livres in addition to 1,200 on the *maison du roi*[9]), Saint-Lambert (requested 1,053 livres, decision delayed), Bernardin de Saint-Pierre (1,000 livres), Cailhava (1,000 livres), Keralio, Garat, Piis, Cubières, Des Essarts, Aubert, and Lemierre.

Blin de Sainmore, a solid citizen in the republic of letters' lesser ranks, exemplified the qualities required for getting a pension. He was a royal censor, *historiographe de l'Ordre du Saint-Esprit,* and protégé of the Princesse de Rochefort. "I will further add, Monseigneur, that I am the head of a family, that I was born without fortune, and that I have nothing for the support and education of my family except the post of historiogra-

---

[8]Controller-general of finance and chief minister of Louis XVI, 1783 to 1787.
[9]King's household account.

pher of the king's orders, whose income is barely sufficient for me alone to live in a decent style." Thus the pensions went for charity as well as good works. Saurin's widow applied because his death had left her destitute, since he had lived entirely from "the beneficence of the government." And Mme. Saurin specified:

Pension of the Académie Française	2,000
Pension on the General Farms[10]	3,000
As the son of a converted [Protestant] minister	800
As a censor	400
On an office of *trésorier du pavé de Paris*[11]	2,400
Total	8,600

This beneficence generally went to serious, deserving writers but not to anyone unconnected with *le monde.* Academicians were first on the government's list—to such an extent that one ministerial aide jotted in a margin, "There is some danger that the title of academician might become a synonym for pensioner of the King." Ducis demanded 1,000 livres a year for life on the grounds that "most of our confrères, either of the Académie Française or the Académie des Inscriptions, have obtained pensions that have the character of a permanent grace." This favoritism offended Caraccioli, who wrote testily,

> I am pretentious enough to believe that you will have heard of my works, all of which have religion and sound morality as their object. I have been writing in this genre for thirty-five years; and despite the frivolity of the century, [my works] have spread everywhere and have been translated into various languages. Nevertheless, under ministers who preceded you and who made me the most beautiful promises, I never obtained anything, although living in a modest state that might well be called indigence. And I have seen *gratifications* as well as pensions pour down.

As Caraccioli's comments suggest, "sound" opinions were considered a necessary qualification for a pension. In some cases the government subsidized writers who had produced propaganda for it. It looked favorably on the Abbé Soulavie, because "he has submitted some manuscripts on financial matters to M. le Contrôleur Général." Conversely, the government avoided making payments to anyone whose loyalties were in doubt. It turned down J.-C.-N. Dumont de Sainte-Croix, a minor author on jurisprudence, because, according to the marginal note next to his name, "All

---

[10]A taxing area for the collection of certain customs duties.
[11]Treasurer of the roadway of Paris.

the new systems of this genre would merit some encouragement, if they were made only to be known by the government and not by the public, which is incited to rebel against the established laws instead of becoming enlightened as to the means of making them better." Then, in another hand: "Nothing." Rivarol also received nothing, but only because he already had a secret pension of 4,000 livres: "He is very clever, and an encouragement, which could be paid to him each year, if he remains faithful to sound principles, would be a way of preventing him from following his inclination toward those which are dangerous."

So several considerations determined the state's patronage. As in the case of modern institutions like the French Centre National de la Recherche Scientifique, the monarchy supported serious savants, perhaps even with the intention of recruiting a fresh intellectual elite. It also dispensed charity. And it used its funds to encourage writing that would make the regime look good. In each instance, however, it restricted its subsidies to men with some standing in the world of letters. A few fringe characters like Delisle de Sales, Mercier, and Carra presumed to apply for the pensions; but they received nothing. Lenoir later revealed that he and his colleagues had turned down Carra, Gorsas, and Fabre d'Eglantine because "the academicians described them as the excrement of literature." While the literary rabble held out its hands to the government, the government gave its handouts to writers situated safely within *le monde.*

It dispensed them on a large scale. A note by a subordinate official put the total payments at 256,300 livres per year, to which 83,153 livres were added in 1786. But that sum represented only the direct dole from the royal treasuries. Far more money flowed into the purses of "sound" writers from the appointments at the government's disposal. Journals, for example, provided an important source of income for the privileged few in the literal sense of the word. Royal privileges reserved certain subjects for the quasi-official periodicals like the *Mercure, Gazette de France,* and *Journal des savants,* which exploited their monopolies without worrying about competitors (the government permitted some discreet foreign journals to circulate, provided they passed the censorship and paid compensation to a privileged journal) and turned over part of the take to writers named by the government. In 1762 the *Mercure* paid out 30,400 livres to twenty subluminaries of the High Enlightenment. Then there were many sinecures. Not only did the king require an official historiographer, he also subsidized *historiographes de la marine, des bâtiments royaux, des menus-plaisirs,* and *de l'Ordre du Saint-Esprit.*[12] The branches of the royal family were loaded with readers, secretaries, and librarians—more or less honorific posts that one had to work

---

[12]Historiographers of the navy, the royal buildings, the common diversions, and the Order of the Holy Spirit.

for but not *at,* that one acquired by waiting in antechambers, improvising eulogies, cultivating acquaintances in salons, and knowing the right people. Of course it always helped to be a member of the Académie Française.

The dozens of volumes about the history and *petite histoire* of the academy in the eighteenth century, whether written in love or in hatred, reveal a dominant theme: the Enlightenment's successful campaign to win over the French elite. After the *chasse aux Pompignans*[13] of 1760, the election of Marmontel in 1763, and d'Alembert's elevation to the perpetual secretaryship in 1772, the academy fell to the philosophes. It became a sort of clubhouse for them, an ideal forum for launching attacks against *l'infâme,*[14] proclaiming the advent of reason, and co-opting new philosophes as fast as the old-guard academicians would die off. This last function, virtually a monopoly of the philosophic salons, assured that only party men would make it to the top. And so Voltaire's church was besieged by converts. The spectacle of a new generation taking up the torch warmed the old man's heart. When he congratulated Suard on his election, Voltaire exulted, "Voilà, God be thanked, a new career assured . . . At last I see the real fruits of philosophy, and I begin to believe that I shall die content." Thus Suard and his circle, the high priests of the High Enlightenment, took over the summit of the literary world, while the mid-century philosophes declined and died. The new men included both writers like Thomas, Marmontel, Gaillard, La Harpe, Delille, Arnaud, Lemierre, Chamfort, and Rulhière, and philosophically minded *grands,* powerful courtiers and clergymen, like the Marquis de Chastellux; the Maréchal de Duras; Boisgelin, Archbishop of Aix; and Loménie de Brienne, Archbishop of Sens.

The fusion of *gens de lettres*[15] and *grands* had been a favorite theme of philosophic writing since the mid-century. Duclos had proclaimed it triumphantly in his *Considérations sur les moeurs de ce siècle*[16] (1750). Writing had become a new "profession," which conferred a distinguished "estate" upon men of great talent but modest birth, he explained. Such writers became integrated into a society of courtiers and wealthy patrons, and everyone benefited from the process: the *gens du monde* gained amusement and instruction, and the *gens de lettres* acquired polish and standing. It went without saying that promotion into high society produced some commitment to the social hierarchy. Duclos had a keen eye for all the subtleties of status and rank; and although he took pride in the man of

---

[13]In 1760 the bishop Lefranc de Pompignan was elected to the Académie Française. In his first speech he attacked the Enlightenment. The response was extremely critical, and public opinion harassed and embarrassed him.

[14]Religious intolerence.

[15]Men of letters.

[16]*Considerations on the Morals of this Century.*

letter's ability to rise by sheer talent, he showed equal respect for what made a man of *le monde:* "One is an *homme du monde* by birth and by position."

Voltaire, the archapologist for *le mondain,*[17] shared the same attitudes. His article entitled "Gens de lettres" in the *Encyclopédie* emphasized that in the eighteenth century "the spirit of the age made them [men of letters] for the most part as suitable for *le monde* as for the study. They were kept out of society until the time of Balzac and Voiture. Since then they have become a necessary part of it." And his article "Goût"[18] in the *Dictionnaire philosophique* revealed the elitist bias in his conception of culture: "Taste is like philosophy. It belongs to a very small number of privileged souls . . . It is unknown in bourgeois families, where one is constantly occupied with the care of one's fortune." Voltaire— who incessantly cultivated courtiers, tried to become one himself, and at least managed to buy his way into the nobility—thought that the Enlightenment should begin with the *grands:* once it had captured society's commanding heights, it could concern itself with the masses—but it should take care to prevent them from learning to read.

D'Alembert believed in essentially the same strategy, but he did not share his "master's" taste for the court. His *Essai sur les gens de lettres et les grands* (1752), published two years before his election to the Académie Française, amounted to a declaration of independence for writers and writing as a proud new profession (not in the present sociological sense of the term, but as it was used by Duclos). Yet despite some strong language advocating a "democratic" republic of letters in contrast to the humiliating practices of patronage, d'Alembert stressed that society was and ought to be hierarchical and that the *grands* belonged on top. By the time he wrote his *Histoire des membres de l'Académie française* (1787), when he ruled the academy as Duclos's successor in the perpetual secretaryship, d'Alembert reformulated Duclos's theme in a conservative vein. He castigated the "horde of literary rebels" (*frondeurs littéraires*) for venting their frustrated ambitions in attacks on the academy. He defended the academy's mixture of *grands seigneurs* and writers. And he emphasized the role of courtiers, as experts in the realm of taste and language, in a very elitist Enlightenment —a process of gradual, downward diffusion of knowledge, in which the principle of social equality could play no part.

> Is a great effort of philosophy necessary to understand that in society, and especially in a large state, it is indispensable to have rank defined by clear distinctions, that if virtue and talent alone have a claim to our true homage,

---

[17]The worldly.
[18]Taste.

the superiority of birth and position commands our deference and our respect . . . ? And how could men of letters envy or misconstrue the so legitimate prerogatives of other estates?

As spokesmen for the writer's new estate (but not for the brand of philosophe represented by Diderot and d'Holbach), Duclos, Voltaire, and d'Alembert urged their "brethren" to profit from the mobility available to them in order to join the elite. Rather than challenge the social order, they offered a prop to it.

But what was the meaning of this process? Was the establishment becoming enlightened or the Enlightenment established? Probably both, although it might be best to avoid the overworked term "establishment" and to fall back on the eighteenth-century expression already cited, *le monde.* After fighting for their principles in the mid-century and consolidating their victories during the last years of Louis XV's reign, the great philosophes faced the problem that has plagued every victorious ideology: they needed to find acolytes worthy of the cause among the next generation. Admittedly, "generation" is a vague concept. Perhaps there are no real generations but only demographic "classes." Still, the great philosophes form a fairly neat demographic unit: Montesquieu 1689-1755, Voltaire 1694-1778; and then Buffon 1707-1788, Mably 1709-1785, Rousseau 1712-1778, Diderot 1713-1784, Condillac 1715-1780, and d'Alembert 1717-1783. Contemporaries were naturally struck by the deaths, not the births, of great men. Voltaire, Rousseau, Diderot, Condillac, d'Alembert, and Mably all died between 1778 and 1785; and their deaths left important places to be filled by younger men, who were born, for the most part, in the 1720s and 1730s.

As age overcame them, the great philosophes made the rounds of the salons, searching for successors. They tried to find another d'Alembert— and came up with Marmontel, the champion of *Gluckisme.*[19] They tried to persuade themselves that Thomas could thunder like Diderot and La Harpe bite like Voltaire. But it was no use. With the death of the old Bolsheviks, the Enlightenment passed into the hands of nonentities like Suard: it lost its fire and became a mere tranquil diffusion of light, a comfortable ascent toward progress. The transition from the heroic to the High Enlightenment domesticated the movement, integrating it with *le monde* and bathing it in the *douceur de vivre*[20] of the Old Regime's dying years. As Mme. Suard remarked after reporting the receipt of their last pension, "I have no more events to recount, other than the continuation of a soft and varied life, until that horrible and disastrous epoch [the Revolu-

---

[19]Composer Christopher Willibald Gluck (1714-1787) who employed Enlightenment ideals in his music.

[20]Sweetness of life.

tion]." Her husband, turned censor, refused to approve Beaumarchais's not so very revolutionary play, *Le Mariage de Figaro*. And Beaumarchais put most of his energy into speculation, and ultimately into building the biggest townhouse in Paris—"a house that is talked about"—the arriviste's dream.

The establishment of the Enlightenment did not blunt its radical edge, however, because just as a generation gap separated the high philosophes from their predecessors, a generation split cut them off from the low-life of literature, from their contemporaries who failed to make it to the top and fell back into Grub Street.

Perhaps the literary world has always divided into a hierarchy whose extremes might be labeled a *monde* of mandarins on the one hand and Grub Street on the other. Such milieux existed in the seventeenth century and exist today. But the social and economic conditions of the High Enlightenment opened up an unusual gulf between the two groups during the last twenty-five years of the Old Regime, and this split, if examined in depth, ought to reveal something about one of the standard questions posed by the prerevolutionary era: what was the relation between the Enlightenment and the Revolution?

At first glance, it seems that the writer's lot should have improved substantially by the reign of Louis XVI. The relevant data, flimsy as they are, all point in the same direction: a considerable expansion in demand for the printed word. Literacy probably doubled in the course of the century, and the general upward swing of the economy, combined with improvements in the educational system, very likely produced a larger, wealthier, and more leisured reading public. Certainly book production soared, whether measured by demands for privileges and *permissions tacites* or indirectly by the number of censors, booksellers, and printers. But there is little evidence that writers benefited from any publishing boom. On the contrary, everything indicates that while the mandarins fattened themselves on pensions, most authors sank into a sort of literary proletariat.

Admittedly, information about the growth of Grub Street comes from anecdotal sources, not statistics. Mallet du Pan claimed that three hundred writers, including a heavy dose of hacks, applied for Calonne's pensions, and he concluded, "Paris is full of young men who take a little facility to be talent, of clerks, accountants, lawyers, soldiers, who make themselves into authors, die of hunger, even beg, and turn out pamphlets." Crébillon fils, who reportedly gave out *permissions de police* for 40,000–50,000 verses of pamphlet poetry every year, was besieged by a "multitude of versifiers and would-be authors" who flooded into Paris from the provinces. Mercier found these "famished scribblers," "these poor hacks" (*écrivailleurs affamés, ces pauvres barbouilleurs*) everywhere, and Voltaire constantly hammered at the theme of the "ragged rabble" (*peuple crotté*) crowding the bottom of the literary world. He placed "the miserable species that writes for a living"—the "dregs of humanity," "the riff-raff of literature" (*lie du genre humain, canaille de la littérature*)—at a social level below prostitutes. Writing in the same spirit, Rivarol and Champcenetz published a mock census of the undiscovered Voltaires and d'Alemberts crammed into the garrets and gutters of Paris. They produced articles on well over five hundred of these poor hacks, who scribbled for a while in obscurity, and then vanished like their dreams of glory, except for a few: Carra, Gorsas, Mercier, Restif de la Bretonne, Manuel, Desmoulins, Collot d'Herbois, and Fabre d'Eglantine. The names of those future revolutionaries look strange in Rivarol's roll-call of "the five or six hundred poets" lost in the legions of "la basse littérature," but Rivarol put them rightly in their place.

That place was Grub Street, and its population, combustible at any time, was exploding during the last twenty-five years of the Old Regime. Of course the interpretation may be only a demographic fantasy based on subjective literary sources, but the sources seem suggestive enough to warrant giving the fantasy rein. They continually stress the theme of the provincial lad who reads some Voltaire, burns with the ambition to become a philosophe, and leaves home only to smolder helplessly and expire down and out in Paris. Even Duclos worried about this corollary to his formula for success. And Voltaire, obsessed by the overpopulation of young writers in Paris ("Egypt of old had fewer locusts"), claimed that he attacked Grub Street in order to warn youth away from it. "The number of those who are lost as a result of this passion [for the "career of letters"] is prodigious. They render themselves incapable of any useful work ... They live off rhymes and hopes and die in destitution." Voltaire's attacks wounded Mercier, who rose to the defense of the "poor devils" in opposition to the pampered, pensioned darlings of the academies and salons. Mercier protested that the "poor" of the "low literature" (*basse littérature*) in the Faubourg Saint-Germain had more talent and integrity than the "rich" in the "high literature" (*haute littérature*) of the Faubourg Saint-Honoré. But even he concluded pessimistically, "Ah! keep away from this career you who do not want to know poverty and humiliation." Linguet, another anti-voltairean, devoted a whole book to the same theme. A constant target of would-be authors in search of a protector, he had reason to lament that "secondary schools have become a seedbed of child authors, who hurriedly scribble tragedies, novels, histories, and works of all sorts" and then "spend the rest of their lives in destitution and despair."

The provincials flocked to Paris in search of glory, money, and the improved estate that seemed promised to any writer with sufficient talent. They did not necessarily share the motivations of the early philosophes, who were often nobles and clergymen enjoying enough leisure to write when the spirit moved them and who wrote before the time when "literature became a *métier,*[21] as Meister distastefully observed. J. J. Garnier, a writer with a highly developed sense of professionalism, noted that by 1764 many men of letters were moved by "the hope of gaining reputation, influence, wealth etc. The avenues of advancement having been closed to them because of their humble birth and modest fortunes, they observed that the career of letters, open to everyone, offered another outlet for their ambition." Mercier agreed that the immigrant from the provinces could hope to shake off his humble origins and climb to the top in Paris. But the top of Paris, the *tout Paris,* had little room for ambitious young men on the make, perhaps because, as sociologists claim, rising status groups tend to become exclusive; perhaps because of a literary version of the Malthusian crush; perhaps because France suffered from a common ailment of developing countries: a surplus population of overeducated and underemployed littérateurs and lawyers. In any case, it seems that the attractiveness of the new career celebrated by Duclos and the new church proclaimed by Voltaire resulted in a record crop of potential philosophes, far more than could be absorbed under the archaic system of protections. Of course the lack of statistics and the confusion of social categories in prerevolutionary France (how does one define a "man of letters"?—someone with a literary reputation, someone who has published a book, or someone who lives by his pen?) make these hypotheses unverifiable. But there is no need for a complete census of eighteenth-century writers in order to make sense of the tension between the men of Grub Street and the men of *le monde* on the eve of the Revolution. The facts of literary life at that time speak for themselves.

The most salient fact is that the marketplace could not support many more writers than in the days when Prévost and Le Sage proved that it was possible—barely possible—to live from the pen instead of pensions. Although publishers offered somewhat better terms than earlier in the century, authors were caught between the masters of the publishing-bookselling guilds, who paid little for manuscripts, and pirate publishers, who paid nothing at all. None of the great mid-century philosophes relied much on sales except for Diderot, who never fully extricated himself from Grub Street. Mercier claimed that in his day only thirty hard-core "professionals" supported themselves by writing. The open, "democratic" market that could feed large numbers of enterprising authors did not appear in France until well into the nineteenth century. Before the day of the steam press and the mass reading public, writers lived by the kind of scavenging along the road to riches that worked so well for Suard—or they dropped by the wayside, in the gutter.

Once he had fallen into Grub Street, the provincial youth who had

---

[21]Job.

dreamt of storming Parnassus never extricated himself. As Mercier put it, "He falls and weeps at the foot of an invincible barrier. . . . Forced to renounce the glory for which he so long has sighed, he stops and shudders before the door that closes the career to him." The nephews and grand-nephews of Rameau really faced a double barrier, both social and economic; for after Grub Street had left its mark on them, they could not penetrate into polite society where the plums were passed around. So they cursed the closed world of culture. They survived by doing the dirty work of society—spying for the police and peddling pornography; and they filled their writings with imprecations against the *monde* that humiliated and corrupted them. The prerevolutionary works of men like Marat, Brissot, and Carra do not express some vague, "anti-Establishment" feeling; they seethe with hatred of the literary "aristocrats" who had taken over the egalitarian "republic of letters" and made it into a "despotism." It was in the depths of the intellectual underworld that these men became revolutionaries and that the Jacobinical determination to wipe out the aristocracy of the mind was born.

To explain why Grub Street had no exit and why its prisoners felt such hatred for the *grands* at the top it is necessary to say a word about the cultural modes of production during the late eighteenth century; and that word is the term one meets everywhere in the Old Regime: privilege. Books themselves bore privileges granted by the grace of the king. Privileged guilds, whose organization showed the hand of Colbert himself, monopo-lized the production and distribution of the printed word. Privileged jour-nals exploited royally granted monopolies. The privileged Comédie Française, Académie Royale de Musique, and Académie Royale de Peinture et de Sculpture legally monopolized the stage, opera, and the plastic arts. The Académie Française restricted literary immortality to forty privileged individuals, while privileged bodies like the Académie des Sciences and the Société Royale de Médecine dominated the world of science. And above all these corps rose the supremely privileged cultural elite who kept *le monde* all to themselves.

It may have been appropriate for a corporate society to organize its culture corporately, but such archaic organization constrained the expansive forces that might have opened up the cultural industries and supported more of the overpopulated underworld of letters. As it was, the bookdealers' guilds acted far more effectively than the police in suppressing unprivileged books, and underprivileged youths like Brissot were forced into destitution, not so much because their early works were radical as because the monopolies prevented them from reaching the market. Writers therefore fed their families either from the pensions and sinecures reserved for the members of *le monde* or from the scraps tossed into Grub Street.

The corporate organization of culture was not simply an economic matter, for it contradicted the basic premises under which the young writers had flocked to Paris in the 1770s and 1780s. They had come with the conviction that the republic of letters really existed as it had been described in the works of the great philosophes—as the literary counterpart to the "atomic" individualism of Physiocratic theory, a society of independent but fraternal individuals, in which the best men won but all derived dignity, as well as a living, from service to the common cause. Experience taught them that the real world of letters functioned like everything else in the Old Regime: individuals got ahead as best they could in a labyrinth of baroque institutions. To have an article published in the *Mercure,* to get a play accepted by the Comédie Française, to steer a book through the Direction de la Librairie,[22] to win membership in an academy, entry into a salon, or a sinecure in the bureaucracy required resorting to the old devices of privilege and protection, not merely the demonstration of talent.

Talent certainly carried some to the top. Maury was the son of a poor cobbler in a village of the Venaissain, Marmontel of a poor tailor in the Limousin, Morellet of a small-time paper merchant of Lyons, Rivarol (who called himself a count) of an innkeeper in Languedoc; La Harpe and Thomas were orphans. All rose through skill and scholarships, and they were not the only examples of rapid upward mobility. But as de Tocqueville observed, it was the erratic opening up of mobility, not the absence of it, that produced social tensions. Nowhere was this general phenomenon more important than in the world of letters, because the attractiveness of writing as a new kind of career produced more writers than could be integrated into *le monde* or supported outside of it. To the outsiders, the whole process looked rotten, and they were not inclined to blame their failures on their own inability: on the contrary, they tended to see themselves as successors to Voltaire. They had knocked on the door of Voltaire's church, and the door remained closed. Not only did their status fail to rise as fast as their expectations; it plummeted, dragging them down to a world of opposites and contradictions, a *monde* turned upside down, where estate could not be defined at all, and dignity dissolved in destitution. Seen from the perspective of Grub Street, the republic of letters was a lie.

If the institutional realities of the established literary world contradicted its principles, at least from the viewpoint of those who failed to reach the top, what were the realities of life for those at the bottom? Grub Street had no principles, and it had no institutions of a formal kind. It was a world of free-floating individuals—not Lockean gentlemen abiding by the rules of some implicit game, but Hobbesian brutes struggling to

---

[22]Bureau of the Book Trade.

survive. It was as far removed from *le monde* as was the café from the salon. Despite the democratic play of wit, the salon remained a rather formal institution. It did not allow any putting of elbows on the table or any admission to those without introductions. During the last decades of the Old Regime, the salon became increasingly a preserve for the high philosophes, who generally abandoned the cafés to the lower species of littérateur. The café functioned as the antithesis of the salon. It was open to everyone, just one step from the street, although there were degrees in its closeness to street life. While the great names gathered in the Procope or La Régence, lesser figures congregated in the notorious Caveau of the Palais-Royal, and the humblest hacks frequented the cafés of the boulevards, blending into an underworld of "swindlers, recruiting agents, spies, and pickpockets; here one finds only pimps, buggers, and *bardaches.*"

Grub Street may have lacked the corporate structure of the established culture, but it was not sheer anarchy. It had institutions of a sort. For example, the *musées* and *lycées* that sprang up in such numbers during the 1780s responded to the needs of obscure writers for a place to exhibit their wares, to declaim their works, and to make contacts. These clubhouses formalized the functions of the cafés. The *musées* of Court de Gébelin and P. C. de La Blancherie seem even to have served as counteracademies and antisalons for the multitude of philosophes who could not get a hearing elsewhere. La Blancherie published a journal, *Les Nouvelles de la République des lettres et des arts,* which vented some of the frustrations of the *musée* members both by sniping at academicians and by reviewing works that were beneath the notice of the *Journal de Paris* and the *Mercure.* But the most effective sniper and the most influential outsider of prerevolutionary France was Simon-Henri Linguet. While respecting the crown and the church, Linguet blasted at France's most prestigious institutions, especially the Parisian bar and the Académie Française. His polemical genius made his pamphlets, judicial *mémoires,* and journals best-sellers; and his tirades against aristocratic and despotic corporateness reverberated up and down Grub Street, setting the tone for some of the antielitist propaganda of the Revolution.

Grub Street therefore had a few organs and organizations to express itself. Perhaps it even had an inchoate stratification system of its own, for the underground contained several levels. Having cultivated an established philosophe or got some verses published in the *Almanach des muses,* some writers lived just below *le monde.* Mirabeau maintained a mandarin style of life even when in prison and in debt. He kept a stable of pamphleteers (who referred to him simply as *le comte*) to produce the works published under his name. Lesser figures put together the encyclopedias, dictionaries, digests, and anthologies that circulated in such profusion in the last half of the eighteenth century. Even cruder hack work could be relatively respectable— writing for ministers, pamphleteering for the *bais-*

siers fighting the *haussiers* on the Bourse,[23] and producing *nouvelles à la main*,[24] or it could be demeaning—manufacturing smut, peddling prohibited works, and spying for the police. Many writers lived on the fringes of the law, calling themselves lawyers or law clerks and taking on the odd jobs available in the *basoche*[25] of the Palais de Justice. Some, at the bottom of the literary underworld, sank into criminality. Charles Théveneau de Morande, one of Grub Street's most violent and virulent pamphleteers, lived in a demimonde of prostitutes, pimps, blackmailers, pickpockets, swindlers, and murderers. He tried his hand at more than one of these professions and gathered material for his pamphlets by skimming the scum around him. As a result, his works smeared everything, good and bad alike, with a spirit of such total depravity and alienation that Voltaire cried out in horror, "There has just appeared one of those satanic works [Morande's *Gazetier cuirassé*[26]] where everyone from the monarch to the last citizen is insulted with furor; where the most atrocious and most absurd calumny spreads a horrible poison on everything one respects and loves."

Grub Street stifled respect and love. Its grim struggle for survival brought out baser sentiments, as is suggested by the following excerpts from reports submitted to the Parisian police by its legions of spies and secret agents, many of them underworld writers themselves with their own dossiers in the archives of the police.

GORSAS: proper for all kinds of vile jobs. Run out of Versailles and put in Bicêtre [a jail for especially disreputable criminals] by personal order of the king for having corrupted children whom he had taken in as lodgers, he has withdrawn to a fifth floor on the rue Tictone. Gorsas produces *libelles*. He has an arrangement with an apprentice printer of the Imprimerie Polytype, who has been fired from other printing shops. He [Gorsas] is suspected of having printed obscene works there. He peddles prohibited books.

AUDOUIN: calls himself a lawyer, writes *nouvelles à la main,* peddler of forbidden books; he is connected with Prudhomme, Manuel, and other disreputable authors and book peddlers. He does all kinds of work; he will be a spy when one wants.

DUPORT DU TERTRE: solicits a position in the offices of the police; is a lawyer who is not often employed in the Palais, although he is not without merit. He failed to get a position in the Domaines. He lives in a modest, fourth-story

---

[23]Bears fighting the bulls in the Stock Market.
[24]News sheets.
[25]Community of clerks.
[26]*The Steel-Plated Gazetteer.* The title refers to Morande's hope that his enemies' barbs would simply bounce away.

apartment; he hardly gives off an air of wealth [*il ne respire pas l'opulence*]. He is generally well spoken of; he has a good reputation in his neighborhood.

DELACROIX: lawyer, writer, expelled from the bar. He produces [judicial] *mémoires* for shady cases; and when he has no *mémoires* to write, he writes scurrilous works.

MERCIER: lawyer, a fierce, bizarre man; he neither pleads in court nor consults. He hasn't been admitted to the bar, but he takes the title of lawyer. He has written the *Tableau de Paris,* in four volumes, and other works. Fearing the Bastille, he left the country, then returned and wants to become attached to the police.

MARAT: bold charlatan. M. Vicq d'Azir asks, in the name of the Société Royale de Médecine, that he be run out of Paris. He is from Neuchâtel in Switzerland. Many sick persons have died in his hands, but he has a doctor's degree, which was bought for him.

CHENIER: insolent and violent poet. He lives with Beauménil of the Opéra, who, in the decline of her charms, fell in love with him. He mistreats her and beats her—so much that her neighbors report that he would have killed her had they not come to her rescue. She accuses him of having taken her jewels; she describes him as a man capable of any crime and doesn't hide her regrets at having let herself be bewitched by him.

FRERON: who has neither the wit nor the pen of his father, is generally despised. It is not he who writes the *Année littéraire,* although he has its privilege. He hires young unemployed lawyers. He's an insolent coward, who has received his share of beatings—and doesn't boast about it—most recently from the hand of the actor Desessarts, whom he had called a "ventriloquist" in one of his issues. He is connected with Mouvel, who was expelled from the Comédie for pederasty.

PANIS: young lawyer of the Palais, protected by M. le Président d'Ormesson because of Panis's parents, who are his [d'Ormesson's] *fermiers*[27]; is employed by Fréron on the *Année littéraire.* Panis has as a mistress a woman branded by the hand of the executioner.

Life in Grub Street was hard, and it took a psychological toll, because "the excrement of literature" had to face not merely failure but degradation, and they had to face it alone. Failure breeds loneliness, and the conditions of Grub Street were peculiarly suited to isolate its inhabitants. Ironically, the basic unit of life in *la basse littérature* was the garret (stratification went more by story than by neighborhood in eighteenth-century Paris). In their fourth- and fifth-floor *mansardes,* before Balzac had romanticized their lot, the undiscovered philosophes learned that they were what Voltaire

---

[27]Tenants.

had called them: the *canaille de la littérature.* But how could they come to terms with such knowledge?

Fabre d'Eglantine is a case in point. A drifter and a déclassé who saw himself as the successor of Molière, he went down in the police dossiers as a "poor poet, who drags about in shame and destitution; he is despised everywhere; among men of letters he is considered an execrable subject" (*poète médiocre qui traîne sa honte et sa misère; il est partout honni; il passe parmi les gens de lettres pour un exécrable sujet*). Sometime before the Revolution, Fabre wrote a play that reads like an escapist fantasy of an author trapped in Grub Street. The hero, an unappreciated twenty-eight-year-old genius from the provinces, writes his heart out in a Parisian garret, mocked and exploited by the evil elite that dominates French literature: mercenary publishers, crass journal editors, and the perfidious *beaux-esprits*[28] who monopolize the salons. He is about to succumb to disease and poverty when, by a stroke of good fortune, a virtuous bourgeois tycoon discovers him, appreciates his talent and superior morality, and carries him off to the provinces, where he writes masterpieces happily ever after. The play breathes hatred of the cultural elite and a fierce egalitarianism, which confirms La Harpe's description of the prerevolutionary Fabre as an embittered failure, "envenomed with hatred, like all the persons of his sort, against everyone who called himself an *homme du monde,* against every-thing that had a rank in society—a rank that he did not have and should not have had."

Others probably sought refuge in similar fantasies. Marat dreamed of being whisked away to preside over an academy of sciences in Madrid. Both he and Carra found solace in imagining that they had outstripped Newton, despite society's failure to appreciate them. But no amount of fantasy could erase the contradictions between life at the top and the bottom of the world of letters and between what those at the bottom were and what they wanted to be. The established writers enjoyed an estate; they derived honor and wealth from the established cultural institutions. But the literary proletariat had no social location. Its ragged pamphleteers could not call themselves men of letters; they were just *canaille,* condemned to gutters and garrets, working in isolation, poverty, and degradation, and therefore easy prey to the psychology of failure—a vicious combination of hatred of the system and hatred of the self.

The Grub Street mentality made itself heard with exceptional vehe-mence during the last years of the Old Regime. It spoke through the *libelle,* the hack writers' staff of life, their meat, their favorite genre and a genre that deserves to be rescued from the neglect of historians, because it communicates the Grub Street view of the world: a spectacle of knaves

---

[28]Dandies.

and fools buying and selling one another and forever falling victim to *les grands*. The *grand monde* was the real target of the *libelles*. They slandered the court, the church, the aristocracy, the academies, the salons, everything elevated and respectable, including the monarchy itself, with a scurrility that is difficult to imagine today, although it has had a long career in underground literature. For pamphleteers had lived by libel since the time of Aretino. They had exploited all the great crises in French history, in the propaganda produced by the Catholic League during the religious wars, for example, and in the *Mazarinades* of the Fronde.[29] But the ultimate crisis of the Old Regime gave them an unusual opportunity, and they rose to the occasion with what seems to have been their greatest barrage of antisocial smut.

Although a survey of *libelles* published between 1770 and 1789 cannot be undertaken here, it should be possible to capture some of their flavor by explicating one of their texts. Perhaps the most outspoken *libelle*—a pamphlet so sensational and so widely read that it became virtually a prototype of the genre—was the work that especially horrified Voltaire: *Le Gazetier cuirassé* by Charles Théveneau de Morande. Morande mixed specific calumny and general declamation in brief, punchy paragraphs, which anticipated the style of gossip columnists in the modern yellow press. He promised to reveal "behind-the-scenes secrets" (*secrets des coulisses*) in the tradition of the *chronique scandaleuse*. But he provided more than scandal:

> The devout wife of a certain Maréchal de France (who suffers from an imaginary lung disease), finding a husband of that species too delicate, considers it her religious duty to spare him and so condemns herself to the crude caresses of her butler, who would still be a lackey if he hadn't proven himself so robust.

This sexual sensationalism conveyed a social message: the aristocracy had degenerated to the point of being unable to reproduce itself; the great nobles were either impotent or deviant; their wives were forced to seek satisfaction from their servants, representatives of the more virile lower classes; and everywhere among *les grands* incest and venereal disease had extinguished the last sparks of humanity. Vivid detail communicated the message more effectively than abstractions; for although the reader might at first merely be shocked by a particular incident,

> The Count of Noail——, having taken some scandalous liberties with one of his lackeys, this country bumpkin knocked over Monseigneur with a slap that kept his lordship in bed for eight days. . . . The lackey . . . is a Picard of the first

---

[29] A vast number of pamphlets attacking the prime minister of France who held that office from 1643 to 1661. The Fronde was a period of great political turmoil, which most accounts date from 1648 to 1652.

order who had not yet been instructed how to serve a Spanish grandee, Knight of the Royal Orders, Lieutenant General, Governor of Vers——, Prince of P——, Lord of Arpa——, Grand Cross of Malta, Knight of the Golden Fleece, and secular member of the Society of Jesus, etc., etc., etc., etc.

he would know what to conclude after he had recovered from the shock. Morande led the reader toward general conclusions by piling up anecdotes and slanting them in the same direction—against *le monde*. He showed that the summit of society had decayed beyond the point of recovery, both morally and physically:

> The public is warned that an epidemic disease is raging among the girls of the Opera, that it has begun to reach the ladies of the court, and that it has even been communicated to their lackeys. This disease elongates the face, destroys the complexion, reduces the weight, and causes horrible ravages where it becomes situated. There are ladies without teeth, others without eyebrows, and some completely paralyzed.

Morande's chronicle of cuckoldry, buggery, incest, and impotence in high places therefore reads as an indictment of the social order. And Morande did not merely leave the reader with a general impression of corruption. He associated the aristocracy's decadence with its inability to fulfill its functions in the army, the church, and the state.

> Of approximately two hundred colonels in the infantry, cavalry, and dragoons in France, one hundred and eighty know how to dance and to sing little songs; about the same number wear lace and red heels; at least half can read and sign their names; and in addition not four of them know the first elements of their craft.

> As the king's confessor was disgraced for having been discovered flirting with some pages, there is now open competition for that position, which will go to the prelate who will be easiest on the king's conscience. The Archbishop of R—— has been proposed but rejected, because of the scandalous relations he has maintained for such a long time with one of his grand vicars. The cardinals of Gèv—— and of Luy—— were designated to serve by alternate semesters; but since the first doesn't know how to read and the second hasn't recovered from being slapped [a reference to a scandal involving homosexuality], one can't be sure of His Majesty's decision.

Morande constantly stressed the connection between sexual and political corruption by news flashes like the following: "Having a pretty wife of whom he was very jealous, the unfortunate Baron of Vaxen was sent to prison by a *lettre de cachet*[30] in order to learn the customs of *le monde*, while the duke [La Vrillière, one of Louis XV's favorite ministers] sleeps

---

[30]A royal order to imprison an individual, which could be issued without submitting the case to a law court.

with his wife." The monarchy had degenerated into despotism, this message stood out on every page: the ministers have hired an extra team of secretaries just to sign *lettres de cachet;* the Bastille and Vincennes are so overcrowded that tents have been set up inside their walls to house the guards; a new elite police corps, modeled on Louis XIV's dragonades, has been created to terrorize the provinces; the government is experimenting with a new machine that can hang ten men at a time; and the public executioner has resigned, not because he is worried about automation, but because the new Maupeou ministry offends his sense of justice. In case any reader could possibly miss the point, Morande stated it explicitly: "According to Chancellor Maupeou, a monarchical state is a state where the prince has the right of life and death over all his subjects, where he is proprietor of all the wealth in the kingdom, where honor and equity are founded on arbitrary principles, which must always conform with the interests of the sovereign."

What was the king's place in this political system? "The chancellor and the Duke d'Aiguillon have come to dominate the king so much that they leave him only the liberty of sleeping with his mistress, petting his dogs, and signing marriage contracts." Deriding the idea of a divine origin to royal sovereignty, Morande reduced the king to the level of the ignorant, crapulous court. He made Louis XV look ridiculous, a trivial figure even in his despotism: "A notice has been published in the hopes of finding the scepter of one of the greatest kings of Europe. After a very long search, it was found in the *toilette* of a pretty woman called a countess, who uses it for playing with her cat." The real rulers of France and the villains of the book were the Countess DuBarry and the ministerial triumvirate of Maupeou, Terray, and d'Aiguillon. Seizing on Mme. DuBarry as a symbol of the regime, Morande dwelt on every detail about her that he could fabricate or extract from café gossip: her supposedly illegitimate birth to a servant girl who had been seduced by a monk, her career as a common whore, her use of the king's power to help her former colleagues by forbidding the police to set foot in brothels, her lesbianic relations with her maid, and so on. Similarly, Morande showed that the ministers used their authority to fatten their purses, procure mistresses, or simply enjoy villainy for its own sake.

Grotesque, inaccurate, and simplistic as it was, this version of political news should not be dismissed as merely mythical, because myth making and unmaking proved to be powerful forces in the last years of a regime, which, though absolutist in theory, had become increasingly vulnerable in practice to the vagaries of public opinion. To be sure, the eighteenth-century French "public" did not exist in any coherent form; and insofar as it did exist, it was excluded from direct participation in politics. But its exclusion produced a political naiveté that made it all the more vulnerable to Morande's style of gazeteering. For instead of discussing issues, the *Gazetier cuirassé* defamed individuals. He buried Maupeou's reforms— probably the regime's last chance to survive by destroying some of the vested interests that were devouring it—in a torrent of mudslinging. That the Maupeou program would have benefited the common people did not matter to Morande, because he and his fellow hacks had no interest in reform. They hated the system in itself; and they expressed their hatred by desanctifying its symbols, destroying the myths that gave it legitimacy in the eyes of the public, and perpetrating the countermyth of degenerate despotism.

Far from being limited to Morande's works, these themes became increasingly important in *libelle* literature as the Old Regime approached its finale. *Le Gazetier cuirassé* merely set the tone for an outpouring of antigovernment pamphlets that extended from the "Maupeouana" of the early 1770s to the "Calonniana" of the late 1780s. The most prolific producer of the latter was Jean-Louis Carra, an outcast from the closed circles of established science, who stated frankly that his efforts to damn the ministry had been provoked by the refusal of one of Calonne's pensions. Morande's motives had not been nobler. He meant to make money, both by exploiting the market for sensationalism and by blackmailing the persons he libeled.

Did slander on such a scale, its crass motivation notwithstanding, amount to a call for revolution? Not really, because the *libelles* lacked a program. They not only failed to give the reader any idea of what sort of society should replace the Old Regime; they hardly contained any abstract ideas at all. In denouncing despotism, Morande cried out for liberty; and in fulminating against aristocratic decadence, he seemed to advocate bourgeois standards of decency, if only by contrast. But he did not defend any clear set of principles. He referred to himself as *le philosophe cynique* and slandered everything, even the philosophes. The same spirit animated most other *libelles*; it was a spirit of nihilism rather than of ideological commitment.

Yet the *libelles* showed a curious tendency to moralize, even in their pornography. The climax of one of Morande's obscene pamphlets about courtiers and courtesans came in an indignant description of Mme. DuBarry:

> passing directly from the brothel to the throne, toppling the most powerful and redoubtable minister, overthrowing the constitution of the monarchy, insulting the royal family, the presumptive heir to the throne, and his august consort by her incredible luxury, by her insolent talk, [and insulting] the entire nation, which is dying of hunger, by her vainglorious extravagance and by the well-known depredations of all the *roués*[31] surrounding her, as she sees groveling at her feet not only the *grands* of the kingdom and the ministers, but the princes of the royal blood, foreign ambassadors, and the church itself, which canonizes her scandals and her debauchery.

---

[31]Dissolute people.

This tone of moral outrage was typical of the *libelles* and seems to have been more than a rhetorical pose. It expressed a feeling of total contempt for a totally corrupt elite. So if the *libelles* lacked a coherent ideology, they communicated a revolutionary point of view: they showed that social rot was consuming French society, eating its way downward from the top. And their pornographic details got the point across to a public that could not assimilate the *Social Contract* and that soon would be reading *Le Père Duchesne.*[32]

This gutter Rousseauism—a natural idiom for the *Rousseau du ruisseau*[33] —may have been related to Rousseau's rejection of the culture and morality of France's upper classes. For the men of Grub Street saw Jean-Jacques as one of their own. In following his career, they could not only imagine the realization of their hopes but also find consolation for their failures. *Débourgeoisé* like such typical *libellistes* as Brissot and Manuel, Rousseau had risen from their ranks into *le monde,* seen it for what it was, exposed elitist culture itself as the very agent of social corruption, and returned with his semiliterate, working-class wife to a humble existence in the neighborhood of Grub Street, where he died pure and purged. The hacks respected him and despised Voltaire—Voltaire the *mondain,* who had stigmatized Rousseau as a "poor devil" and who died in the same year, in the bosom of *le monde.*

Is it surprising then that the writers whom Voltaire scorned as *la canaille de la littérature* should have moralized in the manner of Rousseau in their politico-pornography? To them the Old Regime was obscene. In making them its spies and smut-peddlers, it had violated their moral core and desecrated their youthful visions of serving humanity honorably in Voltaire's church. So they became rank atheists and poured out their souls in blasphemies about the society that had driven them down into an underworld of criminals and deviants. The scatology of their pamphlets— their frequent references, for example, to venereal disease passed on from the Cardinal de Rohan to the queen and all the great figures of the court during the Diamond Necklace Affair[34]—communicates a sense of total opposition to an elite so corrupt as to deserve annihilation. No wonder that the government kept secret files on the *libellistes* and consigned the *libelles* to the bottom of its graduated scale of illegality, or that the very catalogues of them circulated secretly, in handwritten notes, like the list of "philosophical books" quoted above. The *libellistes* spoke for a subintelligentsia that was

---

[32]A very radical newspaper of the French Revolution.

[33]*Ruisseau,* pronounced similarly to Rousseau, means gutter, creating a play on words.

[34]In this scandal, the Cardinal de Rohan was arrested for using the Queen's name to procure a very expensive necklace without paying for it.

not merely unintegrated but beyond the pale and that wanted not to reform society in some polite, liberal, Voltairean way, but to overturn it.

There is a danger of using the word "revolutionary" too liberally and of exaggerating the ideological distance between the top and the bottom of the literary world in the Old Regime. The first philosophes were revolutionary in their fashion: they articulated and propagated a value system, or an ideology, that undermined the traditional values Frenchmen inherited from their Catholic and royalist past. The men of Grub Street believed in the message of the philosophes; they wanted nothing more than to become philosophes themselves. It was their attempt to realize this ambition that made them see *philosophie* in a different light and to hold it up to the realities not only of society in general but also of the cultural world. The great philosophes had had a sharp eye for realities also, and their successors of the next generation may have been as realistic as the most hardbitten hacks: nothing suggests that the view from the top is more distorted than the view from the bottom. But the difference in viewpoints was crucial—a difference of perspective not principle, of mentality not philosophy, a difference to be found less in the content of ideas than in their emotional coloring. The emotional thrust of Grub Street literature was revolutionary, although it had no coherent political program nor even any distinctive ideas of its own. Both the philosophes and the *libellistes* were seditious in their own way: in becoming established, the Enlightenment undercut the elite's faith in the legitimacy of the social order; and in attacking the elite, the *libelles* spread disaffection deeper and more widely. Each of the opposing camps deserves its place among the intellectual origins of the Revolution.

Once the Revolution came, the opposition between the high- and low-life of literature had to be resolved. Grub Street rose, overthrew *le monde,* and requisitioned the positions of power and prestige. It was a cultural revolution, which created a new elite and gave them new jobs. While Suard, Marmontel, and Morellet found themselves stripped of their income, Brissot, Carra, Gorsas, Manuel, Mercier, Desmoulins, Prudhomme, Loustalot, Louvet, Hébert, Maret, Marat, and many more of the old literary proletariat led new lives as journalists and bureaucrats. The Revolution turned the cultural world upside down. It destroyed the academies, scattered the salons, retracted the pensions, abolished the privileges, and obliterated the agencies and vested interests that had strangled the book trade before 1789. Newspapers and theaters sprang up at such a rate that one could even speak of an industrial revolution within the cultural revolution. And in destroying the old institutions, the new elite meted out a crude, revolutionary justice: Manuel took over the police department that had once hired him secretly for the suppression of *libelles,* and he published its archives in *libelle* form (carefully purging all references to his and Brissot's careers as police spies); Marat, a victim of academic persecution before the Revolution, led the movement that eventually destroyed the academies; and Fabre and Collot, frustrated actor-playwrights in the Old Regime, struck down the monopoly of the *comédiens du roi* and very nearly struck off their heads. In a sequel to his prerevolutionary census, Rivarol interpreted the Revolution as the work of the status-hungry surplus population of men who had failed to make it in the old order.

Of course the cultural revolution did not fit perfectly into the pattern of Rivarol's counterrevolutionary propaganda any more than it corresponded to Taine's counterrevolutionary history. Many of the old elite, even academicians like Condorcet, Bailly, Chamfort, and La Harpe, did not oppose the destruction of the institutions in which they had prospered. The literary hacks scattered in a dozen directions, supporting different factions in different phases of the conflict. Some of them, particularly during the Girondist period and the Directory, showed that they wanted nothing more than to participate in a revival of *le monde*. And at least during the years 1789–1791, the Revolution realized many of the ideas propagated by the High Enlightenment. But the Revolution at its most revolutionary expressed the antielitist passions of Grub Street. It would be wrong to interpret hatred of mandarins. The Jacobin pamphleteers believed in their propaganda. They wanted to slough off their corrupt old selves and to become new men, newly integrated in a republic of virtue. As cultural revolutionaries, they wanted to destroy "the aristocracy of the mind" in order to create an egalitarian republic of letters in an egalitarian republic. In calling for the abolition of academies, Lanjuinais put their case perfectly: "The academies and all other literary corps must be free and not privileged; to authorize their formation under any kind of protection would be to make them into veritable guilds. Privileged academies are always seedbeds of a literary aristocracy." From there it was but one step to Grégoire's injunction: "We must look for merit dwelling impoverished in basements and in seventh-story garrets. . . . True genius is almost always *sans-culotte.* "[35] Perhaps the propagandists of the garrets functioned as the ideological carriers who injected the crude, Jacobinical version of Rousseauism into the Parisian *sans-culotterie.* Hébert certainly played that role—Hébert, who had rotted in obscurity before the Revolution and, at one point, had tried to persuade the Variétés to perform one of his plays only to get a job checking seat tickets in the *loges.*

It would seem to be necessary, therefore, in looking for the connection between the Enlightenment and the Revolution, to examine the structure of the cultural world under the Old Regime, to descend from the heights of metaphysics and to enter Grub Street. At this low level of analysis, the High Enlightenment looks relatively tame. Voltaire's *Lettres philosophiques*

---

[35]The artisans.

may have exploded like a "bomb" in 1734, but by the time of Voltaire's apotheosis in 1778, France had absorbed the shock. There was nothing shocking at all in the works of his successors, for *they* had been absorbed, fully integrated into *le monde*. Of course one must allow for exceptions like Condorcet, but the Suard generation of philosophes had remarkably little to say. They argued over Gluck and Piccini,[36] dabbled in pre-Romanticism, chanted the old litanies about legal reform and *l'infâme,* and collected their tithes. And while they grew fat in Voltaire's church, the revolutionary spirit passed to the lean and hungry men of Grub Street, to the cultural pariahs who, through poverty and humiliation, produced the Jacobinical version of Rousseauism. The crude pamphleteering of Grub Street was revolutionary in feeling as well as in message. It expressed the passion of men who hated the Old Regime in their guts, who ached with hatred of it. It was from such visceral hatred, not from the refined abstractions of the contented cultural elite, that the extreme Jacobin revolution found its authentic voice.

---

[36]Niccola Piccini (1728–1800), an Italian composer and competitor of Gluck.

A Script for
a French Revolution:
The Political Consciousness of
the Abbé Mably*

Keith Michael Baker

In this article, Keith Baker, one of the leading analysts of eighteenth-century French political thought, focuses upon a work written in reaction to the political events of the late 1750s by the abbé Mably. Extracting what Mably has to say about appropriate political choices, Baker shows how this intellectual mounted a critique of French society. Mably launched his attack, not from a point of view associated with the Enlightenment, but from classical republicanism or, as the English termed it, Commonwealthman ideology. The central tenet of this point of view was that limiting the power of the monarchy and of business preserves liberty. Applied to France, this perspective first required that people act and not fear change. Mably even endorsed revolutions, as long as they were properly prepared. For this to occur, however, Mably posited, the French must mobilize the judiciary who would ultimately invoke traditional forms of representative government. The members of this ancient and reinvigorated body would then restructure the government to further national rights, but would retain the monarchy as a sign of commitment to hierarchy against extremes of equality.

What is so remarkable about Mably's treatise is the way its recommendations actually corresponded to future events. Indeed, just as he suggested, the French in the late 1780s followed his outline of activity. Baker, however, clearly does not wish to maintain that the revolutionaries were so influenced by Mably that they were merely carrying out his commands. In fact, the author posits that only by understanding all the political viewpoints and seeing how contemporaries understood them can we truly comprehend how ideas influenced the Revolution. Baker does, however, wish to use the

Eighteenth Century Studies, no. 14 (1981), pp. 235–40, 243–45, 247–63. Published with permission.

existence of Mably's text to indicate that classical republicanism ought to be included among the competing ideologies.

M y aim in this paper is to draw attention to the political dimensions of Mably's thinking. I do not wish to review his doctrines concerning the nature of man, government and society—that broad range of issues traditionally subsumed under the capacious category of "political thought." I mean rather to argue that he thought about such matters 'politically' in a more direct and strictly defined sense of the term, that he framed an analysis of French government and society in an explicitly political mode for a consciously political purpose.

What do I mean by a specifically political mode of thinking? I mean a representation of the social field that emphasizes will, contingency, choice, participation. In this mode of thinking, social existence—be it orderly or chaotic, just or unjust—is seen as the expression of will, whether exercised unilaterally by a sovereign power (de jure or de facto) or multilaterally by the conflict or concurrence of any number of competing bodies. As a result, social life is thought of as contingent, in that its state at any particular point in time depends upon the exercise of some will (or wills) and can be changed by it. Analytical emphasis is therefore placed upon such categories of action as choice, defined as the exercise of individual or collective will, and participation, defined in terms of the relationship of individual will to public will.

I offer this account of Mably's thinking as an example (but it is only one example) of the political idiom in French discourse about public life at the end of the Old Regime and as an attempt to move toward a fuller characterization of it. To avoid misunderstanding, let me emphasize at the outset that I am not trying here to make a case for Mably's "influence," though it is true that his arguments were frequently cited in the Pre-Revolution and beyond. Instead, I am interested in exploring his work as exemplary of a certain political vocabulary—a vocabulary whose full place in the political discourse of the late Old Regime remains to be determined— rather than responsible for it. Nor am I trying to suggest that Mably saw more clearly than others the objective nature (or real logic) of the prerevolutionary political situation. That would be to reify the situation in a misleading way and to misrepresent his position as an actor within it. In framing his account of social life and his analysis of French institutions, Mably was exercising a conscious, and consciously political, choice. His aim was to create a definition of the situation in which public order in France was perceived not as the expression of tradition or prescription, custom or law, but as the outcome of willful action. If his thinking exemplifies only one of the ways in which the issues in French public life could be (and were) construed, it also suggests the kind of language that could endow the events of 1789 with explosive force by offering a representation of the social order framed in terms of the exercise of political choice and the assertion of revolutionary will.

In the following discussion, I shall concentrate on one of the earliest of Mably's works, *Des droits et des devoirs du citoyen,*[1] apparently written in 1758. I find this a quite remarkable work, for reasons that I hope will become evident in what follows. Indeed, it is hard at first encounter not to credit the suspicion expressed when it was published early in 1789 that the text had been revised by the editors after Mably's death to meet the circumstances of its publication. That suspicion is fed by what appears to be an almost uncanny anticipation of the confrontation of the Pre-Revolution, thirty years before its occurrence. Yet it seems to be belied by the history of the manuscript. The existence of the work was public knowledge at the time of Mably's death in 1785; and the autograph manuscript itself, presented to the National Assembly in 1790 by Mably's executors, apparently bears few alterations. There appear to be no specific references in the text that would demand a later date of composition than 1758 (a date accepted by Mably's modern editors) and many details that would seem redundant if the work had been written much later. It seems clear, then, that Mably's aim was to cast the constitutional conflicts of the 1750s into a dramatically political light; to represent the tensions that divided crown and parlements[2] during that decade as offering a strategy for a revolutionary confrontation; to embed their conflicts into a script for revolutionary action. Historians familiar with the political discourse of the Pre-Revolution must feel uneasy in reading this work: we have accustomed ourselves not to expect such language thirty years before the event. For that reason, it may be all the more useful to read Mably attentively as a way of approaching some of the questions about the ideological origins of the French Revolution that have been largely neglected by historians in recent years.

Des droits et des devoirs du citoyen takes the form of letters reporting a series of discussions between the author and an English visitor as they walk in the gardens of the palace of Marly during the summer of 1758. It is clear from the outset that the visitor, Lord Stanhope, is one of those eighteenth-century Commonwealthmen whose model of political life and civic action was grounded in the experience of the classical republics. In the course of these conversations, he sketches a program for political reform in England that constitutes a repertory of civic humanist themes. Emphasizing the threat to civic virtue and political liberty inherent in the

---

[1] *The Rights and Duties of the Citizen.*
[2] See the glossary entry *parlements.*

growth of finance and commerce, in the increasing power of the executive to corrupt through ministerial patronage, and in the creation of a standing army, he insists on the need to safeguard English liberty by limiting royal prerogative and extending the separation between the legislative and executive powers. Nevertheless, his principal interest in this discussion lies not in England—nor in the other European states in which the classical republicans found the perennial conflict between liberty and despotism being played out—but in the political implications of the constitutional conflicts occurring in France as a result of the protracted disputes over *billets de confession*.[3]

The significance of this conflict for the ideological origins of the French Revolution has yet to be fully explored by modern scholars. But contemporaries were in no doubt as to the importance of this most explosive of issues: the right of ecclesiastical authorities, on the order of the archbishop of Paris, to withhold the sacraments from persons suspected of Jansenism, even when ordered to desist from doing so by the magistrates of the parlement of Paris. As ecclesiastical *mandements*[4] clashed with judicial *arrêts*,[5] royal authority found itself powerless to resolve this dispute by imposing authoritative definitions of the language in which it was conducted, or to end it by enacting and upholding a law of silence. As parlementary defiance and archiepiscopal intransigence were answered by *lettres de cachet*[6] ordering the exile, first of the magistrates, then of the archbishop himself, the issue of ecclesiastical tyranny broadened into that of despotism in church and state. And as parlementary remonstrances couched in an increasingly radical language circulated in unprecedented numbers, as pamphlets issued on all sides, a new category appeared in French political discourse: the category of public opinion. The "tribunal du public" became the court of final appeal, for monarchical authority as for its critics.

Mably's Commonwealthman is well aware of this transformation in French political culture. "I have heard that the practice of publishing the *arrêts* and remonstrances of your parlements, introduced in the course of your recent contestations, has been an occasion for you to think, to reflect, and to instruct yourselves," he remarks to his French companion. "You learn English, you translate our works and appreciate them; some of your writers occupy themselves with politics, and this is proof that this kind of study is no longer a matter of indifference to your nation." The Commonwealthman gives no direct indication of the English works to which he is

---

[3]Literally translated, confessional tickets. These were proofs required before a dying Catholic might receive the last rites. They were initiated to discriminate against Jansenists. For more on Jansenism, see the glossary.

[4]Orders.

[5]Decisions.

[6]Royal orders that could cause an individual to be imprisoned without legal process.

referring, though it may come as no surprise that he praises Locke's *Second Treatise,* French editions of which appeared in 1749, 1754, and 1755.

Nor was this work the most radical of English political writings to find its way into French in the 1750s. Most evidently important for *Des droits et des devoirs du citoyen* were Sidney's *Discourses on Government* (translated in 1702, republished in 1755), upon whose arguments in defense of civil war Mably's Commonwealthman draws freely; and Gordon's discourses on Tacitus (translated in 1742, republished in 1749, and enjoying two editions in 1751), whose keen political anticlericalism he also invokes. These, in turn, were among a number of English works associated with the tradition of classical republicanism which appeared (or reappeared) in French at midcentury.

We turn, then, to the gardens of the palace of Marly, where a dialogue is in progress between an English Commonwealthman and a Frenchman no less receptive than Mably himself to the lessons and implications of classical political experience. In the eyes of the English visitor, the sumptuous gardens of Marly symbolize luxury, corruption, servitude, and (above all) the concomitant despotism that is threatening to infect the whole of Europe. His host replies that these magnificent gardens are at least some consolation for the irretrievable loss of liberty in France: surely good philosophy consists in accepting that consolation and bearing patiently what cannot be changed.

> While you [English] torment yourselves to preserve your liberty, is there not a kind of wisdom to be found in rendering oneself insensible to one's situation when it cannot be changed? We French were once free as you are today in England; we had Estates which never did any good and passed out of fashion with ruffs and farthingales. Our fathers sold, gave away or acquiesced in the destruction of their liberty; we will not recover it by regretting it. The world proceeds by continual revolutions; we have arrived at the point of obedience that you will reach in your turn. We abandon ourselves frankly to the fatality that governs all things human. What use would it be to complain and balk at the yoke? Then we would feel it more; in frightening our master we would make our government more harsh.

Not surprisingly, this halfhearted defense of political lethargy is immediately repudiated by the Commonwealthman, who proceeds to a vigorous refutation of the arguments of continental natural law theorists (adduced by his host) that the citizen is bound to respect the laws of the country in which he finds himself situated. Grotius, Wolff, Pufendorf[7] speak of the profound respect due to the laws, taking care not to remind the reader that if there are just laws suited for our nature, there are also unjust laws "that cannot be obeyed without humiliating humanity and

---

[7]Hugo Grotius (1583-1684), Christian Wolff (1679-1754), and Samuel Pufendorf (1632-1694), all political theorists and philosophers.

preparing the decadence and ruin of the State." Because some form of government diametrically opposed to the nature and goal of society has happened to produce a temporary or apparent good, they contend that it is a marvelous institution whose harmony must not be disturbed. They demonstrate that the law must be blindly obeyed by exaggerating the supposed dangers of examining it, and by invoking the specter of disturbances, anarchy, and civil wars. With such arguments, these writers conspire to "deprive the citizen of his most legitimate rights." It is the Commonwealth's intention, in contrast, to convince his French host that "despotism with its prisons, its gibbets, its pillage, its silent devastation and its imbecile and cruel ineptitudes, is the inevitable result of the principles of your jurisconsults."

The argument begins with the assertion that man is endowed by nature with reason, liberty, and the "invincible desire for happiness." He therefore has the constant right and duty to exercise the former faculties in pursuit of the latter end, by seeking the reform of existing institutions. Thus "a citizen is neither a conspirator nor a disturber of the public peace if he proposes to his fellow citizens a form of politics wiser than that which they have freely adopted, or which events, passions and circumstances have by insensible degrees established." For the Commonwealthman, love of the laws must be an expression of the love of liberty, not a substitute for it; there is no middle ground between liberty and despotism. Under the logic of this argument, his French interlocutor is obliged to admit that the idea of a monarchy grounded in law—whether in the version propounded by the defenders of monarchical absolutism or that invoked by the parlementary magistrates in opposition to it—is nothing but a contradiction in terms:

> ...we have imagined, contrary to the nature of things and for our consolation, a chimerical monarchy, a kind of abstract being, which, according to us, holds the mean between free government and arbitrary power. We say that the prince is sovereign legislator, and this is to recognize him as our master; but in adding that he is obliged to govern in conformity with the laws, we flatter ourselves that we are in fact only obeying the laws and believe that we have set up an impenetrable barrier between despotism and ourselves. All that is, at bottom, completely ridiculous.

This repudiation of the idea of the French monarchy as constituted by law, and of royal power as sustained and/or limited by it, was a central theme in Mably's political thinking. It was reiterated in no less radical terms in his *Observations sur l'histoire de France.* Indeed, the *Observations* must be read as a systematic historical attack on the very existence of a traditional French constitution defined in terms of fundamental laws: this *galimathias*[8] by which the French lulled themselves into thinking that they could distinguish their monarchy from despotism.

Like the narrator of the *Observations sur l'histoire de France,* the Commonwealthman of *Des droits et des devoirs du citoyen* offered a representation of political life in which the fabric of law was dissolved into the exercise of will. Since there was no middle ground between liberty and despotism, no form of government could be defended that was not sustained by the active will of the people. Nor could it be argued on behalf of monarchy that a people was free—as in Denmark—to entrust its happiness irrevocably to the good pleasure of a monarch. No such act could be binding upon a sovereign people, because it would be contrary to the goal of society and inconsistent with the nature of sovereignty. Neither a primitive contract, nor historical prescription, nor tacit consent, could properly be regarded as depriving a people of the exercise of its will.

> The people, in whom sovereign power originally resides; the people, as sole author of political government and distributor of the power entrusted as a whole or in different parts to its magistrates, is thus eternally endowed with the right to interpret its contract, or rather its gifts, to modify the clauses, annul them, and establish a new order of things.

Faced with these arguments, Mably's Frenchman found himself ready to be convinced of the right of a people to transform its government, but equally fearful of the perpetual anarchy this "fatal right" seemed to imply. For the Commonwealthman, however, this French fear of anarchy—implicit in every defense of absolutism since the Wars of Religion—was but another indication of the extent of that nation's political corruption. Just as they never arrive in London without imagining that they have experienced a tempest on the crossing from Calais to Dover, so the French never experience the slightest political disturbance without imagining that they are about to tear themselves apart by civil war. Yet civil war, the Commonwealthman argues in the language of Sidney's *Discourses,*[9] is often the result of a prior failure to establish liberty effectively, rather than of a present attempt to do so. Nor is it necessarily an evil, when it is prompted by love of the *patrie,*[10] respect for the laws, and the legitimate defense of the rights of the nation. The wars between Caesar and Pompey, Octavian and Antony, were evil and stupid: they were the wars between prospective tyrants that marked the agony of an expiring republic destroyed by the corruption of civic virtue. By contrast, the war of the United Provinces

---

[8]Pompous nonsense.

[9]Algernon Sidney (1622-1683) completed *Discourses Concerning Government* toward the end of his life.

[10]Homeland.

against Philip II[11] was the necessary remedy for despotism: if the remedy was harsh, it was no less salutary given the nature of the disease.

> Thus civil war is a good, when society, without the help of this sad operation, would be in danger of perishing from gangrene, and, not to speak metaphorically, would run the risk of dying from despotism.

The Commonwealthman hastens to point out that the French are not yet among those nations that can be reinvigorated by civil war: lacking the knowledge of the rights and duties of the citizen, they would be unable to bring this radical operation to a salutary conclusion. But he has nevertheless convinced his French host that it is only political sleight of hand that enables oppressors to "persuade us that it is in our interest not to disturb the order of their usurpations and injustices; and that civil war, for a people still virtuous enough to be able to profit from it, is yet a greater scourge than the tyranny which threatens it."

Repose, then, is a state to be sought only by despots and their slaves. The benefits produced in Rome by the eternal quarrels between the patricians and the plebeians offer but one illustration of that truth.

> If the people had preferred repose above all, they would soon have been enslaved by the Nobility, and today we would not even know the name of the Romans. On the contrary, their divisions brought the government to the highest degree of perfection by exciting competition among the citizens.

Contestation is at the heart of healthy political life. "There must be movement in the political Body, or it is nothing but a Corpse." Thus every free people must continually affirm its liberty, repairing the insensible damage inflicted upon its constitution, and contesting the minor abuses that accumulate and combine to produce arbitrary power. French absolutism, the Commonwealthman contends, was exactly such a growth, expanding by the accretion of minor infringements into a mass crushing all beneath its weight. "Your clergy, your Nobility, your Third Estate[12] have always said: it is not worth contesting, disputing, resisting so small a matter; and with that admirable prudence, they were gradually weakened and are now nothing."

How, then, can a nation such as France, "accustomed to regarding despotism as the wisest of governments and liberty as an inconvenience," overthrow the yoke and recover its freedom? For Mably's Commonwealthman, the answer to this question is clear. "Choose between a revolution and slavery, there is no middle point." But what did Mably mean by "revolution" in this context? Are we dealing here with a "modern" idea of

---

[11]King of Spain, 1556–1598.
[12]Commoners.

revolution characterized by notions of novelty and new beginnings, by the appeal to violence and the sense of historical inevitability? Or are we dealing with more traditional notions of revolution as the mere succession of events, or as the return to an old constitution that closes a cycle of governments? The answer appears to lie in neither of these characterizations; or, perhaps more precisely, it lies somewhere between them. In *Des droits et des devoirs du citoyen,* the term 'revolution' seems to enjoy several meanings. In the plural, it is used to describe the expression of contingency in human history; the *mutatio rerum*[13] that threatens the stability of human affairs in general; the cycle of fortune that governs all things human. It was to this contingency that the Gauls succumbed when, their ancient spirit corrupted by their fortune and Roman manners, "too ignorant to fear or foresee anything, they allowed themselves to be pushed by events from revolutions to revolutions." In the singular, the term is also used to describe the profound transformation in human nature ("une révolution singulière,") that accompanied the birth of civil society. But Mably employs the term most frequently in this dialogue to characterize the agitations, commotions, disorders, and shocks that are the work of the passions in political life. In a nation (like Turkey) that has been subjected for several generations to the debilitating yoke of despotism, no such revolution can occur: minds are dulled by ignorance, discontent is stifled by fear, energy is sapped by the annihilation of civic status. But wherever this extreme point has yet to be reached, sovereign power is still susceptible to the "shocks" that are "the fruit of the passions of the citizen, the magistrates or the monarch, and the more or less efficacious measures that the government has taken to perpetuate and strengthen its authority." If sovereign power can still extend its grasp, it can also meet new obstacles; its growth can be hindered; it can be shaken and displaced. "Thus I believe revolutions are still possible; a good citizen must therefore hope, and he is obliged, according to his position, his power and his talents, to work to render these revolutions useful to the *patrie.*"

In this sense, a revolution is an outbreak of disorder, a period of agitation, that can be used for various ends. If the nation is enlightened, it will have the opportunity at such a point to advance the cause of liberty; where it is not, "despotism will always profit from revolutions to extend its yoke over the stupid and the ignorant." From this point of view, then, there is a fundamental distinction to be made between revolutions that are fruitful and those that are not. The outcome of any particular case will depend upon the enlightenment and political will of the nation involved.

---

[13]Changes in things.

An ignorant people will in vain experience the most favorable events; it will not know how to profit from anything. In the midst of the movements necessary to make revolutions and produce good effects it will obey fortune instead of directing it and it will merely be weary, bored and tired.

An enlightened and determined nation, on the contrary, will not merely experience revolution as a fact; it will seek to appropriate it as an act. Revolution in this sense is not simply or necessarily a return to former principles of government (though Mably is prepared to discuss such a return as a revolutionary strategy that is usually more compelling than radical attempts at innovation): it is the opportunity, through the exercise of political will, for a nation to assert its inalienable right to "establish a new order of things." Thus the final usage of the term in *Des droits et des devoirs* seems a particularly modern one: "for a number of years *after the revolution,*" Mably's Frenchman argues, the form of government will still contain defects, irregularities and prejudices from the present constitution. But "as soon as our nation, rescued from annihilation, has recovered the right to assemble," it will be able to create regular periodical commissions to perfect the work of liberty, strengthen the political character of the nation, and prevent it from slipping back imperceptibly into its earlier *vomissement*.[14] Only then will the transformation of French politics be complete.

But a revolution that is to produce systematic political change does not simply occur by chance; nor is it the work of a moment. To succeed, it requires the elaboration of a revolutionary strategy and the creation of a revolutionary political consciousness.

Politics, Milord continued, prescribes a certain order in the conduct of peoples who wish to throw off the yoke. All circumstances are not equal for the success of such an enterprise; and if one does not consult them to dare more or less, one will necessarily go wrong. There are moments of fermentation among all peoples, but one must be careful not to be misled by them. Is the movement sudden and occasioned by a passing incident? Hope for nothing from it. Is it the fruit of long discontent? Have minds only been aroused slowly and with difficulty? Then I will count on their firmness; and they would wish to be free if I made them recognize that liberty alone can make them happy.

In accordance with this observation, the second half of *Des droits et des devoirs du citoyen* was devoted to a discussion of what can only be called a program for revolution: an attempt, given the political conditions of eighteenth-century France, to construct a scenario for what Mably called "une révolution ménagée." Such a revolution would be "ménagée," in the sense that it would be carefully contrived and consciously conducted. It would be "ménagée," too, in the sense that it would be sparingly carried out according to orderly

---

[14]Vomit.

principles and not in the name of "a licentious liberty" that would lead to violence. "I distrust a liberty whose avengers are military men," the Commonwealthman insists; "if they oppress the tyrant, it is rare that they do not usurp the tyranny; Cromwell will always have imitators." The program laid out in *Des droits et des devoirs du citoyen* therefore involved two strategies: constitutional resistance and political contestation. It was necessary, first of all, to resist any attempts by the royal administration to destroy vestiges of the traditional rights and privileges of individuals, communities, and corporations in the name of "reform." These vestiges were all that remained to distinguish the social geography of France from the devastated landscape of despotic Turkey. If they constituted abuses in themselves, they nevertheless served as remedies against still greater vices.

> Restore everything to that wise equality to which a free people must aspire, before wishing to establish freedom of government; and all will become base, abject and rampant in France, as all is base, abject and rampant in Turkey. Everyone will be reduced to the level of the people, and everyone will be consequently a slave; and your ministers, believing themselves Vizirs, will commit their injustices without fear.

Thus Mably was severely critical of the kinds of proposals for administrative reform suggested by the abbé Saint-Pierre.[15] "The most zealous Frenchman of his time for the public good," Saint-Pierre had proposed nothing that was not "contrary to our liberty and favorable to despotism." Wherever he found abuses, he proposed to crush them under the weight of royal authority, without recognizing that abuse of this authority was itself the source of the evils afflicting French society. Nothing was more pernicious than thus to accustom a nation to slavery under the guise of reform. In a nation not yet free, the Commonwealthman insisted, any administrative claim to reform abuses was to be resisted as a further means for the extension of despotism. "Read the history of all the monarchies, and you see everywhere that it is by repressing minor abuses in the nation that the intolerable abuse of arbitrary power has been born."

Resistance to "enlightened" administrative reform remained a constant theme in Mably's political discourse throughout his life. Machault was a "tyrant," whose attempt in 1749 to deprive the clergy of its tax privileges (under the pretext that every citizen should contribute equally) Mably denounced as an act of encroaching despotism. Turgot, twenty-five years later, was a well-meaning quack treating the corns of a man with a malignant fever. Necker, in his turn, was a renegade from Genevan liberty, whose experiment with provincial assemblies was calculated to extend political lethargy. For each of these ministerial reformers Mably had criti-

---

[15]A reformer associated with the Enlightenment.

cism in good measure. But he saved his most sustained attack for a work which went beyond specific reforms to the systematic elaboration of an administrative ideology: Le Mercier de la Rivière's *De l'ordre naturel et essentiel des sociétés politiques*[16] (1768). There are many aspects of Mably's critique of this work that are worthy of attention. But there is one which is central for the present discussion. True to the physiocratic[17] impulse, Le Mercier transposed the problem of public order into the language of social science. He offered the vision of a society reconstituted in the light of rationally demonstrable principles: a domain of action in which the assertion of political will would give way to the transparent exercise and acceptance of rational authority grounded in the natural order of things. For Mably (as for Rousseau) nothing was more directly antithetical to a properly political mode of discourse than this quasi-administrative language. His *Doutes proposés aux philosophes économistes*[18] invoked the experience of the ancients and record of history against the metaphysics of physiocracy. It was not *évidence* but the passions that ruled the world, Mably insisted in that work. Public order depended not on the self-necessitating rule of reason but on the political assertion of will. Liberty could be secured only by the balancing of wills in a political system of *contreforces* that Le Mercier had rejected for the fantasy of legal despotism. In the face of this eighteenth-century version of the withering away of the state, Mably reiterated the primacy of politics and the centrality of political will for the creation and maintenance of public order.

It followed from this political analysis that traditionally constituted corporate bodies[19]—those debris of ancient liberties now floating in an ocean of arbitrary power—should seek every means to resist further incursions upon their rights and privileges in the name of reform, not simply in order to retard the further progress of despotism, but to foster the hatred of arbitrary power that is the beginning of liberty. Their acts of resistance, the Commonwealthman insisted, should nevertheless be understood as a means of advancing the political interests of the entire nation.

> Otherwise they will be disputing with the oppressor of the state over the exclusive right to oppress all. Wishing themselves to be despots, they will alienate the heart of the nation; it will no longer appear behind them as an auxiliary body, and defending themselves only with their own strength, they will necessarily succumb.

---

[16]*On the Natural and Essential Order of Political Societies.*

[17]A system of economic thought, often considered part of the Enlightenment. The central idea of this theory was that true value lay in the land and its products.

[18]*Doubts Proposed to the Economist Philosophers.* "Economist" referred to the physiocrats.

[19]Most of society in the Old Regime was organized into corporate bodies (groups of individuals sharing the same occupation and legally bound together).

This warning was aimed principally at the parlements, the only traditional bodies Mably thought capable of moving beyond resistance to the
contestation that would be necessary to effect fundamental political change.
The vestigial provincial Estates, the Commonwealthman argued, were too
weak for this purpose; the nobility too lacking in corporate solidarity; the
clergy characteristically too hostile to liberty. It would be an illusion for the
nation to expect a new Charlemagne, a monarch who would choose once
again to become the first magistrate of a free people. Nor would it be
practical to await a situation in which a monarch would be forced by
accidental misfortunes to call the Estates-General[20] of his own accord,
thereby opening the possibility of forcing political change. In such a
situation, the Commonwealthman insisted, the meeting of the Estates-
General would in any case be inadequate to such a purpose, because the
opportunity for revolutionary change would not have been prepared by
"the fermentation that alone can give enlightenment and courage." This
fermentation, the necessary prolegomenon to liberty, could only be created
by the concerted action of the parlements.

Thus while Mably was profoundly critical of the language of fundamental law invoked by parlementary activists, he was convinced that confrontation between these bodies and monarchical authority represented the only
available means of developing the political conditions for revolution, fostering
public political consciousness by a strategy of constitutional confrontation.
The conflict over *billets de confession*, the Commonwealthman insisted,
had already created an unprecedented political awareness in France:

> agree that in the past few years you have been roused to indignation against
> despotism; that you desire to see an end to its abuses; and that in the current
> state of intellectual fermentation [*fermentation des esprits*] you today express
> yourselves, even publicly, in discourse that is much more daring than your
> most secret thoughts were twelve years ago.

But what if the parlement of Paris had demonstrated the same obstinacy
and vigor in tax matters as it had over religious issues? What if it had
refused to register tax edicts, issuing remonstrances asserting the principle
that the nation alone can approve taxation, denouncing the history of royal
usurpation, and demanding the convocation of the Estates-General? "Your
most *petits Bourgeois* would suddenly have regarded themselves as citizens.
The parlement would have seen itself supported by all the orders of the
state; a general cry of approbation would have thrown the court into
consternation . . . ." After a characteristic period of vacillation, the government would have held a *lit de justice*,[21] forcing registration of the tax
edicts. But all need not then have been finished. What if the parlement in

---

[20]See the glossary entry *Estates General.*
[21]See the glossary entry *parlements.*

its turn had protested against this violation of the laws, declared the forced registration null and void, forbidden the levying of the tax, and reiterated its demand for the convocation of the Estates-General? What if it had suspended its judicial functions and refused to disband until that assembly had been called? In a matter of such importance, the parlement of Paris would have been vigorously supported by the other parlements in a display of unity that the government could not resist.

> The greater the confusion, the closer you will be to the resolution that will reestablish order. For my part, I am completely convinced that in these circumstances any harsh measures would serve only to embarrass the government and reveal its feebleness. Your ministers hold the judgment of the public in contempt; but, believe me, they fear its discontent. There is no monarch, no sultan, on earth who is not obliged to yield to the general opinion of his slaves when that is known.

Against this cogent scenario for "une révolution ménagée," Mably's Frenchman offered several crucial objections. The parlementary magistrates, he insisted, were motivated by self-interest rather than any love of the public good. Having worked to render the king all-powerful, they now found themselves threatened by the colossus they had brought into being. Their claims to represent the nation were merely the veil for corporate aggrandizement; and their attention to tax matters extended no further than the interest on their investments in the royal debt. Why then would they seek to diminish their own authority by demanding the convocation of the Estates-General? To these objections, in turn, the Commonwealthman had several responses. He was not prepared entirely to doubt the magistrates' love of the public good. But his essential argument was to insist that, whatever their motivation, they would eventually be forced to call for the Estates-General by the logic of their political position.

"If all the parts of the state are oppressed, will the parlement be miraculously preserved from the general ruin?" the Englishman demanded. Its current strength depended upon the ineptness and timidity of the government, the intensity of public feeling against *billets de confession,* and the willingness of the public to regard it as a barrier against despotism. These phenomena were all temporary. The public would tire of a body that was content simply to make useless remonstrances, or solely concerned with its own interests. And the magistrates knew only too well that they could be silenced by the determined assertion of royal power, forbidden to issue remonstrances, and ordered to transcribe upon their registers whatever suited the royal will. Unless these haughty magistrates, "protectors of the nation," wished to be reduced to the level of village judges, they would eventually recognize the need to assert the cause of liberty against arbitrary power.

> I fully believe that your parlement will not profit from this whiff of power to execute what you and I desire; but as it sees itself falling from its present

position, it will not fail to reflect upon the fragility of its fortune, and it will recognize the necessity of rendering the nation free, if it does not wish always to be under the rod of despotism.

Ultimately, then, the magistrates would be obliged in their own self-defense to demand the calling of the Estates-General. They would also realize that they could enhance their institutional prestige and preserve their investments from the threat of a collapse in public credit by doing so. And if, abandoning all aristocratic prejudices, they were willing to set themselves in such a meeting at the head of the Third Estate, "they would give this order, which is in essence the most powerful, a consideration from which they would derive the principal advantage, and which would affirm the rights and liberty of the Nobility; for note that this order can never be free and powerful in a country where the people is under the yoke."

This latter argument did little to satisfy Mably's Frenchman, for whom the historical record of the Estates-General offered bare promise of effective resistance to the royal will. Even if the Estates-General were convoked, he insisted, the monarch would find ample means to subvert the integrity of the representatives, who would be corrupt, cowardly, and politically inept. The assembly would be a chaos of political confusion lacking any ability to generate the will to impose reforms upon a recalcitrant monarch. In short, it would be more likely to pave the way to greater evils than to effect political benefits. Once again, the Commonwealthman repudiated these objections as lacking political acumen. A monarch forced by sustained opposition to call the Estates-General, he maintained, would clearly be in no position to control the outcome of the elections for that body.

> Do you believe that a monarch obliged to yield to the force of circumstances will be in a position to make himself feared and respected, and that he will fill the provinces with *lettres de cachet* to make himself master of the elections? ... The more your despot has kicked against the spur, the more he has struggled in his harness, the less will he retain the means to debase the Estates; and their zeal for the public good will increase in proportion to the resistance they have encountered.

Equally important, the very act of forcing the convocation of the Estates-General would, in itself, constitute a political education for the nation. Its passions engaged and its political consciousness developed, it would not be willing to settle for forms of representation that would frustrate the national will. "By the time your nation has enough wisdom to demand the holding of the Estates-General, and enough firmness to obtain them," the Commonwealthman insisted, "it will not be imbecile enough to accept a sham representation." On the contrary, "a thousand pamphlets will immediately appear to instruct the public in its interests." The faults of the old Estates-General would be examined and the political lessons implicit in their previous decline clearly established. The sources of French history would be mined for their political truths, and the experience of other nations charted as a guide to the assertion of political will.

Far from fearing that the Estates-General would be too timid, corrupt, or respectful of monarchical authority, then, the Commonwealthman argued that there was a greater danger that it would be impatient and extreme in its demands for reform. It was essential to proceed with circumspection, avoiding the impulse to eliminate all abuses overnight. Above all, it was necessary to avoid jeopardizing the cause of liberty in a premature effort to secure equality. Rather than demanding that the privileged renounce their prerogatives, it was necessary to attach them to the cause of liberty by offering them the hope of even greater distinction and honors in the new order. Social passions should not be inflamed by demands for the suppression of privileges nor the creditors of the state alarmed by threats to repudiate the debts of the crown. Such actions would merely exacerbate evils not to be cured by violent remedies. And they would render the Estates-General hostage (as in 1614) to ministerial attempts to exploit social divisions among the three Estates.

> Each order of the state will make an enormous mistake if it does not yield its particular interest to the general interest. . . . Let our nephews not be the dupes of the suspicions, hatreds and jealousies that the ministers will sow among the different orders to divide them and abort their undertaking. Let one suffer a present evil in the hope of a greater good; in a free state, all the bodies insensibly find their level.

For the Commonwealthman, therefore, the essential goal was to secure liberty by establishing a regular system of national representation. If the Estates-General did not achieve this before disbanding, everything would be lost. All other goals should therefore be sacrificed to this end. The Estates-General should refuse to separate without the promulgation of a fundamental law, a *pragmatic sanction,* ordaining that the representatives of the nation would be assembled every two or three years, subject to no delay for any reason, and without the need to be convoked by any particular will. It should also be established that the Estates-General would be neither dissolved, separated, prorogued, or interrupted in the exercise of their deliberations; and that in disbanding they would be free to call an extraordinary assembly, and to adjourn, as circumstances demanded. This done, the Estates-General would be free to investigate abuses and proceed to the political reforms that the Commonwealthman outlined in considerable detail. Provincial Estates would be instituted, meeting annually to form a perpetual check on arbitrary power in the intervals between assemblies of the Estates-General, and providing a reliable system for the election of representatives to that body. Executive power would be divided and dispersed among a broad variety of magistrates. Judicial authority would be clearly separated from executive by establishing the parlements as courts of final appeal in all matters; and *police* would be vigorously subject to judicial control. The entire administration of finances would be reserved solely to the Estates-General, as would be the right to declare war and make peace, and the administration of the army. In short, everything would be done to curtail the royal prerogative and sustain the rights of the nation.

Why, then, retain a king? Transformed by the Commonwealthman's arguments into "a Republican as proud and as zealous as any . . . in England," Mably's Frenchman pressed his interlocutor for an answer to this question. The response is intriguing: "But let us nevertheless respect the thrones, and try not to run after a chimerical good, as we did two days ago when you wanted to embark for my desert island." The desert island here referred to was a utopian republic founded on the community of goods, where "all equal, all rich, all poor, all free, all brothers, our first law would be to possess nothing as private property." This vision was repudiated by the Commonwealthman as chimerical, on the grounds that corruption had advanced too far in modern societies to make it possible. Abolition of royalty was now repudiated on the same grounds, in terms that made it clear that inequality and royalty were symbiotic vices.

> Royalty is doubtless a vice in a government, but whatever this vice may be, it is necessary in a nation, as soon as it has lost the primitive ideas of simplicity and equality that men once had, and that it is incapable of recovering. . . . If the French and the English did not have in their midst a privileged house which occupied the first rank in society, be sure that the state—torn apart by the divisions, hatreds, ambition, rivalry, intrigues and factions of some important families—would soon have a despot: we would inevitably experience the fate of the Roman Republic. . . . In nations that are rich, powerful and extended through large provinces, one cannot have the *bourgeois* moderation that is the soul and support of liberty. The Swedes have thought very wisely in wishing to have a kind of king, which prevents a true one from arising among them.

With this conclusion, the limits of Mably's proposed revolution become clear. If his civic humanism sustained a powerful script for political contestation and the destruction of despotic power, it did not issue here in an equally radical program for social transformation. The ideal of social equality, which depended upon the community of goods, was not to be claimed in a society irreversibly marked by property, commerce, and luxury. Inequality and corruption could perhaps be tempered in the wake of political revolution—censors would be created to execute sumptuary laws and supervise an educational system that would moderate luxury and inhibit its corrupting effects—but the achievement of liberty would not be mortgaged against the dream of a golden age of social equality.

That liberty depended, of course, upon the readiness of the parlements (from self-interest if not for love of the public good) to force the pattern of contestation outlined in *Des droits et des devoirs du citoyen*. Indeed, it is possible that this work was written with the aim of convincing certain magistrates of the necessity for such a strategy. Be this as it may, it is clear that by 1772, in the wake of the Maupeou coup,[22] Mably was convinced that he had miscalculated in any hopes for parlementary action. The second part of the *Observations sur l'histoire de France* contained a sustained indictment of the attempts made historically by the parlements to establish their own preeminence at the cost of undermining the authority of the Estates-General. To this was added a bitter attack on the self-interested refusal of the parlement of Paris to give consistent support to the revolutionary doctrine of the "union des classes." If the parlements had maintained that principle of unity, Mably argued in 1772, it would have been impossible for Maupeou to suppress them. They had been destroyed not because they threatened arbitrary power, but because they had given personal offence to powerful ministers. In short, Maupeou confirmed what events since the composition of *Des droits et des devoirs du citoyen* had led Mably to fear: that the moment for revolution in France had passed.

> We saw not long ago a sort of intellectual fermentation [*fermentation dans les esprits*]; we saw that in protesting we became alarmed by our protests; discontent was regarded as a disorder more dangerous than the evil occasioning it; and we feared that it would antagonize the government and disrupt its workings. The more empty and puerile this fear, the more certain it is that our character is appropriate to our government, and that we bear in our hearts no principle of revolution.

In retrospect, the conclusion Mably reached in 1772 seems less powerful than the political language in which it was expressed: the language of classical republicanism, in which despotic government could be destroyed and historical contingency contained only by the sustained assertion of national political will. Some fifteen years later, Frenchmen found themselves enacting a political script that was remarkably close to the scenario set forth in *Des droits et des devoirs du citoyen*. If they diverged from this script at the point which Mably most feared and with results that he least anticipated—by failing to maintain the unity of the three Estates in the attack upon despotism—they nevertheless gave force to his historical and political analyses. The representative who in 1790 maintained before the National Assembly that the nobility was older than the feudal system was silenced with the reply: "Lisez Mably.[23]"

What are the implications of this reading of Mably for the problem of the ideological origins of the French Revolution? An adequate approach to

---

[22]An effort to eliminate the Parlement of Paris.
[23]Read Mably.

this problem cannot be couched in terms of the "influence" of particular individual thinkers. On the contrary, it will involve the recovery of an entire field of social and political discourse. Thus it is not my purpose here to make a case for Mably's influence on the events of 1789. Nor is it my intention to argue that he anticipated *the* French Revolution, or that the language of 1789 can be found already complete in his work. On the contrary, the hypothesis underlying the present research is that this language crystallized only in 1789 as a consequence of the emergence, elaboration, and interpenetration of several competing discourses, each of which offered an alternative representation of French public life to resolve the institutional and ideological conflicts of the Old Regime. From this perspective, Mably's script for *a* French Revolution offers a particularly clear example of what I have called the "political" discourse, the discourse of will. He offered a representation of political life in which the legal and administrative fabric of the monarchy was dissolved into the exercise of will, in which historical contingency could be contained only by a nation capable of revolutionary action, in which there was no middle ground between liberty and despotism.

The force of the events of 1789 depended on the creation of a language that cast many different kinds of behaviors—from aristocratic resistance to popular terrors—into the same symbolic order: an order defined in terms of the exercise of political choice and the assertion of revolutionary will. Thus the most pressing task for the historiography of the French Revolution, François Furet has recently argued, is precisely to "rediscover the analysis of the political as such. But the price to pay for this is a double one: on the one hand, we must stop thinking of the revolutionary consciousness as a more or less 'natural' result of oppression and discontent; on the other, we must be able to conceptualize this strange offspring of *philosophie* (its offspring, at least, in chronological terms)." The evidence of Mably's writings suggests that this enterprise will need to begin with the transformation of French political culture that occurred in the course of the constitutional conflicts of the 1750s. The political language that began to emerge in the course of those disputes drew on many sources. Not all of them were secular: the revival of arguments for national sovereignty in a language that had its roots in late medieval conciliarism is a phenomenon of the 1750s that is only now being explored. But if Mably is a reliable informant, it seems that we shall also need to gauge the force in France of the language of classical republicanism that proved so powerful elsewhere.

Church, State, and
the Ideological Origins of
the French Revolution:
The Debate over
the General Assembly of
the Gallican Clergy in 1765*

Dale Van Kley

Dale Van Kley has had a major impact on current thinking about the politics of Old-Regime France. Most often, scholars had maintained that much of the political disagreement of the eighteenth century stemmed from the conflict between the king and the supreme court of France, the Parlement of Paris. For the most part, however, historians had characterized this court's activities as selfish and obstructionist. However, Van Kley and other scholars have found purpose and morality in the parlement.

Van Kley's perspective has been to investigate the parlement by examining the battle over the direction and regulation of the Catholic church. In order to encourage religious orthodoxy, the king supported the established church, whose ties to the Pope were strong. The parlement resisted, in part out of a sense of national opposition to Italian influences. Also, the religious fervor of Jansenist judges, adherents of a rather strict form of Catholicism and opponents of the papacy (for more information, see the glossary entry *Jansenism*), was instrumental in shaping the parlement's tendency to oppose ecclesiastical authority. A variety of principles emerged over the second half of the eighteenth century from this continuing struggle, which, according to Van Kley, undermined the Old Regime. Furthermore, he suggests that these same ideas foreshadowed and may have greatly influenced the future ideological encounter between revolutionaries and the monarchy. By focusing on the controversy over the church, Van Kley

Journal of Modern History, 51 (1979), pp. 630–34, 646–55, 656–57, 662–64. Reprinted with permission of the University of Chicago Press.

has thus given coherence to parlementary ideas. The author also has pin-pointed a very unusual source—Jansenists in the Parlement of Paris rather than Enlightenment thinkers—as the driving force for revolutionary thinking.

In the article excerpted here, some of Van Kley's general themes emerge. His analysis focuses upon an effort by the hierarchy of the Catholic church in 1765 to assert its independence from judicial interference. As Van Kley has found elsewhere, the king supported the church against the parlement. Van Kley investigates less the actual confrontation than the issues that emerged in the ensuing pamphlet war. There appear to have been two waves of pamphlets, the first of which is analyzed in pages not included in this abridgment of the article. In that section, which would directly follow the "Introduction," the author described pamphlets on both sides of the issue that depended on fairly traditional forms of argument including religious and historical precedent. The second wave included pamphlets which were both less traditional and more sharply worded. On the parlement's side, pamphleteers urged the supremacy of the state over the church. One even suggested that if the state needed funds, it might seize the assets of the church—a solution eventually adopted during the Revolution. The ecclesiastical and monarchist side retorted by insisting that the existence of the church revealed a tacit contract between it and society to exercise an important function.

Van Kley draws two conclusions from his findings. First, this intellec-tual struggle possessed many of the contours of revolutionary and counter-revolutionary rhetoric. By implication, Van Kley would appear to locate the revolutionary battle in prerevolutionary political conflict. Second, both sides heavily used the language of the Enlightenment with its emphasis on contracts and secular authority. This suggests that, rather than causing the Revolution, the Enlightenment provided a store of ideas that the entire political spectrum appropriated. In addition, because these pamphlets possessed more vigor than those relying on tradition, Van Kley speculates that the special role of the Enlightenment was to radicalize all sorts of arguments. By providing a set of rationales more universal and elastic than the categories put forward by the past, the Enlightenment gave intellectuals and polemicists enhanced weapons.

INTRODUCTION

It was most unusual for a general assembly of the Gallican Clergy[1] to prom-ulgate a doctrinal statement in its *Actes,*[2] or proceedings. For the general

---

[1]The French clergy.
[2]*Acts of the General Assembly of the Clergy of France on Religion, Extracted from the.*

assembly was not strictly speaking a Church council, but rather a delegation of the clergy in its temporal capacity as first order of the realm. Its origin was fairly recent, as Old Regime institutions go: the monarchy virtually created it at the Colloquy of Poissy in 1561 when it guaranteed the clergy's corporate autonomy and fiscal immunities in return for a large financial contribution. Since then the first estate's[3] assembly had ordinarily met every five years in order to renegotiate this contract, verify its financial accounts, and present remonstrances to the king. All the same, the assembly had occasionally made doctrinal judgments, most notably in 1682 when, cajoled by Louis XIV and guided by Bishop Bossuet, it defined the four famous "liberties" of the Gallican Church uniting adherence to the Council of Constance's assertion of the ecumenical council's supremacy in matters of faith to a declaration of the monarchy's complete independence of any ecclesiastical authority in temporal affairs. But on this and other occasions the assembly had acted at the behest or at least with the blessings of the monarchy. In contrast, what the assembly first did timidly in 1760 and 1762, then with great fanfare in 1765, was quite without precedent: it published a doctrinal statement against the "temporal power" in spite of the unexpressed but sufficiently known displeasure of its crowned head. It was indeed, as one historian has called it, an act of "almost revolutionary audacity."

The circumstances accounting for the clergy's belligerence in 1765 are not obscure. In the course of the previous decade, the macabre campaign by a group of episcopal zealots to deny the Eucharist and extreme unction to penitents suspected of Jansenism had broken against the inflexible resistance of the parlements[4] which, led by that of Paris, defended the right of all Catholics to public participation in the sacraments. At first the king had seemed to side with the episcopacy against his Parisian magistrates, who sustained the unmistakable marks of royal displeasure in 1753 and again in 1757. But in September of that year the parlement returned triumphant and, under cover of the king's Law of Silence, thereafter ordered priests to administer the sacraments to appellants of *Unigenitus*[5] and harried them out of the land if they refused. In sum, not only had the parlement "Thrust its hand into the censer" and seized ultimate jurisdictional authority over the Church's most "august" sacraments, but it had seriously undermined the episcopacy's control over its parish priests. Then came the parlement's suppression of the Jesuit Order, entailing two additional pro-

---

Proceedings of that Assembly, Held at Paris, by Permission of the King, at the Convent of the Grands-Augustins, in Seventeen Hundred and Sixty Five.

[3]Clergy.

[4]See the glossary entry *parlements*.

[5]A papal bull issued in 1713, condemning Jansenism as heresy.

fane tramplings upon the holy ground of ecclesiastical jurisdiction. First, the parlement annulled the Jesuits' vows as abusive and pronounced the whole order to be "perverse." Then, not content with having arrogated to itself a purely spiritual authority by condemning a collection of extracts from Jesuits' theological treatises—the infamous *Assertions dangereuses* —the parlement added the effrontery of sending this collection to all the realm's bishops, not for their judgment, but for their instruction and edification. Decidedly, by 1765 the bishops had had enough. For them the time had again come, as it had for Saint Flavian in the fifth century, "to raise our voices and proclaim our doctrine."

So proclaim they did. The resultant "Exposition of the Rights of the Spiritual Power" began innocuously enough with a proclamation of Gallican banalities. Two powers had been established to govern man: "the sacred authority of priests and that of kings"; both came from God, from whom emanated all "well-ordered power on the earth." The goal of the second of these powers was man's wellbeing in the present life; the object of the first was to prepare him for eternity. In establishing these two powers, God had intended not their strife but their cooperation, so that they might lend mutual aid and support. But neither power was to be subordinate to the other, for each was "sovereign, independent and absolute" in its own domain. For that reason "the Clergy of France" had always taught that the Church's power was confined to "spiritual things," and that kings were "not subordinate to any ecclesiastical power . . . in temporal things," because they held their power from God himself. But if kings commanded in temporal affairs, "the universal Church" had always taught that they were "obliged to obey priests in the order of Religion," to whom "alone the government of the Church belongs."

But it was not so much the glittering teeth of its principles as the tailend whiplash of their applications that constituted the *Actes'* chief force. " . . . Silence," the *Actes* for example proclaimed, "can never be imposed upon those whom God had instituted as His mouthpiece." This was a not very covert condemnation of Louis XV's Law of Silence of September 2, 1754, which had forbidden mention of the bull *Unigenitus* and polemical terms such as Jansenist and Molinist.[6] Again, " . . . The Civil Power . . . cannot . . . be permitted to contradict the Doctrine received by the Church, to suspend the execution of her judgments, or to elude their effects. . . . " Instead read: the parlement of Paris flagrantly exceeded its authority on April 18, 1752, when it declared that no one could be refused the sacraments by virtue of opposition to *Unigenitus.* Moreover, "the Laws of the Church can receive no qualifications except from the authority which pronounced them." In other words, even Louis XV exceeded his

---

[6]An accommodating moral system linked to the Jesuits.

authority in his Declaration of December 10, 1756, by saying that *Unigenitus* was not a "rule of faith," thereby implying that the bull's opponents were not really heretics. Further, "The Keys of the Kingdom of Heaven would have been remitted to [the Church] in vain, were she able to authorize a corrupt ethic . . . , and the judgment she pronounces on moral truths, is just as independent of Princes and their Ministers, as that which she makes concerning the objects of belief." That is to say that the parlement's condemnation of lax casuistical propositions taken from Jesuit authors was both unnecessary and jurisdictionally illicit. And finally, " . . . The refusal of the most august of our sacraments can never be the object of the competence of the civil authority." This passage speaks clearly enough for itself.

The general assembly's *Actes* were no sooner printed than the parlement of Paris declared them "null" and condemned an accompanying circular letter as "fanatical and seditious" in judgments on September 4 and 5. These judgments in turn initiated a spectacle of jurisdictional and corporate anarchy—a three-cornered slugfest between the parlement, the episcopacy, and the royal council—to which the realm had grown strangely accustomed since 1750. Not wholly devoid, for its part, of means of "temporal" persuasion—the clergy had been dragging its feet on the 12 million *don gratuit*[7] requested by the government—the general assembly promptly solicited and on September 15 obtained a royal order in council annulling the parlementary judgments. The royal action predictably enraged the parlement of Paris, which set to work on remonstrances, but also left the clergy imperfectly avenged by reserving for the king the cognizance of the contested matters. The provincial parlements now entered the fray: in the parlement of Aix-en-Provence, the solicitor general Le Blanc de Castillon delivered a *réquisitoire*[8] so virulent against the *Actes* that the general assembly felt obliged to ask the king to disavow it. A conciliar[9] order obligingly did so on May 24, 1766, but not strongly enough to suit the clergy: the same day, another conciliar order articulated the royal position on the proper boundaries between Sacerdoce and Empire, which predictably satisfied neither side. A parlementary judgment on July 8, which outlawed episcopal attempts to solicit adhesions to the *Actes,* provoked yet another conciliar order of annullment on November 25, which nonetheless displeased the clergy by adding its own prohibition of soliciting signatures. The controversy slowly melted away during the spring and early summer of 1767, then disappeared altogether beneath the avalanche of the La Chalotais-d'Aiguillon

---

[7]Voluntary offering made by the clergy.
[8]Indictment.
[9]Royal Council.

affair[10] in the following years. Before disappearing altogether, however, the controversy over the general assembly of 1765 set off a minor avalanche of its own in the form of anonymous polemical pamphlets and a few full-scale treatises, the great majority of which took the side of the the parlements.

REASON, CONTRACT, AND THE PURSUIT OF HAPPINESS

Lefranc de Pompignán[11] however seemed less upset by the mass of pamphlets discussed thus far[12] than by a few treatise-like productions which appeared later than the others, and which to his mind displayed an affinity to the principles of the "so-called *esprits forts*[13] of our days," in particular Rousseau. Nor were the worthy bishop's fears in this matter uniquely the figment of a paranoid episcopal imagination. The productions in question indeed differ from the others in their more frequent appeals to "reason," in their employment of the concept of political and social contract, in their easier acceptance of human nature and the pursuit of terrestrial happiness—intellectual traits one associates automatically with the Enlightenment in France. This "enlightened" conceptual apparatus perhaps enabled these pamphleteers to go somewhat further than the others in subordinating religious (or at least ecclesiastical) to purely political and social considerations.

Lefranc de Pompignan directed the bulk of his fire against a two-volume treatise entitled *On the Authority of the Clergy and the Power of the Political Magistrate in the Exercise of the Functions of the Ecclesiastical Ministry,* written by the lawyer François Richer and published in 1766. Like the Rousseau of the *Social Contract,* Richer began with the question of why, given his natural liberty, man had everywhere accepted the restraints of society. Richer found the answer not so much in man's technological prowess as in the long period of helplessness preceding his maturity, rendering stable and authoritarian families indispensable. Large and extended families had therefore been the first sorts of societies. But after these had broken up due to the death of patriarchal chiefs, the "passions and the inherent vices of humanity" had created a state of

---

[10]D'Aiguillon, the royal representative in Brittany, and La Chalotais, the leader of that province's parlement, were the chief protagonists in a struggle over the power of the monarch to coerce the judiciary.

[11]Bishop of Le Puy.

[12]Van Kley refers here to the section of his article [*Journal of Modern History* 51 (1971), pp. 635–45] omitted here, which details the more moderate pamphlets issuing from the debates over the *Actes.*

[13]Hot heads.

perpetual war, whence the need to appoint a "conventional chief" in place of the "natural chief," thereby creating society. In the resulting social contract, the chief or "sovereign" agreed to promulgate "the most suitable rules" for the general welfare, in return for which the "nation" promised "the most prompt and blind obedience." The Hobbesian[14] rigor of the contract's terms was nonetheless softened by their apparent compatibility with the sovereign's divine right—he accounted to God alone— and with his quality as a "representative" and even "mandatory" of the "nation."

This somewhat precarious balance of constitutional authorities was revealed to the author by a combination of "reason," "nature," and the "essence of things," although it was also confirmed by biblical authority. These sources of inspiration again collaborated to produce another principle, that the "conservation and the agreements of terrestrial life" had been the "unique motive" behind the formation of civil societies. . . . " Religion had had no hand in it. For "the cult inspired by enlightened nature and guided by reason" (the only one which the Supreme Being had demanded before revealing "a more particular one") was not dependent upon society for its celebration. "Each man," in Emile-like[15] fashion, had fulfilled all he owed to his Creator "within the most profound solitude and without any sort of communication with his fellows." Classical history here came to his aid by revealing that the "first legislators" had been almost solely occupied with temporal concerns; to the small extent that the "religious cult" had distracted them, it was "only as a subordinate dimension of politics. . . . " They were "almost always observed to accommodate the exterior ceremonies to the civil order they established."

The intended effect of all this was obviously to give priority to the interests of civil society over those of religion, at least so far as temporal arrangements were concerned. Nor had the advent of Christianity much altered this primitive state of affairs. For Christianity had established an altogether different sort of society—the Church—consisting of a "corps of travelers on earth" en route to their "other country" or "the bosom of God himself." In contrast to the State, which employed physical force to rule corporeal bodies, the Church employed the gentler arms of grace and reason to persuade "our souls, or pure spirits" to accept its authority. The Church could proceed in no other fashion because our souls were "essentially free"; it was a "formal heresy" to suppose that even God coerced them. Such spiritual authority as the Church rightfully possessed was moreover the property of the whole Church, or the assembly of all the faithful; the ecclesiastical hierarchy only administered the power of the keys. Though it

---

[14]Thomas Hobbes (1588–1679), a political philosopher.
[15]Rousseau wrote *Emile* to discuss techniques which he advocated for child raising.

was true that priests received their ministry directly from Christ, it was "no less true," Richer insisted, that they exercised it "only in the name of the Church" and could undertake nothing "without its presumed consent." The ministers were "only representatives" and could only do "what the represented would do if he were acting upon his own."

Despite the un-Jansenist emphasis upon the freedom of will, much of this seems vaguely familiar. It is as if Richer had imperceptibly strayed from the stark, austere heights of simple contracts and states of nature into a thickening forest of scriptural and early Church precedents below. Before descending any further, however, the ascent of another contract intervened, this one between the Church and the prince become Christian. For when the band of travelers which was the Church had first asked the prince for the "liberty of passage" through his lands, the prince's duty to maintain "good order" had obliged him to undertake a detailed examination of "all the views and intentions of these foreigners," including their doctrine, morals, liturgy, and government. None of this meant, to believe the author, that the prince had actually judged dogma; he had only ascertained that the "good order of the State" was in no way compromised. Now if as a result of this examination the travelers had obtained a safe conduct, they for their part had agreed to abide strictly by the Scriptures and the tradition of the early Church, while the Sovereign for his part had sworn "to maintain them in the free exercise of the dogmas, moral code and discipline" which formed "the basis of the contract" and its essential "clauses."

With the conclusion of this second contract, however, the truth finally emerges. Like the Church he defines, our author has all along been a stranger in a foreign land, that of philosophical states of nature and natural religions.[16] Yet far from impeding his homeward course, the last contract rather plummets him headlong toward the promised land of Gallicano-Jansenist conclusions. For this contract, not as two-sided as it might appear, has already put the "Sovereign" as "political magistrate" in control of everything affecting "good order," therefore everything external about the Church. The prince's promise to protect the Church's doctrine and discipline— read; his rights as "outside bishop" and "protector of the canons"—further entitles him to protect these rules against the ministers themselves. Hence, for example, the prince's obligation to oppose any novel doctrine—the bull *Unigenitus?*—that an ecclesiastical cabal might attempt to foist upon the Church. Hence, too, his obligation to examine all the exterior circumstances of the Church council to ascertain its ecumenicity, as well as his right to impose

---

[16]Van Kley refers here to the essayist's reliance, despite his interest in religion and thus God, upon Enlightenment concepts of nature.

silence on religious disputes, invalidate unjust excommunications, prevent public refusals of sacraments—all this and more, without ever infringing upon the spiritual. But whether holy or not, most of this is familiar ground.

Not so entirely, however. For the treatise's enlightened social contracts and states of nature do not simply serve as neutral containers of Jansenist and Gallican contents. They display, rather, a cocoon-like effect, in some cases making more explicit what was implicit before; in others, metamorphosing the contents altogether. More explicit are the author's transformation of the Catholic priest into moral henchman for the State—"the organ of those charged with announcing the divine word ought always to be at the orders of the government"—as well as his starker statement of Gallicano-Jansenism's criteria for infallibility on the part of Church councils—"only when human passions are silent" and "the necessary liberty to receive the Holy Spirit" obtains. Some examples of metamorphosis are his advocacy of the marriage of priests—the "good order" of the State included the propagation of the human species—and his willingness to legalize divorce, which he justified by distinguishing between the civil contract, or "matter," and the inessential sacrament or its "benediction." Under the same heading falls his attack upon ecclesiastical property as a contradiction in terms. The "improperly called property of the Church," he maintained, belonged not to the Church but to some clerics, and to these in turn not as clerics, but only as a privileged order of citizens. Having desacralized the property, he then subjected it to the "fundamental law" that all property was taxable. The "general will" of the "Sovereign" therefore demanded that the "particular interest" of these citizens cede, and that their property be, if not confiscated for the benefit of the State, at least taxed like "secular" property.

It was this particular distillation of Richer's unique blend of Gallicano-Jansenism and "enlightened" concepts that several anonymously published pamphlets seized upon in their turn. The most spectacular of these, entitled *The Right of the Sovereign over the Property of the Clergy and Monks, and the Usage to Which He Can Put This Property for the Happiness of the Citizens,* appeared in 1770. Unlike Richer, this pamphleteer began his pilgrimage in the forest of Gallicano-Jansenist appeals to the authority of the New Testament, especially the gospels and Saint Paul, and to the example of "the first centuries of the Church." Thoroughly within this tradition, too, are his subordination of the clergy to the Church defined as the assembly of all the faithful and his insistence that the Church was purely spiritual and "not of this world"—all this, of course, to the familiar purpose of establishing the State's control over everything external, temporal, and factual. Christ's precept to "sell everything you have, give it to the poor, and come follow me" was a formal condemnation in advance, he thought, of "every kind of [temporal] pretension on the part of members of the Sacerdoce,"[17] most especially including the possession of property. Anyway, he argued, since the Church could not by definition possess property, all donations of property to priests "under the borrowed name of God or the Church" were legally invalid because they involved "an error of persons."

Yet one might well enquire why he restricted the application of Christ's precept to the clergy alone. If the Church is the assembly of all the faithful, and if the faithful are the followers of Christ, then should not laymen and clergy alike sell all they have and give to the poor—or at least to the Church which succors the poor? Sensing this difficulty all the more acutely because ecclesiastical property constituted the grail-like object of his unholy quest, he retreated the better to advance. Having all but obscured the distinction between clergy and laity with the one hand, he then stealthily reintroduced it with the other, for we learn with surprise that "sell all you have" is not a precept after all, but rather a "counsel" applicable to the Church's "Holy Ministers" alone. Yet his left hand knew very well what his right hand was up to—Christ's injunction to the contrary was undoubtedly just another counsel—for he was also aware that his task was now to justify the acquisition of property in particular and the pursuit of physical well-being in general.

His strategic retreat completed, he now jumps—indeed fairly catapults himself—onto the high ground of Enlightenment rhetoric. Like Rousseau's, his remaining "letters" are written from the mountain; the air grows abruptly chilly with appeals to "reason" and its "imprescriptible rights." Jolted, first of all, with the most un-Jansenist comment that it is not really necessary for a Christian to relate all his actions to God, that some actions are "indifferent in themselves," we are next astonished to hear that *"le bonheur physique"*[18] is a gift of heaven, "that happiness and unhappiness are the results of our conduct," and that "the springs, producers of one as well as the other of these two states, are purely physical." Nor is that all. The proposition that society's "inspection extends even to the precepts of Religion, not to contradict them, but in order to turn then to the profit of the State" may sound familiar enough, but not so the lengths to which it is taken. For not only is the Church's "exterior cult" purely "ceremonial and commemorative," but the State could eliminate it altogether and "restrict the Christian's cult to an interior act and the recitation of Dominical prayer, without forcing him to violate his religious obligations." Now if the State may do all that, can the Church legitimately resist the "Supreme Legislator" should he cast covetous eyes upon ecclesiastical property, especially when "armed with the equitable and transcendent motive of the public good . . . ?"

----

[17]Clergy.
[18]Physical happiness.

The answer is clearly no. The author then proceeded to imagine precisely the situation in which the monarchy and the National Assembly successively found themselves in 1789. The State owed 3 billion livres, and the payment of the interest on this debt, which consumed nearly half of the annual revenues, did not leave enough to meet the State's ordinary expenses. Taxes could not be augmented because of the "*cherté*[19] of nearly all sorts of goods. . . . " What was then to be done? After considering and dismissing sundry alternatives, such as bankruptcy, economy measures, and additional loans, he opted for the "surgical, decisive," and "simple" solution also adopted in 1789, namely, the confiscation of all ecclesiastical property and its sale to private citizens, together with the transformation of ecclesiastics into paid "pensionaries of the State." Nowhere, not even in the literature immediately preceding the Revolution, was the revolutionary solution to the State's financial problems more clearly anticipated than here.

TOWARD THRONE AND ALTAR

Quantitatively, at least, the episcopal cause mustered no more than a Noah's ark-like response to the deluge of writings submerging its *Actes:* the anonymous *Respective Rights of the State and the Church Reminded of Their Principles* (1766), the bishop of Grenoble's uninteresting *Dissertation* (1767), and the bishop of Le Puy's monumental *Defense of the Acts of the Clergy of France concerning Religion* (1769). Taken together, however, these responses are not without some interesting features, one of which is a marked preference for explicitly engaging the more "enlightened" of their opponents. In doing so, moreover, they proved themselves as adept at manipulating "enlightened" vocabulary and concepts in defense of their own cause as some of their enemies had been in attacking it.

Take, for example, the anonymous reminder of *The Respective Rights,* apparently an aristocratic defender of the first order rather than a member of it himself. His system, like that of the episcopacy's more "enlightened" opponents, made "civil" or "social" laws both chronologically and anthropologically prior to "religious" and "ecclesiastical" laws because of the more imperious character of physical needs. Further, these civil laws originated in "first conventions" based on natural law, more readily perceived, he thought, by "the vivacity of sentiments" than by some "method of reasoning." The resultant State, at first enlightened by means of natural religion alone, had accepted Christianity and the Church only subsequently, and on condition—a second contract, this—that its "ecclesiastical laws" did not run counter to its own. The State therefore reserved the right to inspect, approve, or reject ecclesiastical legislation, since it exercised an

---

[19]High price.

influence over "exterior morals" which in turn formed part of the State's *"haute police."* The Church, although not expressly the ecumenical council, the author defined as the assembly of all the faithful, and he insisted that the clergy's functions had been "originally entirely spiritual."

So far the author seemed headed down the path carved out by François Richer in *On the Authority of the Clergy and the Power of the Civil Magistrate,* which was published the same year. But at precisely this juncture his path diverged sharply. This was perhaps due in part to his accent on "sentiment" as opposed to reason, but mainly to his Montesquieuian, empirical, yet unimpeachably "enlightened" emphasis on the "strange circumstantial vicissitudes" and "conjunctural whimsicalities" encountered by different peoples. The main effect of these, in his view, had been to refract the application of natural law into the bewildering variety of particular laws we observe. Though natural law had inspired the formation of all constitutions, each "legislator" had had to adjust it according to the nation's physical and climactic circumstances, "factitious inclinations," and even errors, but infallibly with a view toward the "best possible condition." Even the most apparently bizarre laws were therefore "nonetheless respectable" because the "idea of the best possible" had dictated their formation; to understand them a detailed empirical examination of the circumstances which produced them was necessary. And the science of politics was therefore not reducible to a "system of geometrical order," but was rather a "calculus of proximities and simple approximations."

The author's more empirical cast of mind thus led him to a proto-Burkean[20] veneration for the delicately complex and infinitely variegated texture of all positive law, seen as the embodiment of the wisdom of the past. Consistent with himself, he did not exclude the clergy's privileged constitutional position from his all-embracing ken. The existence of a separate and even coercive ecclesiastical jurisdiction, the clergy's "titles of honor" and "exterior prerogatives," the Church's extensive property holdings— all these represented "universal reason's" infallible application of "natural law" to achieve the "best possible," which included the respect due to the ministers of a religion serving as spiritual foundation to the State. For "if in order to assure the repose of society, it was necessary to fortify the observation of human laws by means of a principle of religion and a motive of conscience," was it not "equally advantageous," he rhetorically asked, "to imprint on the people's soul a particular sentiment of respect for the censors of their conscience and the ministers of their religion . . . ?"

Whereas the anonymous author of *The Respective Rights* thus antici-

---

[20]The Englishman Edmund Burke believed that the best governments developed by evolving slowly over time.

pated counter-Revolutionary conservatism's veneration for traditional law and historic wisdom, Lefranc de Pompignan, in his monumental *Defense,* pointed no less clearly toward its theocratic and ultramonarchical tendencies. Yet he too, by pitting himself specifically against Richer's *On the Authority of the Clergy,* chose to do battle on unmistakably "enlightened" terrain. Though complaining throughout his treatise about "the false and modern philosophy" of "our day" and its addiction to states of nature and reciprocal contracts, he nonetheless accepted these concepts for practical purposes, and contrived to maneuver within their constraints.

This maneuvering is not unimpressive, in a purely forensic way. Tactically postulating society's emergence from a state of nature, the future bishop of Vienne first argued the "enlightened" utility of religion by contesting the principle that mundane considerations alone could have effected such a transition. It was to "outrage providence," he protested, "to suppose that civil societies were formed without her, or that her principal purpose in presiding over their formation was not to unite men so that they could render the sovereign arbiter of their destinies the common duties required of them." Although he conceded that terrestrial considerations might have been the occasion for the formation of civil societies, the deeper cause, he clearly implied, was religious. From Adam through Noah, the "first men" had indeed been recipients of a "particular revelation" which, however distorted with the passage of time in all but God's chosen race, made the father of every family at once a sacrificer and priest, rights inherited by the eldest son. Just as each family, then, had been basically a "religious association," so also the body politic, after men's "unchained passions" had led them to unite in civil society. Religion therefore entered into the very "constitution of every body politic, and it would have been impossible to associate men under a civil government if Religion, anterior to these human establishments, had not been the foundation and the tie." The redoubtable bishop thought it "easy to prove that, far from accommodating the exterior ceremonies of the religious cult to the civil order they established," the first legislators had more often "accommodated their political laws to the religious ideas established before them."

That religion was fundamental to the formation of civil societies, that God alone was the source of political sovereignty—neither of these principles led necessarily in a monarchical direction. The bishop acknowledged as much, and allowed that "all the nations of the earth [had] originally possessed the liberty to choose the form of government which suited them best." To the nations which had opted for monarchy he further allowed the choice of their first monarch, as well as between elective and hereditary monarchy. But could a nation so constituted subsequently rescind its original choice? Or could it ever dethrone a particular monarch by virtue of the nonfulfillment of some reciprocal contract? De Pompignan could hardly deny that some monarchical nations possessed such contracts, but he emphatically denied that these derived from natural law. He further failed to see how they could derive from the original liberty by which God had allowed men to choose their governments if this same liberty, "a gift of God's providence," could become the "germ of inexhaustible discords and intestine factions, of revolutions and catastrophes." Obviously, the bishop wanted to say no; the whole discussion put him out of sorts. What he clearly wished to affirm, on the contrary, was that the founders of heredi-tary monarchies could have very well tied the hands of their descendants and that, for the governance of their kingdoms, monarchs answered "to God alone."

In thus defending "divine right" monarchy against the threat of national sovereignty, the bishop was opposing the parlementary constitutionalism of the great majority of his opponents as much as the *"école de nos prétendus esprits forts,"*[21] Le Paige[22] as much as Rousseau. That this was the case he made clear by an off-handed and less than reverent reference to the "fundamental laws" of the Realm, a key phrase in the parlementary consti-tutional rhetoric of the time. Not, of course, that in 1765 either the parlement of Paris or the Gallicano-Jansenist press was publicly espousing a theory of national sovereignty or reciprocal political contract. But de Pompignan was not ignorant of the fact that the parlement, in its remon-strances, was then styling itself as "born with the monarchy" and the temple of its fundamental laws; or defining its duty as the defense of the "national constitution" against the "absolute power" of misguided monarchs, for which it was accountable to the "nation." In view of this rhetoric, it was a calculated provocation on the bishop's part to define the French monarch as "absolute" and to add that his magistrates were "his first subjects, and nothing more" who "received his orders and gave none except in his name."

CONCLUSION

The controversy over the general assembly of the Gallican clergy in 1765 was really the last in a series of mixed religious, ecclesiastical, and political disputes which had dominated the eighteenth-century French domestic scene until then. The coming of the bull *Unigenitus* in 1713, the "miracles" of Saint-Médard in the early 1730s,[23] the refusal of sacraments to Jansenists in the 1750s, the expulsion of the Jesuits in the 1760s—these

---

[21]The school of our so-called radicals.

[22]Louis-Adrien le Paige, a Jansenist spokesman and canon lawyer.

[23]The Jansenists believed that the miracles in Saint-Médard cemetery were actually occurring. The efforts of the ecclesiastical authorities and the state to undermine these beliefs or convictions led to a significant battle between the Jansenists and the Old-Regime establishment.

were the major landmarks on a polemical road which gradually bifurcated toward both Revolution and counter-Revolution. By 1765 these directions were well established and clear enough. Not only had the Jansenist, Gallican, and parlementary syndrome conceived of the Civil Constitution of the Clergy and contemplated the confiscation of ecclesiastical property, but is it wholly fanciful to recognize the lineaments of future "liberalism" in its constitutionalism, protonationalism, and the thoroughgoing laicism of its ecclesiastical conceptions? And does it, again, stretch the imagination unduly to discern the basic contours of counter-Revolution—indeed, of early nineteenth-century "conservatism" generally—within the episcopal defenders' veneration for the past, theocratic social conceptions, and synthesis of anticonstitutional royalism and ultramontanism?[24] Most conspicuously missing, at this stage, is aristocracy as such as a bone of contention. But the anti-aristocratic egalitarianism which played so important a role in the revolutionary mentality of the 1790s was a latecomer to the eighteenth-century scene; it was nowhere to be found in concentrated form during its middle decades.

If there is anything to this, then the marquis d'Argenson[25] was not far wrong—in fact, much righter than he knew—when he observed of these midcentury ecclesiastical and religious controversies that they no longer so much pitted Jansenists against Molinists as "nationals" (*nationaux*) against "sacerdotals" (*sacerdotaux*). It also follows that, at least prior to the Maupeou "revolution" of the 1770s,[26] these mixed religious, ecclesiastical, and political controversies were central, not peripheral, to the unraveling of the Old Regime and the coming of the French Revolution. For they appear to have engendered the ideological and political divisions which later burst forth with greater clarity during the Revolution itself, which was hence as much a product of these divisions as it was a progenitor of them in its turn.

If the 1765 meeting of the general assembly touched off the last major *Unigenitus*-related controversy in France, it also occasioned the Gallican clergy's first explicit condemnation of Enlightenment works. This contrast raises the difficult question of the relationship between the Enlightenment and the emerging ideological and political divisions in France, which seem to have arisen quite independently of the celebrated "movement of lights." The question becomes the more difficult in proportion as one associates "Enlightenment" with "unbelief" because, as the study of this particular affair has indicated, these mixed religious, ecclesiastical, and political controversies tended to divide Catholic from Catholic much more than Catholic from unbeliever. Lefranc de Pompignan undoubtedly had doubts

---

[24]Favoring increased papal authority.

[25]Royal provincial official, ambassador, and foreign minister.

[26]An effort to eliminate the Parlement of Paris.

about the Catholicity of some of his opponents whom he called "enemies of the clergy," but he still distinguished between these and "unbelievers," and professed to respect the sincerity of the former who, he acknowledged, "call themselves Christians." Not a single participant in this controversy fully qualifies as a member of Peter Gay's "little flock"[27] of the truly enlightened, whose distinguished bleating constitutes in fact no more than the most distant echo in any of these disputes. In the debate over the general assembly of 1765 there is moreover across-the-board agreement among all participants that Catholicism should function as the moral and spiritual foundation of the State. This much seems to suggest that even the very immediate origins of the ideological divisions of the Revolution and nineteenth-century France lie primarily in the century-long disputes between Catholic and Catholic, at best secondarily in the more loudly sung conflict between Catholic and unbeliever.

If, however, the Enlightenment is understood more broadly as a set of appeals, whether to reason, nature, or sensate experience, which replaced older ones such as to revelation and traditional precedents, then the problem of its relationship to the emerging ideological and political divisions of France is possibly susceptible of solution. And what this small study suggests is that "enlightened" concepts and vocabulary were sufficiently elastic to accommodate themselves to either side of the controversy, not just one, with perhaps a slight tendency for the Enlightenment's empirical side to run in a conservative direction, its natural rights inheritance in a revolutionary one. Can it be said, then, that the mixed religious, ecclesiastical, and political controversies generated the fundamental political and ideological directions of eighteenth-century France; whereas the Enlightenment, a broad cultural movement affecting the thought patterns of all literate groups, provided the conceptual apparatus and vocabulary in which either direction progressively expressed itself?

---

[27]"Little flock," a term found in Peter Gay's important work on the Enlightenment, refers to the band of philosophes trumpeting their point of view.

The Prerevolutionary Origins
of Political Journalism*

Jeremy Popkin

Revolutionaries believed that their own press had little or nothing to do with the Old-Regime periodical. Decayed if not dead, the latter was at best an arm of the monarchy. During the last two centuries few historians have been willing to challenge that contention. Recently, however, a growing band of scholars, with Jeremy Popkin in its vanguard, has been reevaluating the prerevolutionary press.

In the article presented here, Popkin makes the strongest statement to date about the vitality of political journalism during the late eighteenth century. Popkin casts his net wide, examining the governmentally sponsored press, the newspapers circulated in France but published outside her borders, and two political commentaries that were organized as daily chronicles but were likely released sometime later. Popkin finds these last two categories particularly important. The foreign press treated government as a group of ministers, and thus removed the monarch far from the action. Political pundits even attacked these institutions with a great deal of verve. Together, these two manifestations of the press not only exhibited many aspects believed characteristic only of their revolutionary successors, but the very existence of such organs prior to 1789 also suggested that the demise of the monarchy had already become an inevitability. In his reevaluation of the press, Popkin has found it not only a worthy forerunner of the later papers but even an important part of the Revolution.

Very recently published, this article has not yet had time to attract much praise or criticism. Its strong claims, though, will surely raise questions. Some may focus on the commentaries. Can these two reports carry enough weight to make eighteenth century journalism a critical genre? Some of Popkin's contentions seem to rest on a slender base. In addition, it would seem that the propaganda efforts of the monarchy may have diluted the effects of the press. Although these and other questions will certainly be

*Published in Keith Michael Baker, ed., *The Political Culture of the Old Regime* (Oxford, 1987), pp. 203–21. Published with the permission of Pergamon Press.

raised, scholars and students will no doubt find Popkin's article imaginative, exciting, and provocative. Its influence should be felt for some time.

Even those scholars who have most strongly stressed the connections between the prerevolutionary and revolutionary eras have normally accepted the assumption that the events of 1789 gave rise to a new political culture, and to the extent that they have discussed the political press, they have assumed that, as part of that new politics, the revolutionary press, too, had little in common with the periodicals of the Old Regime. The explosion of new publications in 1789, which carried the Parisian press from the level of four titles in 1788 to 184 before the end of the following year, and the unmistakable difference in tone between the best-known prerevolutionary papers, such as the *Gazette de France,* and the best known revolutionary ones, such as the *Ami du Peuple,* seem to rule out any doubt: the revolutionary press can only have been a new departure, a new creation to meet new political needs.

If the gap between the prerevolutionary and the revolutionary press was truly this profound, however, we would clearly face a major difficulty in reconciling the situation in this domain with the increasing recognition of continuities in other aspects of French life. If the barriers between nobles and educated bourgeois were breaking down long before 1789, if the revolution did not mark a major turning point in French economic development, and if the roots of revolutionary political ideology can be found in the conflicts of the previous half-century, it would be surprising to discover that an institution as important as the revolutionary press had no significant prerevolutionary roots. Indeed, such a conclusion would challenge all general interpretations of the Revolution that emphasize the connections between the ancien régime and its successor.

The fact that journalism is, by definition, ephemeral literature has traditionally served to relegate it to a lesser place in historical studies. This has been particularly true with respect to eighteenth-century France, where there has been hardly any serious study of political pamphlet literature or journalism, compared with the meticulous attention lavished on the ambiguous political implications of such books as the *Encyclopédie,* or even with the attempt to extract traces of ideology from such apparently unpromising materials as the *Bibliothèque bleue.*[1] As historians increasingly recognize

---

[1]A series of books published to appeal to the illiterate or barely literate public. Of course, their audiences often heard, rather than read, these volumes.

the necessity of recapturing the sense of the *événementielle*[2] in the past, however, it is clear that we must pay more attention to the literature most closely associated with events themselves. Furthermore, we should be wary of accepting the equation often implied between ephemeral literature and marginal literature, a tendency that can be seen in Robert Darnton's article on Grub Street. The decision to publish an ephemeral text was a conscious decision to try to influence the course of ongoing events, not a necessity imposed on certain classes of writers because of their marginal social situation. The authors of ephemeral literature included the great names of eighteenth-century French literature, such as Voltaire and Condorcet, as well as Darnton's hacks, and even the hacks were often acting on behalf of the rich and powerful. Over the course of the eighteenth century, journalism was becoming an increasingly stable profession, not simply a refuge for the down-and-out.

Although journalism was thus a vital part of the literary and political culture of the Old Regime, it may legitimately be asked whether the distinction between periodical and non-periodical journalistic literature, so evident in the modern world, is equally relevant to the conditions of the eighteenth century. The periodical is different from the pamphlet in two fundamental ways: it creates a two-way circuit between author and reader, since the journalist learns at least something about his audience's reactions and can adjust his aim accordingly, and the news periodical "deals with the ephemeral but specific present moment, clearly located in time and space." But the eighteenth-century political pamphlet was normally just as concerned with immediate events as the news periodical, and, since significant periodicals were usually printed abroad, whereas pamphlets were often produced in Paris itself, the two forms of literature often appeared with equal rapidity. The pamphleteers, particularly those in Paris, lived and worked in the midst of their audience and had a good sense of its response, and there is no question that the readership of the two genres overlapped heavily. Indeed, from the point of view of the readers, periodicals and pamphlets were clearly complementary: the periodical news press announced events, the pamphlets interpreted them. Furthermore, the two genres were not always distinct: excerpts from pamphlets often appeared in the newspapers and pamphlet authors explicitly presumed that their readers had seen the accounts of the events they discussed in the press. News periodicals such as those I will discuss here thus need to be interpreted as part of a larger complex of communications media, including not only pamphlets but a variety of other written and oral channels by which political news and ideas were communicated.

There are many aspects to the problem of continuity between pre-

---

[2]History that depends on the narration of events.

revolutionary and revolutionary journalism in France. In some respects, there is no doubt that there was a dramatic rupture with the past in 1789. Although many prerevolutionary titles continued to appear, they either changed their content completely or were submerged by the flood of new publications without prerevolutionary ancestors, ranging from the *Moniteur* to the *Ami du Peuple*. On the other hand, there were important aspects of the periodical press which hardly changed at all, such as the printing technology used to produce newspapers. In what follows, I shall concentrate on continuities in two important dimensions of the press: the voices or personae journalists used to address their readers, and the manner in which prerevolutionary periodicals structured the flow of time. I will argue that these are two essential aspects of the power of the revolutionary press, and that both represented the application of lessons already learned in the prerevolutionary years.

There is no doubt that one of the effects of the Revolution was to favor the development of periodical newspapers at the expense of pamphlets. Many journalistic techniques primarily associated with pamphlets before 1789 became commonplace in the newspapers, and it is thus of particular interest to examine the forms of prerevolutionary periodical journalism to see how far this process had advanced before the Revolution. Recent research has demonstrated that this periodical press was far livelier and more extensive than has normally been recognized. Gilles Feyel's work on the provincial reprints of the *Gazette de France* has shown that the newspaper reached the French provinces much earlier than had been thought, and in his provocative contribution to the recent *Histoire de l'Edition française,* Jean Sgard has argued that periodicals represented the most dynamic sector of French publishing during the age of the Enlightenment. Old Regime France may not have enjoyed a totally free marketplace of ideas, but even in the realm of politics, where controls were at their most elaborate, there was a good deal of diversity and competition long before the Revolution.

Like other sectors of the press, the political newspapers had multiplied and diversified throughout the eighteenth century. Among the various species of news periodicals there were representatives of older forms, such as the official *Gazette de France,* as well as new varieties, culminating in publications whose relationship with the revolutionary press is impossible to mistake. Few of the periodicals that appeared in the course of the eighteenth century were completely independent of all state-imposed controls, but few of them were constrained by the formal rules that governed the *Gazette de France* either. The process of evolution in political journalism accelerated tremendously from the time of the Maupeou "coup" of 1771,[3]

---

[3]Maupeou's effort to conquer the judicial opposition to the crown.

and it is on this period of change that I will concentrate in the pages that follow.

It is worth remembering that seemingly archaic forms of news publication, such as the *Gazette de France,* remained important to the very end of the monarchy. Official gazettes of this sort were published in most European countries of the time, including not only the absolutist states on the continent but England as well. To modern eyes, they appear to be of little journalistic interest, but contemporaries saw them as one of the distinguishing features of lawful governments, in contrast to despotic regimes like Turkey where the rulers, bent on keeping their subjects in ignorance, refused even to permit "a public paper, which informs the Nation about the happenings of the time, according to the way the Government sees them." Certainly readers recognized the *Gazette de France* as a tool of government policy, performing a specific function in the context of French state institutions, but it was nevertheless an important part of the French journalistic system. A serious study of the *Gazette de France*'s content remains to be undertaken. It essentially offered French readers two very different kinds of information. The bulk of the paper related news from foreign capitals, provided—under the impetus of repeated proddings from Versailles —by members of the French diplomatic service; the *Gazette* thus enjoyed the services of a correspondence network far more extensive than that of any unofficial periodical of the period and, as the *Encyclopédie* admitted, it was not without value as a source of information. The paper presented foreign news in a neutral tone and with a fair degree of objectivity; even political systems as fundamentally different from the French as England's constitutional monarchy were depicted in objective terms. Jack Censer has found that the percentage of news items reporting revolutions and social violence rose gradually from 1740 to 1780, indicating that the paper reflected faithfully the growth of unrest in the world around it. If this foreign-news section of the *Gazette* had any impact on its readers' views of the world, it was by encouraging them to think of France as part of a system of rival states, and perhaps by stimulating them to identify with their own country, but this effect, if it existed, was purely subliminal: the overt content of the coverage never suggested that the success of France's foreign policies depended on the subjects' identification with them.

When it depicted French domestic affairs, however, the *Gazette* proceeded in an entirely different fashion. It made no effort to describe events in the form of a more or less continuous narrative, as it did in its coverage of other countries: instead, its goal was to build up a very specific image of the French monarch and the monarchy. Like the palace at Versailles, the *Gazette*'s coverage was entirely centered around the king. He alone acted; all others obeyed. The royal will was thus presented as the sole force shaping the events in the kingdom. The king was rarely shown acting as a political figure: the emphasis was on his ceremonial role. As the incarnation of the state he received foreign ambassadors and he met with his council; occasionally, he issued an edict, although the text was not always published in the *Gazette,* which was not an ancestor of the revolutionary *Bulletin officiel.* The paper reflected the existence of political institutions other than the king, but only insofar as they participated in the world of royal ceremonies. A typical item consisted of the report that the king had received a deputation from some corporate body, such as the Estates of Cambrai; the item would mention the names of the delegates and the court figures who had presented them, but would give no hint of what had been discussed.

The publication of even this much news about political affairs had some significance, of course: in effect, the public got to see the king's appointment calendar. But that calendar was not composed primarily of political events, or rather the reception of deputies from provincial estates and the naming and dismissal of ministers were simply a few of the many acts the king regularly performed to exhibit himself to his subjects as king. Such political acts were interspersed with mentions of the king's attendance at church, his meetings with members of his family, his benevolence to his royal academies, and the victories of his armies. Whatever the subject, however, the *Gazette* touched on French news only insofar as it concerned the king. The real political life of the country penetrated into its columns only in a veiled and incomplete manner. The ministers were mentioned occasionally, but they were never depicted as acting on their own, and no explanation for their nomination, their actions or their dismissal was ever furnished. The virulent quarrels between crown and parlements were reflected only in the bare announcements of formal ceremonies such as *lits de justice.* In a curious reversal of the normal function of a newspaper, the *Gazette* thus provided reports whose significance was only evident to those who already knew the news, and who could hence translate images of ceremony into measures of the strength of contending forces. The two most activist ministers of the outgoing ancien régime, Maupeou and Turgot, did on occasion bend the rules governing the *Gazette* and use it more directly to promote their policies: under the former, for example, the paper uncharacteristically announced that the reconstituted Paris parlement's first session had "gone off with the greatest order, the greatest propriety and the greatest tranquillity . . . " suggesting that some people had expected the opposite, and Turgot had the paper print his denunciation of the conspirators he blamed for the *guerre des farines*[4] in 1775. But such uses of the *Gazette* were exceptional, and after Turgot's fall, the paper reverted firmly to its court-centered tradition.

The picture of French domestic affairs the *Gazette de France* conveyed

---

[4]A series of bread riots.

was thus structured to fit the requirements of the absolutist myth. It was an apolitical depiction of politics, from which all elements of conflict had been removed. And the *Gazette de France*'s coverage of France was delivered in an absolutely impersonal voice. The editorial "nous" which figured so prominently in the same paper's reports from foreign capitals, implying the existence of an observer registering events, was absent from the French news coverage: even a fictitious passive witness was not to come between the king and the readers of the *Gazette,* which behaved as though the king's actions reported themselves. And, curiously in view of the fact that the newspaper medium's special quality is the depiction of events as they unfold in time, the logic of this absolutist imagery required that French affairs be depicted neither as a temporal sequence nor as a continuous narrative. Each royal action was described as complete in itself; since the royal will was by definition omnipotent, there could be no sense of journalistic tension caused by the necessity of waiting for events to unfold and determine whether a given policy had been successful. Nor could the crown's decisions be presented as choices whose logical consequences the king himself had to accept: such a conception would have amounted to arguing that the royal will of today was constrained by that of the day before. In the *Gazette,* the King's will created a realm of arbitrary freedom and his actions had no binding consequences for the future. To the end of the Old Regime, the *Gazette de France* remained an example of what Jürgen Habermas has defined as "repräsentative Öffentlichkeit,"[5] in which the king as public person stood for or represented the entire society he governed.

Clearly the *Gazette de France* was not a model for the revolutionary press. Even the quasi-official newspapers published at the height of the Terror never depicted the omnipotence of the republic in the way in which the *Gazette* celebrated that of the king. Indeed, both the notion that the Convention's acts were the outcome of reasoned discussion in what Habermas has called a civil or "bürgerliche" public sphere—validated through the press's publication of excerpts from its debates—and the heroic image of the Republic overcoming its enemies by struggle were intrinsic elements of Jacobin propaganda. The sovereign republic, unlike the monarch, could never stand still; the static quality of the *Gazette de France*'s representations had to yield to something dynamic.

Long before 1789, readers who wanted to know at least as much about French politics as the *Gazette de France* told them about the affairs of foreign countries had sought other sources of information. From the seventeenth century onward, manuscript news bulletins circulated to satisfy part of this demand for news. These bulletins continued to exist

---

[5]Representative publicity.

down to the time of the Revolution, but throughout the eighteenth century, they faced competition from printed news publications that also succeeded in getting around the restrictions imposed on the *Gazette de France,* while enjoying the technical benefits of mechanical reproduction and hence the ability to reach a much wider audience than the handwritten *nouvelles.*

These printed publications were the "gazettes de Hollande" and their imitators in other countries: newspapers printed in French but published outside France's borders, intended for sale to an international audience. The earliest enterprises of this sort pre-dated the appearance of the *Gazette de France*; French translations of the early Dutch *corantos*[6] appeared in the early 1620s. In the seventeenth century, their content was similar to that of the manuscript *nouvelles,* a collection of rumors and short announcements strung together in no apparent order. A typical excerpt from the *Gazette de Leyde*[7] in the 1680s reads, "le jour precedent quatorze prisonniers se sauverent des prisons de l'Abbaye, après avoir bien rossé le Geolier & les Guichetiers. Il arriva hier un Courrier qui aporta la nouvelle, que le Grand Doyen de Liège en avoit esté éleu Evêque. On asseure qu'on va faire une levée 5,000 de Chevaux et de 10 mille hommes de pied. Le Roy fut hier à la Chasse aux environs de Meudon."[8] As with the manuscript *nouvelles,* it is difficult to discern a narrative strategy behind this sort of presentation of materials.

In the course of the eighteenth century, however, the news coverage in the extraterritorial gazettes evolved toward a more structured form of journalism. The news bulletins from major capitals, particularly London and Paris, became longer, and if they still tended to pass from subject to subject with no apparent transition, at least the individual items became extensive enough to make their significance more comprehensible. To accommodate this growing volume of news, the papers expanded: by the 1770s, most were at least eight quarto pages per bi-weekly issue. Since they invariably used very small type, they could convey almost as much information per week as did the average daily newspaper during the Revolution, and considerably more than the *Gazette de France.* In the 1770s and 1780s, sales of individual titles reached 4,000 copies or more in France, and there is no doubt that the total circulation of such publications equalled or

---

[6]Periodicals, then called courants.

[7]Gazette of Leiden.

[8]Yesterday fourteen prisoners escaped from the prisons of the Abbaye, after having thrashed the jailer and the turnkeys. Yesterday a courier brought the news that the Grand Doyen of Liège has been elected a bishop. We are assured that 5,000 horsemen and 1,000 foot soldiers will be raised. Yesterday the King hunted near Meudon.

exceeded that of the *Gazette de France* and the other privileged news publications in the kingdom.

What did French readers find in these publications that they did not get in the official press? Not an equivalent to the British opposition newspapers of the period: these papers printed no scurrilous personal attacks on the king or the ministers. But if the *Gazette de France* represented the kingdom as an absolutist state, in which everything depended on the king's will alone, the international press depicted instead a constitutional monarchy in which the royal will was exercised indirectly, through ministers, and hedged about with restrictions enforced by a variety of traditional institutions, above all the parlements.[9] Those bodies, which were reduced to silence in the pages of the *Gazette de France,* used the foreign press to make their votes echo throughout the country and indeed the entire French-speaking world. Papers like the *Gazette de Leyde* and the *Courier du Bas-Rhin* regularly printed the full texts of the supposedly secret remonstrances by which the parlements conducted their ideological campaign against the crown from the 1750s onward, and they summarized the internal debates of the Parlement of Paris, thus giving it the appearance of a legislative body. They extended similar coverage to many other corporate bodies, including the provincial Estates, particularly those of Bretagne, the Assembly of the Clergy and a number of other institutions. The pamphlet press of the period might weaken royal authority by arguing that France had been a constitutional monarchy in the time of Charlemagne; the international gazettes implied that it continued to be one in the age of Louis XV and Louis XVI.

Even in their coverage of the king's own government, the international gazettes differed sharply from the *Gazette de France.* The king, the centre of the official paper's system of imagery, was virtually invisible in the foreign papers. This was partly because disparaging references to foreign sovereigns were the one offense most likely to land publishers in trouble with their own governments, but it was due more to these papers' concentration on the dynamic aspect of politics as opposed to the representational and ceremonial aspects that the *Gazette de France* had to stress. Hence the foreign papers' coverage focused on ministers rather than monarchs. This coverage was generally uncritical and always incomplete, since news about rivalries among ministers and speculations on the degree of royal favor they enjoyed were always suppressed. Nonetheless these reports gave a very different image of how French politics worked than that provided in the officially licensed papers. Policies were identified as the work of specific ministers, and there was some effort to explain the rationale behind decisions as well as to publicize the edicts in which they were

---

[9]See the glossary entry *parlements.*

embodied. The papers often offered judgments and prognostications about major initiatives, even if they were rarely very probing. Thus the *Gazette de Leyde* welcomed Terray's appointment in 1770 with the comment that "he has only accepted this difficult position in the hope of sparing the people the burden of new taxes," and it later endorsed Turgot's efforts to liberate the grain trade, remarking that "no fair-minded man can help being convinced of the Controller-General's patriotic intentions and wise views." Without any hostile intent, then, the foreign gazettes depicted a political system very different from that portrayed in the regime's own publications: indeed, in their pages France appeared to be a constitutional monarchy in which the king reigned but did not govern, and in which the Parlement of Paris bore an uncanny resemblance to the British Parliament, whose sessions all the papers routinely summarized.

As has been noted, the international gazettes were in no sense clandestine or subversive publications. In a long memorandum written during his service as Directeur-Général de la librairie,[10] Malesherbes outlined the various policies the government might adopt towards these publications. Although he recognized that they contributed to domestic criticism of the government by airing opposition, he concluded that an effective ban on the papers was unenforceable and suggested that the best policy was to offer their editors positive encouragements to restrain themselves within certain limits. Whether or not they had read his mémoire, subsequent French ministers down to the Revolution adopted his advice. Indeed, they frequently used the papers themselves: thus the *Gazette de Leyde* and the *Courier du Bas-Rhin* published a purported conversation among Louis XVI, Marie Antoinette, and the Cardinal Rohan designed to establish his guilt in the Diamond Necklace affair in 1785.[11] But this cooperation between the press and the ministers did not mean that the papers were simply disguised means of official propaganda. Thanks to their sales in other countries, they were able to risk displeasing Versailles from time to time without courting instant ruin, and they clearly understood that their success depended on occasional demonstrations of their independence. As Etienne Luzac, editor of the *Gazette de Leyde,* wrote to the French ambassador to the Netherlands in 1772, if he was truly compelled to limit himself to official news, "the French public would notice this reticence, which would produce the opposite effect from what is expected. . . . Now, Sir, in that case, what respect would you give my gazette? What respect would it have left among those who simply want the present state of the world's affairs?" Even for the French government's own purposes, it was

---

[10]General Director of the Book Trade.

[11]Rohan claimed that he was duped into trying to acquire without purchase an expensive diamond necklace for Queen Marie Antoinette.

important that the newspapers at least appear to be uncontrolled, lest they lose their persuasive power.

The position of the international gazettes was thus somewhat analogous to that of the French parlements, as William Doyle has analyzed it in a well known article: they gave the appearance of being independent checks on the monarchy, although in fact they had no tangible way of blocking a determined minister. But one can argue in both cases that the regime's bargain with these institutions was a Faustian one: having allowed the French public to become accustomed to the appearance of an informal constitution limiting the king's power, the ministers found it increasingly difficult to act as if they could wilfully disregard those limitations. One can argue, as Doyle does, that the attempts to eliminate the parlements' opposition in 1771 and 1788 could have been carried through, but the fact is that they were not. As for the quasi-independent foreign-based papers, there is some evidence of a plan to try to supplant them with a domestically published news organ during the Maupeou coup, but the idea was never really tested. Malesherbes's conclusion that the uncensored press was an unavoidable evil seems to have been accepted.

The result of this toleration of the international news press was that French readers became accustomed to a more or less accurate narrative of political events in their country long before the Revolution. This press abundantly publicized the existence of opposition to royal policies, and accustomed the French public to the forms of parlementary journalism long before the summoning of the Estates General. Given that the power to impose a certain image of reality is an aspect of political power in general, there is no doubt that the foreign-based gazettes were a significant factor in pre-revolutionary politics, and that they worked to push France in the direction of representative government.

There is no doubt that the international gazettes also had a definite influence on the forms and practices of French revolutionary journalism. A number of revolutionary journalists had reported for or edited such papers before 1789, including Brissot and Théveneau de Morande, who had worked for the *Courrier de l'Europe,* and Antoine Cerisier and Pascal Boyer, both associated with the *Gazette de Leyde,* who became founders of the extremely successful *Gazette universelle.* Although Brissot exercised a different kind of journalism in his *Patriote françois,* many Parisian journalists imitated the sober, seemingly neutral style that had characterized the international gazettes, in which the author affected to be no more than an "impartial narrator" of events that were beyond his control. Like all other forms of journalism, this "objectivity" in fact reflected a definite strategy of persuasion: readers were to be won over to a certain interpretation of events through the belief that the writer was simply giving them the facts and allowing them to interpret them for themselves. In fact, both the international gazettes and the revolutionary papers that imitated their reporting style often had distinct biases, but in general these papers eschewed the techniques of partisan journalism, as they had developed, for example, in the British press. They made no explicit declarations of party preferences, they did not engage in polemical exchanges with journalistic opponents, and they claimed to present all sides of public controversies. Such rhetorical strategies are not normally considered characteristic of the French revolutionary press, but in fact they were more prevalent than is normally realized: newspapers of information such as the *Moniteur,* the *Logographe,* and the *Gazette universelle* were often among the most widely read titles.

In addition to elaborating an important narrative mode later taken over by the revolutionary press, the foreign-based papers did more than the *Gazette de France* to accustom newspaper readers to the modern relationship between journalism and the flow of time. As we have seen, the *Gazette de France* was characterized by the atemporality of its reporting: events in France were depicted as complete in themselves, without origins or implications, and there was no sense of a continuing story. In the international gazettes, on the other hand, the reader's attention was kept firmly focused on what was going to happen in the next issue. Acutely aware that time had already marched on, even before they had succeeded in getting their latest bulletins from Paris set up in type, these journalists engaged in constant speculation about the outcome of the situations they were narrating. "Nous sommes toujours dans l'incertitude . . . "[12] was a phrase that could have been their collective motto, so frequently did it appear. While awaiting "la suite au numero suivant,"[13] the reader was left in suspense and thus encouraged to engage in the process of speculation himself. Pulled along in the flux of temporal events in this fashion, newspaper readers developed a sense of time geared to the rhythm of their publication's appearance, as they eagerly anticipated the arrival of each issue to find out how ongoing events had developed and to begin discussion and speculation anew on the basis of additional information. This method of engaging the reader anticipated the techniques of revolutionary journalism, in which writers learned to cultivate a sense of tension about impending events in their readers, and it is an integral aspect of all modern journalism—a basic technique for compelling readers to return to their paper issue after issue. From this point of view, as from several others, the international political gazettes were clearly forerunners of the revolutionary press.

Although one can find important traits of the revolutionary press in the international gazettes, there is no denying that there were also important differences between the two groups of papers. The absence in the international gazettes of overt ideological polemics published in the paper's

---

[12]We remain always in uncertainty.
[13]The remainder in the next issue.

own name (as opposed to being imbedded in documents such as parlementary remonstrances that were published as "materials for history") and the refusal to adopt explicit partisan positions clearly indicated that the international papers operated along different lines from those followed by journalists like Brissot, Marat, or the abbé Royou. To find the prerevolutionary origins of these aspects of revolutionary journalism, one must examine other genres of eighteenth-century newswriting.

The strongest stimulus to these mutations came from the political crisis associated with the "Maupeou coup" of 1771. Whatever the actual intentions of Maupeou and his associates, this thoroughgoing attempt to eliminate the parlementaire opposition upset the traditional institutional balance in France. Both sides in the dispute felt compelled to find effective ways to present their case to the reading public. Of course, each had its time-honored journalistic outlets: the ministers, as has been noted, made somewhat freer use of the *Gazette de France* than their predecessors, and the parlementaire party filled the columns of the foreign gazettes with its protests until the government suspended their sale in France. Among the "patriot" opponents of Maupeou, however, the coup was the impetus for the creation of something more closely resembling a genuinely political newspaper, highly professional in its collection and presentation of information and openly partisan in its interpretation of what it reported. The series of journalistic publications I refer to have virtually escaped the attention of press historians, however, because although they read like a newspaper and act like a newspaper, they apparently never were a newspaper: they were first published, as far as we know, considerably after the events they describe, and in the form of books rather than as a periodical. Nevertheless, they prove to be a highly significant development in the history of French journalism.

The publications in question, though overlooked by press historians, are well known to specialists in the period. Attributed to the *nouvelliste,*[14] royal censor, and stock speculator Pidansat de Mairobert, they were published under the titles of the *Journal historique de la Révolution opérée dans la Constitution de la Monarchie Françoise, par M. de Maupeou, Chancelier de France,* and the *Observateur anglois, ou Correspondance secrète entre Milord All'Eye et Milord All'Ear.*[15] The chronological sequences of these works (they also contain other kinds of material) constitute a detailed political history running from January 1771 to December 1776. In the *Journal historique,* the material is in the form of day-by-day

---

[14]Newswriter.

[15]*Historical Journal of the Revolution Made in the Constitution of the French Monarchy by M. de Maupeou, Chancellor of France* and the *English Observer or Secret Correspondence between Milord All'Eye and Milord All'Ear.*

notes, similar in style to the manuscript *nouvelles* but distinguished by its careful selection; almost all the items relate directly to the crisis of the parlements. The *Observateur anglois* is divided into irregular installments, written, as the author indicates, "less often and with more coherence." The exact origin of these texts and their relationship to the other anti-Maupeou news sources of the period such as the so-called *Mémoires secrets de Bachaumont* still needs to be sorted out, as does the publishing history of the works in question. Compared to these other texts, however, the *Journal historique* and the *Observateur anglois* are much more finished journalistic products, so persuasive that they have often been accepted at face value by historians. Whereas the printed *Mémoires de Bachaumont* and the manuscript *nouvelles* are fascinating but unstructured collections of gossip and information, these two texts are highly polished journalistic narrative, shaped by a keen political mind; they are among the outstanding political texts of the period. What cannot be said with assurance is that they actually circulated as journalism at the time of the events they describe.

Whether printed at the time or not, the texts in this series are all presented as though written in the midst of events. The author of the *Journal historique* proceeds day to day and acts as though he has no foreknowledge of impending occurrences. He writes as if to persuade specific political actors: thus, when reporting the first stages of the negotiations that led the Princes of the Blood to drop their public opposition to Maupeou, he writes, "it is feared that, tired of remaining so completely inactive, they may let themselves be misled . . . ," an obvious attempt to influence the Princes to stand firm. But there are no definite references to the circulation of these pages, either in manuscript form or in print, prior to the appearance of the first printed edition of the *Journal historique*'s first three volumes in 1774, other than a cryptic reference in the work itself, dated 19 Dec. 1774, which mentions the appearance of a three-volume edition in Geneva and claims that it is based on an earlier English edition printed "in more critical times." We cannot be certain, then, whether the texts as we have them represent journalism or an elaborate simulacrum of journalism. In either case, however, they richly repay analysis from the point of view of the pre-history of revolutionary journalistic techniques.

The Mairobert texts, in their chronological sections, share the same method of presenting events in chronological sequence as the international gazettes, but they differ from those publications and anticipate the journalistic methods of the revolutionary press in at least three important ways. In the first place, Mairobert, who criticized the international papers for the self-censorship they engaged in to preserve their access to the French market, was free to make negative as well as positive comments about ministers and even the king; hence he gave a picture of politics with far more depth and realism to it. Secondly, he mastered several key techniques of modern propaganda, in particular the use of simple labels and slogans regularly repeated to drive home major points. Finally, the *Journal historique* and the *Observateur anglois* were structured around an explicit ideology, which served to make sense of all the news they reported and link diverse events together in a coherent way. That this ideology is remarkably radical and in many ways anticipates the ideas of 1789 is significant, particularly given the success of the Mairobert publications, but from the point of view of the evolution of journalistic forms, Mairobert's specific ideas are less important than the way in which he used them to define the criteria by which he selected news he considered relevant.

Like the journalists of the international gazettes, Mairobert was essentially interested in elite politics, the politics of the ministerial bureaux and of the antechambers of Versailles. Within that framework, however, he was free to give a much more complex portrayal of events. That he possessed an impressive "data base" of information about French court politics is evident from the lengthy series of newsletters attributed to a "Dutch observer" and inserted in the first volume of the *Observateur anglois,* a portrait gallery of France's decision-making elite at the end of Louis XV's reign which includes capsule biographies of several hundred personalities. The newsletter in that work recounting the fall of Turgot's ministry, dated just three weeks after the event, mentions the role of 36 different individuals and groups in the affair; of the major participants identified by modern scholarship, only the Queen is not discussed. But the information Mairobert gathered was not primarily the scurrilous gossip which was the stock in trade of the period's pamphleteers; the additional dimension he brought to the representation of politics was essentially a detailed and serious portrayal of the political motives of the characters on the scene. The outstanding example of his method was his depiction of the Chancellor Maupeou himself, the pivot around which the entire seven-volume sequence of the *Journal historique* turns. Undoubtedly Mairobert's Maupeou was largely a fictional character, but he was presented with sufficient skill and ingenuity to make him a worthy peer of Choderlos de Laclos's[16] personnages. For Mairobert, Maupeou was the supreme villain, the architect of a sweeping plan to install a despotic government in France, in which all courts, provincial estates, and corporate assemblies would be abolished, all individuals deprived of their privileges, and all power concentrated in the hands of the ministry. But the author of the *Journal historique* could not repress a certain admiration for the energy and talent with which Maupeou carried out his evil deeds: "He is constantly on the move . . . after having taken care of all the details of the plot, he uses the evening, the night, and the early hours of the morning for his work, which mostly concerns the conspiracy. . . .

---

[16]Famous writer, best known for his bawdy *Les liasons dangereuses.*

Despite his delicate temperament, his never-ceasing ambition and his facile genius allow him to take care of everything."

The methods by which Mairobert built up his portrait of Maupeou were far more refined than those of the most of the pro-parlementaire pamphleteers. Whereas the author of the highly successful anti-Maupeou pamphlet series titled *Correspondance secrète et familière* belabored the accusation that one of Maupeou's distant relatives had murdered his son-in-law in an inheritance quarrel in the 1600s, the *Journal historique* concentrated on its enemy's actual deeds. As it followed him step by step through 1771 and 1772, the *Journal* never suppressed its respect for the Chancellor's political talents. When the king squelched rumors that Maupeou was about to be dismissed, it remarked, "there are political experts who assert that he himself floated the rumor of his dismissal, in a ruse that would be typical of him. . . . " When the Chancellor appeared looking unusually healthy, the chronicler remarked, "it is believed that he puts on make-up, not like a sexpot . . . but as a skilled politician, who knows how important an imposing appearance is." The author of the *Journal historique* thus admitted and explained Maupeou's successes, but at every turn he insinuated that the Chancellor's actions could not be taken at face value, that his professions of good intentions masked a boundless and tyrannical ambition. Mairobert's method was a patient and consistent process of character assassination. He was much subtler than the revolutionary journalists, such as Marat in his pursuit of Lafayette or Brissot, but he exemplified the same journalistic technique: the reduction of politics to personalities, and the development of a demonized but plausible portrait of the chosen enemy.

Like many of the best revolutionary journalists, Mairobert also understood the value of repetition and of simple slogans and labels to make his point. For him, the court with which Maupeou replaced the Parlement of Paris was always "le soi-disant Parlement,"[17] and Maupeou himself was always the author of all evil. The fact that the *Journal historique* paid only peripheral attention to the other two members of the anti-parlementaire triumvirate, the duc d'Aiguillon and the abbé Terray, was partly a political choice—it reflected the *Journal*'s close ties to the parlements, whose quarrel was above all with the Chancellor—but it also had the effect of making the work's theme clearer and more precise and thus promoting its propagandistic effectiveness. Mairobert's appreciation of the value of simplicity is evident also in his summaries of the political pamphlet published on behalf of the parlement. He was a master at compressing their arguments into a few lines and giving to the often overly long and diffuse literature of the period a clarity and pointedness it really did not have. Eliminating anything more than cursory references to the historical argu-

---

[17]The so-called Parlement.

mentation that filled most of the "patriot" pamphlets, Mairobert asserted that their content could really be reduced to "the great principles found in so many works, concerning man's natural liberty, the imprescriptibility of his rights, the origin of kings, the social contract, etc." He reduced even the 1000-page summa of the parlementaire case, the *Maximes du droit public françois,*[18] to a set of catchphrases. So long as most supporters of the good cause knew that such a work existed, they were doubtless content to settle for a one-page summary of its argument.

In addition to providing a dynamic, three-dimensional depiction of political personalities and to simplifying issues into easily comprehensible slogans, Mairobert anticipated revolutionary journalism by orienting his news around explicit ideological principles. There was no doubt in Mairobert's mind that the object of Maupeou's policy was "the establishment of an arbitrary power and . . . the overthrow of the state . . . ," and in that context, he defended the parlements as a check on despotism. But their value was purely relative in his eyes, and he did not simply embrace the magistrates' arguments in their own favor. He criticized the *Maximes du droit public françois,* for example, because its concern was "too focussed on that body, without insisting, as it should have under the circumstances, on the necessity of the Assembly of the Estates-General, the real remedy to restore the threatened Constitution." The author actually blamed the parlements for having usurped the authority to approve taxes, "to have dared to put the nation in chains along with themselves, by letting them suffer under this enormous number of disastrous edicts. . . . " He maintained this critical attitude even after the restoration of the parlements, praising one judge who had protested against the terms of the restoration for having "spoken as the nation would have itself; he called for its imprescriptible rights, he showed the necessity of listening to it, of consulting it, and finally of bringing back those national assemblies, without which everything is irregular and illegal, and which the parlement and the Princes and Peers cannot replace." And he reiterated his belief in national sovereignty in the pages of the *Observateur anglois* in a stinging critique of the coronation ceremony of Louis XVI, claiming that essential parts of the ritual that underlined the king's dependence on the nation had been suppressed.

Mairobert's journalistic enterprises thus exemplified that merging of detailed factual narrative, plausible analysis of human motives, and outspoken ideological argumentation that reappeared in the revolutionary press. Had it actually been published as a periodical, Mairobert's work would have to be recognized as a first-rate radical journal; indeed, as a source of political news, it is superior to most of the revolutionary papers. Its existence demonstrates that pre-revolutionary France already possessed a jour-

---

[18]*Maxims of French Public Law.*

nalistic culture of considerable sophistication, and that it did not take the opportunity of the Revolution to allow writers to discover how to shape an ideological effective narrative, rather than simply presenting "materials for history." Mairobert's work had certainly not been forgotten at the time of the Revolution—the police confiscated a copy of the *Journal historique* from a colporteur in November 1788—and there can hardly be any doubt that many of the revolutionary newsmen had read it. Nevertheless, in the form in which it has survived, Mairobert's work was not yet periodical journalism: he had solved the problem of writing modern political reportage, but not the problem of getting it published and circulated in time to affect the events it covered.

If Mairobert's works represented one line of development toward the revolutionary press, those of one of his bitterest personal enemies exemplified another that contributed at least as much to the journalism of 1789. The writer in question was Simon-Nicolas-Henri Linguet; the journal was his *Annales politiques,* first published in 1777 and carried forward, with frequent interruptions, until the end of 1788. Linguet's *Annales,* begun in London and later carried on from Brussels, were not a newspaper; they had the form of a magazine but they never achieved regular periodicity, both because of Linguet's repeated embroilments with various governments and because of his chronic inability to meet a set schedule. Linguet sometimes wrote about the events of the day, but equally often he used his pages for long essays only remotely connected to the latest news. Although he constantly asserted his independence, he in fact submitted his work for clearance by the French authorities, in order to have permission to circulate it in the country. Nevertheless, there can be no doubt that his journal, despite its irregular form and its submission to unacknowledged censorship, had tremendous impact on the revolutionary press.

What made Linguet the single most important forerunner of the revolutionary press was not so much the explicit content of his message, although that was often radical enough, but rather the manner in which he delivered it. More than any other prerevolutionary writer, Linguet demonstrated the power of journalism to move and stir readers, to appeal to their passions as well as their minds. As one recent biographer has put it, "even if Linguet was not the creator of a genre which already existed, he was certainly the most remarkable and intelligent practitioner of it, the only one capable of making it an effective instrument of political criticism and of the diffusion of ideas." Through his extraordinary use of language, Linguet showed how words could be transmuted into political high explosives, capable of demolishing their targets. Often treated as a marginal figure in prerevolutionary intellectual life, interesting primarily because of his anticipation of nineteenth-century socialist critiques of capitalism, Linguet was in reality one of the most influential writers of his time.

Linguet's unique talents in appealing to public opinion grew out of his unusual career. He began as a would-be man of letters, and quickly learned to draw attention to himself by his outspoken opposition to the self-proclaimed representatives of progress and reform, the Physiocrats and the philosophes, whom he castigated as a self-interested clique bent on suppressing dissent, thus casting himself in the heroic role his opponents had long claimed for themselves. To get his arguments across, Linguet showed a clear recognition of the value of the shock effect: he countered the reasoned propositions of his foes with the most extreme negations, defending Asiatic despotism against the philosophes' ideal of liberty and slavery as preferable to the free enterprise system advocated by the Physiocrats.[19] Linguet's "paradoxes" naturally sabotaged any hope he might have had of making a stable intellectual career, but he refused to resign himself to the role of a marginal hack. In the late 1760s, he turned to the bar, and quickly became one of France's most celebrated trial lawyers. In a series of sensational cases, he revolutionized courtroom *mores,* although the violence of his language scandalized his peers. He was a pioneer in addressing both his written legal *mémoires* and his oral pleadings to the public more than to the judges. His flamboyant conduct brought him into conflict with the *Ordre des avocats,*[20] and Linguet ended up as his own star client, pleading for his right to remain in practice against the opposition of the other lawyers and the Parlement of Paris. During this lengthy dispute, he crafted himself a public persona resembling Rousseau's, depicting himself as a persecuted innocent and inviting his audience to identify emotionally with him.

Forced out of the courtroom, Linguet turned to a new career as a journalist. At first he worked for Panckoucke, editing the latter's *Journal de politique et de littérature,* but his rabid attacks on his personal enemies soon led to his ouster. He thereupon emigrated and set up his own publication. Despite his stinging attacks on various French ministers and institutions, Linguet managed to obtain permission to sell his work in France most of the time; his criticisms of England, of the philosophes, of the parlements, and of other anti-ministerial groups in France were often welcome in Versailles. Though he used violent language, Linguet was no scandalmonger: the only private life he dissected was his own. Like Rousseau, he used a personal, confessional tone to win his readers' trust, and even the *lieutenant de police* Le Noir, who oversaw Linguet's writing, must have appreciated the talent of a propagandist who succeeded in convincing his public that "I had written, as I usually do, without political intent, without bias, letting my pen follow the impulses of my heart, and always depicting things from whatever point of view that struck me." Seduced by Linguet's willingness to

---

[19]Economists whose ideas have been associated with the Enlightenment.
[20]Order of the barristers.

direct most of his fire at officially approved targets, even after his well-publicized stay in the Bastille in 1780–82, the ministers overlooked the passion and the revolutionary tension in the journalist's writings.

In his journalistic work, Linguet used the same techniques he had perfected in his books and his legal briefs. Not only were his ideas always new and shocking, but he deliberately underlined their conflict with received assumptions. Thus, in a discussion of whether warfare could be made more humane, Linguet—anticipating the twentieth century doctrine of mutual assured destruction—called for scientists to develop a weapon that could vaporize an entire army instantly, and then told readers, "You shudder! Don't you see that if war were ever reduced to that point, it wouldn't be waged any more?" Far from backing away from the controversial defenses of despotism and slavery that had made him an outcast among men of letters, he reaffirmed his old stands and buttressed them with ingenious new arguments, as in his anticipation of the modern theory of entitlements as an explanation of hunger crises, in which he rejected the notion that famines resulted from an absolute lack of food and pointed out that "when the price of bread is not in just proportion to the laborer's daily wage, there is dearth. . . . When the balance is thrown off even more . . . there is famine, even if the markets are full."

Linguet's enemies—and they were numerous—charged that he used his undeniable talents as a writer purely to create a scandal and draw attention to himself. In fact, however, there was a consistent ideology underlying Linguet's rejection of the rational and moderate values of the Enlightenment. He saw society as being based on an irreconcilable conflict between rich and poor, and argued that only a completely unrestricted central authority could protect the oppressed lower classes against the rapacity of the wealthy. His famous endorsement of Asiatic despotism was the logical conclusion of this line of argument, and explains how Linguet could anticipate both the ideas of authoritarian conservatism and those of radical socialism. His constant tirades against privileged institutions and corporate bodies in France derived much of their vehemence from Linguet's personal quarrels, but they also fitted with his contention that France needed a monarch unconstrained by such intermediaries between himself and his subjects. The famous engraving prefixed to his lurid *Mémoires sur la Bastille,* representing grateful subjects kneeling before the king while lightning destroys the prison, accurately translated Linguet's view of the king's role, and his vigorous polemics against all the privileged groups in 1788 followed the same lines. In these last issues of the prerevolutionary *Annales politiques,* Linguet produced some of the most thoroughgoing denunciations of the Old Regime published at the time, and his formulations anticipated some of the best known passages in other revolutionary writers. One can see, for instance, a clear foreshadowing of Sieyès's famous statement about the uselessness of the nobility in Linguet's lines about what the king would be without the nobles: "What he would be! He would be what he is, the Sovereign, the beloved ruler of a brave, industrious, civilized, faithful people. The nobility is a distinguished part, no doubt, but would the subtraction of that part annihilate the whole?"

Although Linguet's writings thus had a clear ideological message and indeed had a direct influence on a number of revolutionary thinkers, including Babeuf, his importance for revolutionary journalism came less from his specific ideas than from his style of writing. Like Mairobert, he knew the value of turning conflicts of ideas into conflicts of personalities. His offensive against the academy system was conducted in the form of a perpetual campaign against d'Alembert, whom he blamed for keeping him out of the *Académie française,* and he waged equally bitter warfare against a variety of other personal enemies, including the duc d'Aiguillon and the publisher Panckoucke. Indeed, these personal smear campaigns were much cruder and less sophisticated than Mairobert's artful dissection of Maupeou; driven by his personal paranoia, Linguet could see nothing behind his enemies' conduct but their determination to persecute him. He relied heavily on conspiracy explanations for his own difficulties, another anticipation of much revolutionary rhetoric. Although he had no real gift as a coiner of slogans, he certainly knew the value of repeating the same ideas, both in promoting his favorite ideological hobby horses—the virtues of despotism, the humaneness of slavery— and in conducting his vendettas. Criticized for his obsessive attacks on d'Alembert, he replied that "this success [against d'Alembert] is due to consistency: a moment of silence would put M. d'Alembert back on his pedestal, and the public would relapse into veneration, or at least into uncertainty."

Beyond these matters of journalistic technique, Linguet bequeathed to the revolutionary press the example of his extraordinary rhetoric, and his apocalyptic, revolutionary sense of time. Linguet's highly original use of language stands out in recent statistical studies; while he was obviously part of the broader pre-romantic movement in French literature, he was unique in his use of direct appeals to emotion and sentiment for political purposes. Whether he was urging readers into a fury against the selfish privileged orders or wringing tears from them for his own personal sufferings, Linguet always addressed himself more to the heart than to the head. More sober contemporaries mocked his contorted sentences, with their concatenations of adjectives and pictorial images, but Linguet knew what he was about. It was he who pioneered the new sentimental and serious journalistic style that Robert Darnton has defined as characteristic of prerevolutionary France, in contrast to the rationalistic and satirical tone of Voltaire's generation, and thus opened the way for the political rhetoric of the revolutionary era.

More than any other prerevolutionary writer, Linguet bequeathed to the revolutionary journalists a new way of manipulating the sense of time in their works. Time in his pages was neither the static element of the *Gazette de France*'s formal system of representation nor the linear flow characteristic of the international gazettes and of Mairobert's work. In Linguet's *Annales,* time moved forward in a succession of terrifying lurches, and every crisis brought Europe to the edge of an apocalyptic disaster. But each disaster brought with it at least the possibility of a millenarian redemption. Linguet left no doubt that the times were out of joint, that the eighteenth century was "more full of bizarre occurrences, completely contrary to the ordinary course of events, than any other yet recorded in the annals of the world." If Mairobert's gloomy forebodings hinted that France was descending gradually into a long night of despotism, Linguet foresaw sudden, instantaneous collapse: "A terrifying void in the public revenues; a state of disorder that the government would sincerely like to put right, but that can only be cured if things are calm, whereas the least prolongation of tension will make it incurable; the threat, perhaps, of a foreign invasion which is infinitely to be feared for a number of reasons. . . . " But whereas Mairobert held out only a vague hope of salvation via the Estates-General, Linguet always saw the possibility of a sudden reversal of any situation. In 1778, for instance, he urged all the major powers to declare bankruptcy simultaneously. With this one stroke, "rejuvenated, in a way, by this violent but healthy plunge in the bath, they will find themselves with resources they never had before." In 1788, he urged a union of king and commoners to sweep away all privileged institutions. The combination of his apocalyptic sense of crisis and his millenarian optimism gave to the movement of time an almost unbearable tension, one that was later created in the pages of many of the revolutionary writers as well.

Although much in Linguet looked forward to the era of revolutionary journalism, the importance of his work is primarily the impact it had when it was first published. The *Annales politiques* was neither a clandestine publication nor a marginal one: there are good reasons for believing the contemporary estimate that, with counterfeit editions taken into account, as many as 20,000 copies of each issue may have been printed. This was a figure far surpassing the press runs of any of the international gazettes, or any but the most successful revolutionary pamphlets. Linguet inspired admirers and imitators all over Europe, and many of his acolytes later became revolutionary journalists: Brissot among the radicals, Mallet du Pan among the reactionaries. One cannot mistake the impact of his style on Marat any more than on the most successful thermidorian counter-revolutionary writer, Richer-Serizy. No attempt to understand the development of those revolutionary journals built around what Pierre Rétat has called an author posing as an "enonciateur personnalisé" bent on creating "une relation immediate, passionée ou ludique avec son lecteur.... "[21] can succeed without reference to Linguet. It is thus evident that the Revolution of 1789 did not have to create a completely new journalistic culture to transmit its self-representations: the revolutionary journalists were able to adopt and adapt existing methods. The informational papers followed the reportorial methods and narrative strategies of the international gazettes. The polemical and ideological journals expanded the procedures of Mairobert and Linguet. To be sure, the revolutionary journalists added new forms derived from other sources as well, such as the plebeian journalism represented by the *Père Duchêne*. But the more one examines the full range of journalistic species already flourishing in the last decades of the Old Regime, the more one recognizes how much of the supposedly new fauna of the revolutionary era had already evolved before 1789. And if so many of the characteristics of revolutionary journalism had already appeared earlier, it was because the politics of the French monarchy had already taken on some of the central characteristics of revolutionary politics. Long before 1789, publicity had become a central weapon in political disputes; both ministers and opposition groups recognized the vital importance of imposing their representation of political reality on a public whose opinion was an increasingly essential source of legitimation. The process which François Furet has described within the Revolution, in which the king as symbol of political legitimacy was replaced by symbolic words, was already well under way before the Revolution; only the *Gazette de France* continued to pretend otherwise, but its depiction of politics as ceremony had long since lost whatever persuasive force it might once have had.

In its place, the representation of politics as the play of conflicting forces within a system of constitutional laws, transmitted via the international gazettes, accustomed French readers to a vision of public life virtually without a king. But even this style of journalistic representation, in effect accepted and manipulated by the king's own ministers, could not contain the political tensions in France after 1774. It came under challenge from the radical ideological journalism of Mairobert's works and the emotional apocalypticism of Linguet, both of which showed a much greater potential for arousing and directing public opinion. The result was the evolution of a genuinely subversive journalism, not necessarily in the sense that its content openly called for the overthrow of the existing order— although Mairobert and Linguet, each in his own way, could be said to have done so—but in that French writers had learned to use the printed word to sap the legitimacy of existing institutions. To be sure, radical critiques of French institutions appeared in other media as well, but the unique power

---

[21]A personalized writer, bent on creating an immediate relationship—passionate or playful—with his reader.

of journalism was its ability to underline the temporal instability of the existing order. It alone was a medium suited to a politics of constant change. As the counter-revolutionary journalist Joseph Fiévée argued in 1815, in urging the suppression of the *Moniteur,* it was incongruous for a regime that promised to prevent further change to sponsor a medium whose readers "only continue to subscribe in order to have 'the continuation of the Revolution'." But this powerful means for manipulating the sense of time as a political weapon had been forged before 1789.

Inasmuch as political journalism imposed a new time rhythm on politics, the legacy the Old Regime bequeathed to the Revolution was a profoundly ambiguous one. For it was not the revolutionary legislators' intent to open a perpetual revolution: from the earliest days of the Constituent Assembly, the overriding goal of each successive dominant party was to bring the apocalyptic crisis to a close. As Mona Ozouf has shown in her study of revolutionary festivals, the revolutionaries themselves revived the monumental, ahistorical representation of events that had been typical of the Old Regime and of which the *Gazette de France* had provided a version in printed words. But the revolutionaries could not separate themselves from the time-bound, change-oriented representations of events that dominated the periodical press, and consequently of the sense that ongoing change was inevitable, whether it came peacefully through public discussion as parlementary journalism suggested or abruptly through violence as the journalistic heirs of Linguet urged. Freedom for the periodical press, although it was one of the central tenets of the revolutionary project, posed an obstacle to the creation of a stable new order. The revolutionaries learned that modern politics, which is inescapably dependent on periodical journalism, is in essence a politics built on instability and change. But they were not the first to experience that phenomenon: it was already apparent in the closing decades of the Old Regime. And one can thus conclude that the origins of revolutionary journalism can be found well before 1789, and that vital continuities linked past and present in this domain as in so many other areas of French life.

PART THREE

The Revolution

Only recently have historians of ideas come to study the revolutionary decade, but their impact has been quite significant. Unlike the search for causes in which historians sought to supplement or replace competing interpretations, in this case the scholars have been leading a revival of interest in the post-1789 period. Of course, research on this subject had never entirely ceased, but it had been greatly overshadowed in volume by attention to the origins of the Revolution. In part, historical concern with social history led to this oversight, because that interest pulled scholars away from studying the political world of 1789 to 1799. During the last several years, however, the number of investigations has accelerated, partly in response to some very influential works by researchers of intellectual history in France, the United States, and Germany. One could cite as important examples the efforts of François Furet, Mona Ozouf, Lynn Hunt, and Rolf Reichardt.[1]

Although such scholars have been at the forefront of change, they have seldom agreed on how to study the Revolution. Furthermore, this disparateness of subjects and approaches has yielded few complementary findings. Unlike the scholars examining the causes of the Revolution, those working on the revolutionary decade have not produced enough overlapping studies to yield a hypothesis equivalent to the claim about the importance of thinkers from outside the Enlightenment.

The variety of subjects and techniques available encouraged selecting, for this volume, a range of excellent studies in quite different areas. First, the essays chosen cover the entire ten years chronologically. Two of them address concerns of the national legislators, while two others explore decisions made all across France by ordinary people. This list of differences might be greatly extended.

---

[1]See the contributions by Furet, Ozouf, and Hunt in this volume. For interesting work organized by Rolf Reichardt, see Rolf Reichardt and Eberhard Schmitt, eds., *Handbuch politischsozialer Grandbegriffe in Frankreich, 1680–1820,* vols. 1 and 2 (Munich, 1985); and Reinhart Koselleck and Rolf Reichardt, *Die Französische Revolution als Bruch des gesellschaftlichen Bewusstseins* (Munich, 1988).

Methodologically, the four papers utilize several approaches. First, they disagree on the role of ideas. Tackett's view is complex. In his study of the reasons why the clergy swore, or refused to swear, a required oath of allegiance to the Revolution, he relates the tendencies of groups of priests to social as well as intellectual problems and possibilities dating back to the Old Regime. In this account, these decisions seem to be more or less rationales, in part related to social circumstances. Once made, though, the determinations of a region's clergy exercised considerable influence over the future, as parishioners tended to adhere to or reject orthodoxy according to the choices of the majority of their curés. These patterns endure today. Thus, ideas that were based on circumstances eventually possessed extraordinary power.

All three other scholars treat the power of belief somewhat differently. In particular, Ran Halévi strongly endorses the importance of ideas. He examines the National Assembly's 1789 debates over creating a new form of representation as a clash of ideologies with strong roots in the eighteenth century. Furthermore, he believes that the triumphant ideology forced an interpretation of representation that led directly to the Jacobin dictatorship of 1793 and 1794. As such, beliefs defined political debate and predicated the future. Halévi seems to be somewhat in line with recent literary critics, who posit the ability of images and rhetoric to shape reality.

Lynn Hunt and Mona Ozouf place a very different emphasis on ideas. First, they are uninterested in the impact and origin of ideas, and concentrate on how ideas are articulated and how they communicate societal values. Hunt's study of the selection of Hercules as a national symbol to replace the images of the fallen monarchy focuses on the political values revealed. Ozouf's examination of historical festivals connects them with a general psychological need to purify and create anew. Both of these scholars thus share a conviction contrary to that of Halévi and Tackett, that language represents present, not past, circumstances. Furthermore, their work seems to contend that ideas relate to values, not ideological or political conflicts. In sum, political beliefs do not relate to other formal intellectual systems, and possess neither past nor future. Nevertheless, this should not suggest that Hunt and Ozouf lack interest in ideas, for while focusing on their subjects, both seem to suggest that revolutionary language expressed the deeply held position of the revolutionaries. In this approach, Hunt and Ozouf join a very important group of anthropologists who treat ideas as revelatory of important feelings and values.

Reconsidering this analysis of these essays, one also finds differences among them over the special place of the Revolution in the formation of beliefs. Evidently, Halévi believes the Revolution simply confirmed past tendencies. On the other hand, Hunt and Ozouf evidently find the decade a spawning place for ideas. Tackett actually falls between the two camps. In his description of how the Old Regime sources combined to create a general culture of decision-making, he painstakingly shows that the cauldron of the Revolution apparently reshaped and reconfigured those factors predating 1789. Thus, the clergy acted as it did because of new and complex interactions.

The four analyses presented here do not begin to exhaust the possible techniques currently exploited by intellectual historians. It would be very useful to examine the fundamental contribution of François Furet and compare it, substantively as well as methodologically, with work presented here. To some degree, chapter introductions are intended to aid in this task. Another important area of research has been the history of concepts. Germans have taken the lead in this field, following the meaning of an idea over a long period to chart changes in society's intellectual temperature. Doubtless, other new approaches also will soon follow.

The Constituent Revolution and Its Ambiguities*

Ran Halévi

In this fascinating study of the National Assembly (also known as the Constituent Assembly), Ran Halévi attempts to understand the actions of the deputies on the subject of representation. He argues that, even before the meeting of the Estates General, two absolutely contrary concepts were already competing. The Old Regime traditionally held that individuals represented not other individuals but social and professional groups, constituted by the state. The relationship was very clear, because the legislator was closely bound to the wishes of the constituents. In the contest over the Estates, however, the commoners, led by abbé Sieyès, championed a theory of national sovereignty that made representatives responsive to the nation as a whole. Very early in the Revolution, a month and a half after the convening of the Estates General, the king was forced to accede to the commoners' demand. During the next few months, the Estates General, renamed the National Assembly, debated the implications of this new state of affairs. Some, like Sieyès, wanted legislators to be free agents operating in the best interest of the nation; others, in the tradition demarcated by Rousseau's *Social Contract,* advocated direct democracy, in which constituents controlled deputies. Although the National Assembly formally accepted Sieyès's view of matters, the logic of the situation inevitably gave the Rousseauist concept the upper hand. Installing this relationship of the governed to the government meant, according to Halévi, that the strongest parts of the public would be able to define the public interest. Because this was the state of affairs that existed during the Terror, Halévi views the decisions about representation as foreshadowing early in the Revolution the inexorable slide to the dictatorship of 1793–94.

Among the characteristics that make this interpretation significant is its similarity to the view of François Furet. Despite the seminal nature of the latter's work, few studies have explicitly examined the points he has

---

*A French version of this article is available as "La Revolution constituante: les ambiguités politiques," in Colin Lucas, ed., *The Political Culture of the Revolution* (Pergamon Press, 1988). This version is published here with the permission of Pergamon Press and the author.

raised. This article, though, clearly offers support. Furet has found the heart of the Revolution in prerevolutionary thought; similarly, Halévi grounds his view in the debates going into 1789. Furet believes that Rousseauist-style thinking still had to compete during the Revolution but early emerged victorious; similarly, Halévi believes that the concept of the will of the people triumphed in 1789. Both share the conclusion that those victorious notions provided the theoretical core of the Terror.

The evidence from Halévi's intelligent case study forces scholars to consider even more carefully Furet's broad hypotheses, which explain the Revolution, and the Terror as well, as the result of Rousseauist ideas. This surely undermines the optimistic interpretation of the Revolution as the triumph of high-minded and elevated ideas. To be sure, this approach will receive criticism, and some may question the immediate dominance of Rousseauist ideas in the Revolution. Halévi's piece does acknowledge that, at first, a rather different sort of representation emerged—one in which individual rights might have been better protected. Halévi dismisses the vitality of these notions rapidly because they were not logically connected to the revolutionary momentum. Perhaps, though, the Revolution was not as rigid as he suggests and could have accepted compromise in its principles. The war and the development of internal enemies not some inevitable revolutionary engine, may have doomed a more delicate structure. Others may also doubt that the principle of the will of the people inexorably legitimized the role of the strongest. Such demurrers certainly will be examined and considered in the coming years.

To study the political origins of the Constituent Revolution, in the summer of 1789, is above all to explore what the Revolution was seeking to "revolutionize": that is, the absolute monarchy as an idea if not as a reality, the idea of liberty, the concepts of sovereignty and representation, the foundations of law, and the practices of daily political action.

Curiously, this fundamental chapter of the political history of modern France is the least popular among students—at least French students—of the French Revolution. Perhaps this is because it is—or seems to be—the least problematical; it has never been a subject of controversy. In the historiography of the French Revolution, the Constituent Revolution appears not as a subject but as a period, less as an issue than as a celebration. It is wedged between what precedes—the "origins" and the "causes"—and what follows—the Revolution itself, whose premises this chapter announces, defines, and consecrates.

Several reasons can explain this peculiar situation. The most obvious is that the historiography of the French Revolution has long been inseparable from what the French would call "a project of society," such as 1) the republic from 1870 on; 2) socialism under the stimulus of Jaurès; and 3) the very idea of revolution revived by the Russian Revolution of 1917, which had a tremendous impact on French scholars, under the authoritarian if not always fruitful influence of Albert Mathiez.[1] This "project of society" reshaped the writing of the history of the French Revolution, which had always been an account of origins, a history of French identity. From the very beginning of the Revolution, such tendencies among historians mobilized erudition in France generally when there was disagreement on the nature of the revolutionary process, on the significance of this or that episode, or on the virtue of this or that actor in the drama. After the fierce polemic between Dantonists (Aulard) and Robespierrists (Mathiez),[2] we can see the debate turning successively on the Revolution's consequences, its process, its origins, and its tragic development after 1791, but seldom on its advent and even more rarely on its political advent.

If we turn to the royalist historiography of the period, with its various schools—legitimist, Orleanist, and Bonapartist[3]—we find that the picture does not change significantly. Royalist authors shared with those on the left the same idea, one would say the same conviction, of the Revolution as a "block"; they simply turned it upside down. Influenced and encouraged by Taine,[4] whose erudition and brilliance momentarily legitimized this interpretation, royalist authors and pamphleteers of the 1870s and 1880s saw the French Revolution as definitely compromised before it even began. July 14, to them, was just a spectacular milestone of what Taine called the "spontaneous anarchy" of the years 1788–89: This is the title he gave to the chapters dedicated to that period in his general study of the Revolution. To Louis de Poncin, July 14 was the first day of the Terror, which degenerated progressively during the Revolution. Thus, if 1789 has never been seriously studied, it is mainly because, on the left as on the right, for different but convergent reasons, it has been seen as accomplishing, explaining, and containing the Revolution as a whole.

Behind this conviction lay, in fact, an ideological and a historiographical

---

[1]These are momentous events in the history of France. The modern day republic began in 1870, Jean Jaurès brought socialism into the mainstream of French politics around the turn of the twentieth century, and the Russian Revolution resulted in the left splitting into communist and socialist factions. Albert Mathiez (1874–1932) was a famous historian of the Revolution.

[2]One of the most significant debates among historians of France in the early twentieth century evaluated whether Georges Danton or Maximilien Robespierre best represented the Revolution. Alphonse Aulard (1845–1928) championed the former and Mathiez the latter.

[3]Legitimists sought the return to the throne of the Bourbon dynasty of Louis XVI and his brothers. The Orleanists supported the claims of Louis Philippe's family and Bonapartists those of Napoleon Bonaparte's heirs.

[4]Hippolyte Taine (1823–1893).

necessity to escape the contradictions and confusion of the whole period between 1789 and 1791. For the royalists, as for the republicans, those years were encumbered by "aristocrats" too much in favor of the principles of 1789, by "patriots" who later went astray, and by the "revolutionary spirit," much too contaminated in the eyes of the authors by the idea of "constitutional monarchy," a compromise practically uncontested before June 1791 and carefully buried by the Mathiez school.

I think it is necessary to reassess the "Constituent Revolution" (1789–91) and to rehabilitate the political history of the French Revolution by investigating the revolutionary phenomenon from the perspective of its own fundamental principles. My intention is not to study some abstract ideas and their various and successive interpretations, but rather to analyze the relationships, discrepancies, and contradictions among the revolutionary principles, their different usages, and their successive "socializations" before and during the Revolution. In this article, I will limit myself to three of these ideas—liberty, sovereignty, and representation—analyzing them at the very moment they were about to become revolutionary and trying to see how the men of 1789 appropriated them and interpreted them, in order, as they used to say, to "regenerate France." Let us turn first to the idea of liberty.

We may begin with the succinct and pessimistic sentence that opens Rousseau's *Social Contract:* "Man is born free and everywhere he is in chains." For many years, this precept has taught us how to interpret liberty in Old-Regime France. Is it time to revise that old verdict? Obviously not, if we subscribe to the classical definition of liberty as it prevailed in nineteenth-century Europe. Freedom of speech, economic and social freedoms, and political freedom had no foundation in either the law or the institutions of France before the Revolution. But before the Revolution, the French knew a different kind of liberty, a freedom that was intermittent and without uniformity, a freedom inseparable from the "organic" logic of their society.

What did this liberty mean under the Old Regime, and what was its source? According to Tocqueville,[5] who obviously nourished a certain nostalgia for this liberty, that freedom was simultaneously fragmented and "empirical." It was fragmented because it was linked, not to a unifying general principle, but to the idea of privilege: that is, to a series of contracts between the monarchy and various individuals, groups, towns, professions, and other Old-Regime entities. At the same time it was an "empirical" sort of liberty, because these contracts, in the course of time, ended up creating a broad margin of independence in which liberty could flourish well beyond its formal limits. There, it existed without constraint but also without sanction.

---

[5]Alexis de Tocqueville (1805–1859).

This irregular liberty, taken rather than given, was by no means incompatible with the other theme of Tocqueville's *The Old Regime and the Revolution:* that is, centralization. It was even the product of that centralization. There was, Tocqueville explained, a contradiction between the royal government's desire to centralize and its ability to realize its ambitions, a contradiction that opened to the French a space for freedom both unexpected and lasting, as lasting as the structural imbalances within centralization.

Thus, traditional or "old" liberty relied largely on the initiatives, the determination, and the spirit of independence of the individuals and groups that made up society. From this came its varied character: It was a liberty that preserved more than it created, that owed more to the vices of a system than to the virtues of principle. That is why it perished with the Old Regime that gave it birth. However, before disappearing, concluded Tocqueville, it formed "those vigorous natures, those bold and daring spirits that we will see appear, and who will make the French Revolution the object of both the admiration and the terror of following generations." Tocqueville concluded, " . . . if that irregular and unhealthy sort of liberty prepared the French to overthrow despotism, it rendered them perhaps the least likely nation of all to replace it with the peaceable and free rule of law." François Furet has added a still more striking conclusion to this statement: Deprived of real freedom, incapable of collective political experience, the French went from the ruins of "organic" liberty straight to revolutionary Utopia, bound up in theories of natural rights.

Can we reformulate this statement in order better to understand the origins of Jacobinism? I believe that Rousseau, in the passage referred to previously, can help us. Liberty was both the basis and the guarantee of the social contract. The social contract depends on balance, according to Rousseau—balance and not compromise—between "what the law permits and what interest prescribes." It seems to me that one could write an entire history of the Revolution based on the continual tension between these two elements of the social contract: the general interest expressed in legal restrictions and the freedom of the individual. Indeed, one can say that the dictatorship of the Committee of Public Safety and the Terror illustrated an extraordinary difficulty, an inability to invest an abstract definition of liberty with an exact and durable set of laws. Of course, the Constituent Assembly as early as August 1789 enshrined the rights of man and of the citizen, before elaborating a constitution that the majority believed to be in conformity with those principles. However, the laws of the Constitution and those principles of freedom quickly came into conflict with one another. During the great revolutionary crises, we see both perverted or suspended, sometimes in the name of the law, sometimes in the name of liberty, always in the name of the people. Hence, my contention is that a tension between liberty and society went back to the very beginning of the

Revolution, I would say even to the very first revolutionary moment, that is, to June 17, 1789. Let us attempt to locate it, define it, and understand it.

As soon as the king had called it into session, the Estates General[6] found itself trapped by the conflict between the orders. During six long weeks, the nobility and the Third Estate went from conferences to mediations and from aborted compromises to denunciations, under the watchful eye of the clergy, more conciliatory but no less divided. "The commons," Lally-Tollendal[7] would write later, "wished to conquer; the nobility wanted to conserve; the clergy waited for a conqueror to choose an ally." The effervescence born of this paralysis affected the connections in the heart of the Estates. Problems included the schemes at the Palais-Royal[8]; the rumors circulating at Versailles; and the inaction, especially of the court, interpreted by some as weakness and by others as a maneuver to raise fears of a coming dissolution of the Estates, which would dash all hope of reform.

In fact, the nature of the stakes determined the irreducible character of the disagreement. There was not much margin for maneuvering. The difficulty was fundamental, because it brought up the terms of the social contract and, beyond that, the title to the property of the nation. Two incompatible logics of sovereignty, two irreconcilable modes of political participation, opposed each other. These major questions, which haunted public debate from 1788 and which were not yet regulated when the deputies from the countryside arrived at Versailles, remained unresolved even by the electoral regulations[9] of January 24, 1789.

In reality, these ambiguous and contradictory electoral rules, midway between tradition and innovation, juxtaposed the old system and the new ideas. On one side, the system used the personnel and the form of the former meetings, prescribed the meeting of the inhabitants of the big cities by corporations[10] and communities of professions, and maintained the binding mandate[11] and the traditional procedure of grievances. It multiplied exceptions and exclusions in the name of acquired privileges. It especially conserved the separation of the orders and remained mute on the principal demand of the Third: deliberation in common and vote by head.

On the other side, it accorded to the Third a double representation

---

[6]See the glossary entry *Estates General.*

[7]A noble deputy who sided with the revolutionaries for a time, but later became a staunch monarchist.

[8]A center of radical political activity.

[9]For the Estates General.

[10]Groups of individuals linked by occupation.

[11]The requirement that representatives vote according to the specific dictates of their constituents.

and consecrated the principles of modern politics: the role of the individual, citizenship, and proportionality. In the end, the law designated the deputies to the Estates both as delegates of traditional communities and as representatives of a nation of independent individuals. It institutionalized this confusion, which it left the assembly of the orders to resolve, just as it also abandoned to the assembly's verdict the problems of how meetings and voting would be conducted.

Now, if this debate on the means of representation was unresolvable, this was because, in truth, it left no compromise between the antagonistic electoral rules. The alternatives, the organic[12] tradition and the democratic tradition, fueled the intransigents on both sides and condemned them from the beginning to eternal struggle.

The Third Estate could not drop its major demand of vote by head without losing the benefit of its doubled size. Its entire future depended on it, and many of its members had received on this particular point a binding mandate. The commons could not then separately begin the verification of members, and it neither drew up rules nor kept records, which would have meant acceptance of the vote by order.

The nobility had no means of political existence other than its privileges. It feared, not without reason, that the verification in common would prejudge, once the assembly was constituted, the questions of deliberation in common and then of the joining together of the three orders. It is true that, in this regard, the leaders of the Third Estate would not equivocate. After the publication of the electoral rules, Sieyès,[13] in his celebrated pamphlet, proscribed all thought of accommodation with the privileged. The third order had to recognize "that it can no longer hope for anything except from its own lights and courage. No, there's no longer time to work at conciliating the parties. . . . " Once on the route toward national restoration, even if it were conquered, the Third might never again be what it was. "The circumstances allow no relaxation. *One must advance or retreat.*"[14] For the author of *Qu'est-ce que le Tiers Etat?* this was to say that the rupture between the orders had occurred long before the king had resolved to call the Estates. The privileged had identified too much with their own perogatives to consent to abandoning them and to lose, at the same time, their political, cultural, and symbolic identity. "They fear today the Estates General that they had formerly invoked with too much vivacity."

For Sieyès, the regeneration of France depended on dropping the concept of the nation traditionally linked to the Estates General and

---

[12]Organic refers to the notion that the Old-Regime rules seemed to grow rather than result from specific periods of constitution-making.

[13]Emmanuel-Joseph Sieyès, deputy to the Estates General, and author of the most important pamphlet of the Revolution, *Qu'est-ce que le Tiers Etat? (What Is the Third Estate?)*

[14]Author's italics.

substituting an extraordinary assembly or, if necessary, tearing this old representative organ from its primitive function of serving as an image from which the monarch could decipher the pleas of the *corps* and communities. Rarely had a political essayist outlined so accurately the possible scenarios of the Constituent Revolution. Rarely had a pamphlet resonated so much with the passions of the day. At the time when the old monarchy was seeking public opinion about lost traditions, Sieyès had already submitted for public debate the terms and the means of its end.

No matter how little the nobility held to its perogatives, it still had to oppose the commons by the stubborn refusal of all concessions. "It isn't we," one of its members had said, "who need the Estates General; we are holding it for the people, and if they are difficult, we willingly renounce it." This passage, both ingenious and limited, revealed the open gulf between the two sides.

The meetings of conciliation with the representatives of the commons (they merit, elsewhere, a more comprehensive study) confirmed the nobility in its intransigence. In the course of these sessions, Mounier,[15] rigid as usual, had indicated to his commissioners that "it is a question of ensuring political liberty by a constitution; the joining of all the deputies was necessary for such a great object; it was the wish of the Nation; that one could not resist without being both extremely unjust and extremely imprudent." The Third had neither the right nor the power to negotiate with a fraction of the political body over what belonged to the entire nation. Mounier, like Sieyès, could conceive of no middle ground between the paralysis of the Estates and the surrender of privileges.

Thus, progressively, the idea that was winning was that only a blow of force would unknot the problem. Some expected it from the commoners, others from the court, but Necker[16] regarded all initiatives as unwelcome and would not then explain his reasons. This blow of force, it is often forgotten, came from the nobility, who were the first to attempt it, on two separate occasions. On May 26, 1789, the nobility decided that, at least for the current session of the Estates General, the verification of powers would take place separately. The Third replied the next day, by solemnly proposing to the clergy, "in the name of the God of peace and natural interest . . . ," the combining of their two chambers. Faced with the impatience of their priests, the bishops asked for the mediation of the king, who, by a letter of the twenty-eighth, offered the arbitration of his ministers to the commissioners of the three orders. This expedient, accepted with relief by the clergy, provoked a tumultuous debate in the commons, which ended, however, in the acceptance of new meetings. Even though the nobility acceded to the king's proposition, it swept away the last hope of compromise by declaring that "the right to deliberate by order and the ability to prevent the orders from separating from the whole are the rights of the

---

[15]Jean-Joseph Mounier (1758–1806), deputy and leading constitutional monarchist.

[16]Jacques Necker, chief minister during much of the early Revolution.

monarchy, and the nobility will persevere consistently in the principles that conserve the throne and liberty." It was this resolution, passed 202 to 16, that opened the way to revolution for the Third.

The seventeenth of June is a date more memorable than remembered: It was on that date that the commons, at the instigation of Sieyès and Mirabeau, transformed itself into the National Assembly, alone capable, in the celebrated phrase, "of interpreting and presenting the national will." It was a revolutionary act in the proper sense of the term, because it completely upset the very essence of French public law. At that time, in effect, the divine-right monarchy gave way to the sovereignty of the nation.

The historians of the Revolution have dispatched this transformation in a few triumphant or desolate sentences. Not necessarily have they misunderstood its importance; it is only that they have seen this transformation in the light of later events, inscribed in what preceded, announcing what followed. They celebrated or deplored it without really questioning it, in contrast to, for example, the war, the dictatorship, or the Terror.

This was not the case in 1789. At that time, the sovereignty of the nation was the root of a new political liberty, which would later consecrate the Declaration of the Rights of Man. Article 6 of that Declaration noted, "Every citizen has the right, in person or by representation, to participate in the legislative process." In person or by representation? Directly or by delegation? Those questions would only be raised later.

The fundamental question, though, is to what extent this new political liberty fulfills our modern definition of political freedom. The answer is ambiguous. I will limit the present discussion to the question of political representation. If political liberty means the control of government by the governed, it is very clear that 1789 marked a watershed: The Declaration of Rights and the first articles of the new constitution attested to it. If, on the contrary, one investigates the *way* in which that control was exercised after 1789—its practical forms, its daily language—then doubts predominate. In other words, the new sovereignty of 1789 was modern (it was our own conception of that idea); but the system of representation to which it gave birth was only partly modern. It was modern in appearance but less so in reality, modern in theory, but less so in practice.

What, though, was the meaning of this transfer of sovereignty initiated on June 17? First, the nation was no longer made up of groups, communities, and regions as under the Old Regime: The nation had become on that date an indivisible entity that excluded all forms of partial representation. A second transformation stemmed from the first: After June 17, each deputy no longer represented his district. The entire nation became a universal and indivisible whole, beyond electoral lines. As Thouret[17] affirmed in 1791, each of the sections, in its direct ballot, voted not just for itself but for the whole nation.

---

[17]Deputy to the National Assembly and a member of the committee to write a constitution.

The National Assembly thus had the power to choose for the whole nation; the deputies were the authors of the general will, which only came into existence once the Assembly met and had its credentials verified and accepted. This was, of course, the very opposite of representation under the Old Regime, in which the general will was completely fragmented, not only during, but also before, the meeting of the Assembly. In fact, under the Old Regime, the deputies were only the spokesmen of their electorate to the king, the advocates of a grievance that defined their powers. It was a sort of contractual dependence with precise definitions; if a deputy went beyond the boundaries drawn by the electorate, he was disavowed or even sanctioned.

Thus, the proclamation of June 1789 implied the inevitable elimination of any legal dependence of the deputy on those who elected him. This meant also that the mandate of a deputy, whatever his political affiliation in the Assembly, could no longer be revoked by the electorate or even by the king.

Curiously, this radical break with the binding mandate was rarely found in the pamphlets or *cahiers* published on the eve of the Revolution. I do not know of any demand before 1789 for the suppression of the old form of mandate. In fact, this change appeared less as a goal in itself than as an opportunity, the necessary *sine qua non* for the realization of the Third Estate's two essential demands: deliberation in common as opposed to by order, and voting by head instead of by estate. Even for the most patriotic, the problem was not so much the mandate system itself as the contents of certain mandates.

In fact, from the moment the commons proclaimed itself the National Assembly, the elimination of the old binding mandate was unavoidable for two reasons: Not only was the mandate incompatible with national sovereignty, but it also was the main obstacle that prevented numerous deputies from the privileged orders, forced by their mandates to deliberate and vote separately, from joining the Third Estate. However, it was very rare for the members of the Third Estate to understand, as did Mirabeau and Sieyès, the interdependence of these two explanations. For the majority of the deputies, the most important part of this episode was less the transfer of sovereignty than the royal decision to regard as "unconstitutional" all limitations on the powers of the deputies and to forbid all binding mandates for the future, thus permitting the last recalcitrants of the clergy and the nobility to join the National Assembly.

Hence, an action that was inevitable developed. In June 1789, the unity of the three orders was totally dependent on the will of the monarch, even if the Third Estate requested it in the name of national sovereignty. In eliminating the old form of mandate, though, the king, perhaps without realizing it, removed the contradiction between the old representation and the new sovereignty, which had existed until then.

The question for us, of course, is to know how the deputies to the

Estates General perceived, understood, and interpreted this change. In other words, how did they later reconsider the revolution they had made? In order to answer this question, we have to turn to the debates that followed the revolution of June.

The problem of representation was raised on two occasions before the Assembly moved to Paris in October 1789. First in July, then in September, the deputies discussed the crucial issue of the royal sanction, that is, the power with which the king was to be endowed under the new regime.

The main speaker in July was Talleyrand, bishop of Autun, whose clergy he represented at the Estates General. Talleyrand was a staunch supporter of the revolution of June and a strong opponent of the old binding mandate. For what reasons, though, and with what arguments? Like those of most other deputies, his reasons were practical and did not stem from principles; his arguments were original but indefensible. The idea he supported was that of a limited mandate—limited by the function of its exercise and limited as to the moment it was to become effective. For example, the deputies could be instructed to vote subsidies only after particular demands of their constituents had been satisfied.

Now, if the arguments raised by Talleyrand to sustain this idea of a "limited mandate" are closely examined, there is a constant confusion between the old and the new systems of representation. Talleyrand combined two incompatible notions: the sovereignty of the nation and the right that he recognized of all districts to participate, at least in theory, in the elaboration of the general will. In practice, this participation had to be accomplished exclusively by the deputies, through a free consultation and a free vote. It was the districts, though, which voted and decided, not the nation as a whole. In other words, Talleyrand wanted to change everything in the relations between the monarch and the nation but to change nothing fundamental in the juridicial and political relations between constituents and representatives. In fact, what preoccupied Talleyrand most was not so much principles but political tactics. His opposition to the old mandate expressed the fear, first, that a tiny minority of deputies, sticking to its instructions, might completely paralyze the work of the Assembly—as was the case when the nobility and the clergy refused to join the Third Estate; and, second, that the constituent revolution would be permanently at the mercy of such a small minority that would constantly obstruct its progress.

The crucial debate on sovereignty and representation took place in September 1789. The most important protagonists in this debate were the abbé Sieyès, deputy of the Third Estate of Paris, and Pétion, who was deputy of the Third Estate of Chartres, a future mayor of Paris, and one of the leaders of the Girondin faction.

Pétion, speaking on September 5, put the question bluntly. Who was the ultimate legislator in the new context of national sovereignty: Was it the nation, or was it the representatives of the nation? In other words, according to Pétion, the alternatives were an unlimited mandate, totally independent of the constituents, or a new form of binding mandate, adapted to the new concept of sovereignty.

On that matter, Pétion's opinion was very clear: He refused any representative mandate and favored what we might call a direct democracy "à la Rousseau." He condemned all attempts to prevent the nation from exercising its sovereignty directly and fully by its own judgment and will. The sovereign nation was, according to Pétion, the ultimate arbitrator of French politics.

In a sense, Pétion tried to go even further than Rousseau by elaborating a whole network of intermediary assemblies, destined to discuss and to transmit upward to the National Assembly the terms of the general will. In this respect, Pétion wanted to avert any opposition to direct democracy based on the argument that the people were too ignorant, thus dangerous and unreliable, because they lacked any political experience. Politics and political participation, said Pétion, enlightened even the most ignorant of men.

This optimistic view of progress through education and political apprenticeship was to be flatly rejected by Sieyès when he addressed the Assembly two days later on September 7. Sieyès recognized, of course, the compatibility of national sovereignty and direct democracy. Recognition, though, did not mean acceptance. According to Sieyès, direct democracy had to be rejected from the outset, because it was extremely dangerous to the national as well as the territorial unity of France. The nation could not, ought not, and had no means to express its will other than through the voice of its free and independent representatives, free and independent of their constituents' will and instructions. The national will was not the synthesis of contradictory, or of complementary, demands; the national will was the elaboration of laws and policies by a group of men whose education and well-being had endowed them with the aptitude to understand and make politics.

This was not to say, of course, that Sieyès denied the equality of rights; however, given the universally recognized equality of rights, he was denying an unequal conception of representation that might lead to a property based franchise.

The deputies would debate the new system of representation at length, and in the end they would accept Sieyès' thesis. Hence, Sieyès triumphed over Rousseau, at least on paper. However, what was that victory really worth? The question returns us to our point of departure: that is, to the ambiguities of the Revolution of June, with which I would like to conclude.

The first ambiguity is that in June 1789 the members of the Constituent Assembly abolished, at least on paper, the system of representation that had chosen them as the nation's spokesmen and that had given them their legal legitimacy as deputies. In "revolutionizing" the concept of sovereignty, and by founding their actions on a new right, they themselves destroyed the mandate they had received, while continuing to exercise this very mandate.

The second ambiguity is that in order to reach its goal, the Assembly was forced to have recourse to the authority of the king. By accepting the fact that only the king could annul the old mandates, they made him the titular author, or at least coauthor, of their own revolution.

Finally, the ambiguity that seems the most important to me, is perhaps the least known, and is certainly the most difficult to grasp, is to understand the "explosive potential" of the proclamation of June 17. It is clear that the control of deputies by their constituents was never again as strict, legally speaking, as under the Old Regime. Formerly, however, that control was also limited by the extremely precise terms of the written mandate. The proclamation of June 17, with the help of the king himself, was supposed to free completely the deputies to the Estates General from their constituents.

The combination of archaic practice and modern theory merits attention. From this moment on, the terms of the contract that linked deputies and constituents were no longer fixed by any document. In fact, nowhere were those terms laid down. The actors had to reinvent them every day amid revolutionary turmoil. The slogans, language, and images of the revolutionary Utopia of which Tocqueville wrote installed themselves in this void. "The will of the people" was the most effective; it was never defined, never fixed, all-encompassing, always present, and left entirely to the discretion of those who made use of it, provided they were the strongest.

From 1789, there also existed in the electoral districts committees of correspondence, who imagined they were engaging in direct democracy "à la Rousseau," when in reality they were distorting its meaning through an Old-Regime practice emptied of its original content. These committees controlled their deputies strictly, denounced them, and threatened them in the name of a sovereignty, an ancient system that they thought they had abolished.

Would it be too bold to see in the emergence of direct democracy as the dominant style of representation one of the characteristics of what we might call the origins of Jacobinism, a trait that was perhaps at work in the days after the 17th of June? A reassessment of the Constituent Revolution, inside and outside the Assembly proper, can help us respond. By systematically studying the contradictory, illusory, and sometimes murderous appropriations of the new political legitimacy born at that moment, we can better measure the abyss that separated the political liberty of 1789 from the apologies and illusions to which it was destined to lend its name in the future.

The Meaning of the Oath*

Timothy Tackett

One important activity of the first two years of the Revolution was the reorganization of the Catholic church. The National Assembly seized church lands to pay national debts but promised to sustain the clergy out of the state treasury. The legislature also passed the Civil Constitution of the Clergy, which regulated many of the operations of the church. After debates late in 1790, the Assembly early in 1791 passed and implemented an oath of allegiance to the constitution, required for all bishops, parish clergymen, and clerical teachers. The demand to swear loyalty proved a momentous occasion and even an obsession throughout France during the spring and summer of 1791. Perhaps it was because supporting or opposing the constitution was tantamount to accepting or rejecting the Revolution that so much controversy was generated. Nonetheless, when the dust settled, some fifty-five percent of the fifty thousand clergymen took the oath, but wide regional variations existed.

Timothy Tackett has attempted to explain why some members of the clergy embraced the Revolution while others did not. In his investigation, based on a massive research effort, he systematically correlated numerous factors with rates of adherence and rejection. He evaluated many hypotheses for the extent of their explanatory value.

In the excerpt printed here, which serves as the concluding chapter to his book on the subject, Tackett initially summarizes how well different variables worked. He discovered that it was very difficult to isolate any general factors that would explain the course of any individual clergyman. However, his examination of behavior by regions yielded patterns. He could discern why some areas leaned one way and others the opposite. Perhaps the most important factor was the extent to which the area had been integrated during the Old Regime into the realm. In areas alienated from the center, the clergy tended to refuse the oath. Other variables also mattered, though, and during the Revolution a variety of combinations

*Timothy Tackett, *Religion, Revolution, and Regional Culture in Eighteenth-Century France: The Ecclesiastical Oath of 1791.* Copyright © 1986 by Princeton University Press. (Footnotes to be omitted.) Chapter 12 reprinted with permission of Princeton University Press.

emerged. Consequently, Tackett presents seven different zones and offers a separate rationale for the behavior of each.

In his conclusion, he indicates that the zones that emerged in 1791 retained importance over the next two centuries. Henceforth, French attitudes toward religious practice have proceeded along the lines first articulated during the Revolution.

Perhaps the most important achievement of Tackett's work is an explanation touching so broad a cultural phenomenon. His comprehensive and careful effort is a model for illuminating the decision making of ordinary individuals. It also reminds us that intellectual history needs to continue to branch out to explain the ideas of the many as well as the few.

PATTERNS

Assessing the origins of collective opinion, the wellsprings of social behavior, is a delicate undertaking even in a contemporary setting and even under the most favorable of circumstances. For a historical period such as the French Revolution, a period when many of the norms and stays of authority and allegiance were regularly being put into question, the task is particularly complex. Our efforts to follow and understand one key event in that Revolution, the ecclesiastical oath of 1791, has led us down a surprisingly circuitous and at times frustrating route. Several of the seemingly promising approaches to oath options—the influence of the bishops, the stamp of seminary training, the factors of age or of social origin—ultimately proved to explain very little. Other potentially important elements—like land-tenure patterns, seigneurial structures, or demographic variables—have been largely neglected or only touched upon for lack of sufficient regional information. And, nevertheless, despite its inevitable limitations, our inquiry has uncovered a number of interlocking patterns which, when taken together, would seem to go far in explaining the overall picture of oath-taking.

It is now evident that there was a dialectic constantly at work between the perspectives and attitudes of the clergymen confronting the oath and the opinions of the laity with whom those clergymen lived and worked. Any interpretation which does not take into account the ripples and vibrations of this symbiotic interaction can never be fully successful. But, beyond this general proposition, various facets of explanation are revealed, depending on the magnification of one's lens and the aperture of one's field of vision. From a microscopic perspective, we have found that the particular benefits or disadvantages entailed in a specific position on the oath almost certainly influenced the decisions of some clergymen and some parishioners. There was a certain tendency to accept the oath among those curés gaining the greatest material benefits from the Civil Constitution— particularly those formerly receiving the *portion congrue*[1]—though the *congruistes* now appear to have been much less numerous than was once believed, and though there was no corresponding tendency to refuse the oath among those whose incomes were most reduced. A juring[2] position was also more common among those for whom the loss of a post would have been most economically and psychologically devastating: the elderly priests, the migrant priests living far from their home parishes, and the clerics from the lowest socioeconomic backgrounds—most notably, the sons of artisan families. To these categories, one must add that group of new curés who, having only recently obtained their first permanent status, found it particularly difficult to reject the oath and thus find themselves cast adrift once again. On the side of the laity, we have encountered instances in which the loss of political authority or the threat of economic discomfort occasioned by the new regime may have alienated significant elements of a town or parish, stimulating them to oppose the oath as a demonstration of their opposition to the whole Revolution. Among cases such as these, the disappointment registered by communities dominated by tenant farmers was particularly significant. Finally, we have explored the ongoing political and social dynamics of individual villages as they may have affected local positions: the extent to which the episode of the oath was merely a new installment in a long-term power struggle between clergymen and local notables.

Ultimately, however, local and personal factors such as these do not seem to take us very far toward a general explanation of the oath through- out the country. On closer examination, the hypothesis of the oath as a local referendum on the secular policies of the Revolution appears to be of relatively limited utility. As for the comparison between oath options and the collective biographies of clergymen, percentage variations are often rather marginal, measurable only within samples of several hundred priests. It now appears evident that throughout most of *rural* France, clerical options were related less to individual career experiences than to the broader cultural assumptions and opinions of fellow citizens and fellow clergymen across whole *pays* or provinces.

In order to comprehend the striking and remarkable regional patterns of oath-taking, it has been necessary to put aside the microscope and examine certain factors affecting larger territorial clusters of French men and women. The reception of the oath in a given region was influenced, in

---

[1]A fixed salary, set at a very low minimum rate of 700 *livres* at the end of the Old Regime and paid to parish priests by individuals who had the right to collect the tithe.

[2]To swear to support the oath.

part, by the cultural and political distance between that region and the traditional—and now Revolutionary—core of the country. A whole range of factors combined potentially to increase this distance, factors which included the institutional structures for local political initiative (provincial parlements[3] and estates,[4] most notably), the independence from the Gallican Church,[5] the local traditions of ultramontanism[6] (more powerful in some areas for political and institutional reasons), the use of the *concours,*[7] and, perhaps most essential, the presence of a significant non-French culture and language. But more important, in all likelihood, were those factors which directly impinged on the *religious* perspectives of a region. Thus, reception of the oath was strongly affected in a negative sense by the regional proximity of Calvinist or Lutheran populations, particularly insofar as those populations had a reputation for aggressive confrontations with their Catholic neighbors. It was also affected by the extent to which certain clerical corps had successfully evolved a *modus vivendi* between the "clericalized" Catholicism prescribed by the Tridentine[8] reforms—and which had implicitly come under attack from the National Assembly—and their own popular religious cultures. Though the reasons for the regional success or failure of clericalization remain something of a mystery, it seems commonly to have been associated with the relative density of the rural clergy. A more numerous parish clergy, it has been argued, helped establish in the minds of the laity a sharper sense of a clerical *society,* of a clergy distinct and apart from the secular world. For the priests themselves, faced with the dilemma of the oath, the presence of other clerics in the community created a context of support and emulation, reinforcing their sense of hierarchy and strengthening their resolve to act in uniformity against the oath. By contrast, the regional penetration of Jansenism[9] among the parish clergy had a *positive* influence on the acceptance of the Civil Constitution. In fostering clerical intolerance toward local "superstition," Jansenism hindered the development of a *modus vivendi* with popular religion. More concretely, it tended to create an irreducible kernel of curé opposition toward the episcopal corps, facili-

---

[3]See the glossary entry *parlements.*

[4]Some provinces incorporated more recently into France still retained provincial estates as a governing body. These estates dealt directly with the monarch. They should be clearly distinguished from the Estates General, with which they had no connection. See the glossary entry *Estates General.*

[5]French church.

[6]Sentiments favoring papal authority.

[7]Competitive examinations used to distribute positions.

[8]The reforms, stemming from the councils of Trent in the mid-sixteenth century, which sought to raise the educational and religious level as well as the role of the clergy.

[9]See the glossary entry *Jansenism.*

tating the break with the established hierarchy at the time of the oath. But other sources of clerical politicization were probably even more important than Jansenism. In the two or three zones of the kingdom where a long-standing tradition of clerical unrest was based in the regional economic structures of the Church and in local ecclesiastical institutions, a highly unified parish clergy had declared its independence from its prelates even before the Revolution. In regions such as these, politics might take precedence over everything else.

Yet the complex of forces affecting oath sentiments in the countryside might be strikingly different from those operating in the towns and cities of the kingdom. The urban milieu was a separate universe, with patterns of behavior and relations all its own. If in rural France clergy and laity tended to move in the same general direction on the oath, the two were probably more frequently at odds in the towns. The strong inverse correlation between urban oath-taking and the size of the local population (and to which Paris is the major exception) is remarkable and in need of explanation. In part, no doubt, the correlation was a function of the more dense ecclesiastical presence normally found in the larger towns—and in this sense there was a certain continuity with the situation in the hinterlands. Moreover, the cathedral town—which was usually, though not exclusively, a larger town—was the one site in which the bishop and his assistants seem to have had some measure of success in influencing lower clergy. But, at the same time, many clergymen living in the towns, especially the largest towns, stood to receive distinctly different impressions of the goals of the Revolutionaries in their implementation of the Civil Constitution. There can be little doubt that the large and medium-sized towns of the kingdom had been the principal fields of operation for the manifold forms of eighteenth-century anticlericalism—whether originating in the Parlements or the Jansenist movement or the writings of the *philosophes,* [10] or generated from longstanding rivalries between Church and town fathers. We have seen the growing fears among clerical deputies in the National Assembly that the patriot Left was attacking the clergy, if not religion itself. Similar fears were reflected in the oath explanations of a whole segment of the refractories[11] who announced their conviction that the Civil Constitution had been dictated by godless philosophy. The reality of such clerical perceptions could be debated at length. Yet the openly aggressive and unsympathetic attitude of the patriot administrators in certain towns easily aroused clerical suspicions about the true intentions of the urban Revolutionaries.

In both town and country, contrasting perspectives on the oath have

[10]Intellectuals associated with the Enlightenment.
[11]Those refusing to take the oath.

frequently been associated with two different role models of the parish clergyman—which, for want of better terms, we have come to characterize as the "Tridentine priest" and the "citizen priest." To judge by their oath explanations, many non-jurors had decidedly different conceptions of the nature of their office and their position in society than did their constitutional colleagues. The first saw themselves as bound primarily to spiritual and supernatural functions and as tightly integrated into an ecclesiastical hierarchy of authority, whose opinions they had no choice but to follow; the second viewed themselves rather as the servants of humanity whose identity was shaped primarily by their toils in behalf of the secular society and state. To a certain extent, the image chosen seems related to the personality traits of individual clergymen—though the evidence for this conclusion remains rather thin. But the regional prevalence of one image or another depended most likely on a combination of the factors alluded to above: to the strength of the ultramontane tradition, to the rural clerical density—reinforcing a sense of hierarchy—to the relative success of clericalization, and to the strength and objectives of curé political activities. In the clash of conflicting loyalties which the oath represented, the relative force of one of the two models might well determine whether clergy and laity would heed the local bishop or the local patriots, would be more receptive to the demands of Rome or to those of the National Assembly.

A TOUR DE FRANCE

Obviously, then, in any explanation of oath reactions, it is essential to take note of the specific geographic settings in which the crisis was confronted, of the particular constellation of forces at play in the various regions of the country. The number and definition of such regions could be debated at length. As certain historians have noted, every village, every hamlet, in the traditional society of the Old Regime was a unique world in itself. In the present context, we can make only a rapid journey through the France of 1791, through a series of seven zones defined pragmatically and very approximately around similar clusters of oath tendencies. We must confine ourselves here to the major attractions, the principal landmarks. Detailed accounts of the backroads and lesser-known sites will have to be left to local explorers.

The first and the largest single zone was centered on the "Parisian Basin," in the broadest sense of the term. But it included extensive projections north and east toward Picardy and Champagne, and south and west toward Berry, Bourbonnais, Upper Poitou, and perhaps even Bordelais: a sweep of provinces entirely dominated by the constitutional clergy, cutting diagonally across the historic core of the country from the border of the Austrian Lowlands to the mouth of the Gironde. Throughout most of the region, it has been suggested, the seventeenth-century efforts toward clericalization may have achieved a rather mediocre success. Local clerical recruitment was meager, especially from the rural areas, and for this reason a significant proportion—sometimes over half—of the parish clergy were "outsiders" arriving from the towns or from other provinces. But, despite such importations, the clerical presence remained sparse, and most parishes were manned by a single curé, without the assistance of vicaires or chaplains or other priests. The regions closer to Paris had also been marked by a strong Jansenist tradition among the rural clergy, a tradition which contributed both in alienating the curés from their bishops and in alienating the lay parishioners from their clergy. As for the urban populations, the longstanding legacy of anticlericalism, mediated in the eighteenth century by Parlementarians, Jansenists, and the men of the Enlightenment, had undoubtedly had an effect. Entries into the clergy fell more rapidly in Paris than in any other urban area. In their cahier[12] demands concerning religion and the clergy, the notables in the greater Parisian Basin were among the more progressive, even radical, in the country. Those in bailliages[13] from Picardy to Bourbonnais and in the region near Bordeaux were among the few in the kingdom proposing the reorganization of popular religious festivities for the sake of economic efficiency. Later, in the Year II, much of the zone would be fertile ground for vigorous de-Christianizing activities. Not surprisingly, the image of the citizen priest was dominant in a great many of the oath explanations of this region. One suspects that many priests, finding themselves only marginally appreciated as dominant sacral figures and necessary intermediaries to the supernatural, opted for a more viable role model, adopting the alternative pushed with such fervor by the philosophers and converting themselves into *social* intermediaries, the educated servants and tutors of the community. In this role—at least for the time being—they seem to have been generally accepted by the population, a population which would subsequently remain relatively indifferent to the loss of that small number of priests who chose to refuse the oath.

Traveling north from the capital, crossing Picardy into the small frontier provinces of Artois, Boulonnais, Flanders, Hainaut, and Cambrésis, one entered into a starkly different cultural milieu, a milieu in which both clergy and laity massively rejected the Civil Constitution. Outside the institutional structures of the Gallican Church, strongly marked by a heritage of Spanish dominance and by the Jesuit control of the local university of Douai, the clergy harbored strong ultramontane ties and

---

[12]A list of grievances compiled throughout France as part of the elections to the Estates General.
[13]Bailiwicks.

looked askance at the importation of Jansenism. Indeed, a certain number of priests reacted against the Civil Constitution specifically because they found it "tainted" with Jansenism. To a far greater extent, the priests in question were home-grown products. Substantial local entries into the secular clergy were supplemented, moreover, by a strong tradition of recruitment to various of the regular orders, present in great strength throughout the zone. Perhaps these recruitment patterns, coupled with the Jesuit influence, facilitated the development of a successful working relationship between popular culture and a clericalized religion. Significantly, this northern zone was one of the few regions in France in which a portion of the population took the defense of the regulars[14] and their landholdings in 1790. The clergy's attachment to the ecclesiastical hierarchy had been reinforced by the widespread use of the *concours,* and was revealed in the oath explanations of parish clergymen and in the readiness with which they responded to the bishops' appeals for joint petitions opposing the oath. As for the laity, the urban notables revealed themselves particularly conservative in their cahier statements regarding the Church and the clergy. The relatively late entrance of the zone into the kingdom, the maintenance of local estates and a *conseil souverain,*[15] and, in the case of Flanders, the barrier of language: all helped to promote a sense of distance and separation from the Paris Revolution and its religious legislation.

Skirting the border farther to the east, beyond the Ardennes, one entered into another frontier zone, a zone which stretched from Lorraine and Alsace southward to Franche-Comté and which perhaps included portions of Burgundy (a transition province cut into several different zones). This eastern periphery shared many characteristics with its northern counterpart, including a propensity on the part of most of the clergy to refuse the oath. Here, too, there was a strong historical and institutional basis for separatist sentiments toward the Parisian core. Here too, a vigorous ultramontane legacy—especially in Alsace and Franche-Comté—and the use of the *concours* contributed in fixing a hierarchical sentiment among the clergy, a clergy which was generally quite numerous and recruited locally. In addition, perhaps one half of the population of Lorraine and the vast majority of the Alsatians had little or no facility with the French language. But, unlike the northern frontier, this zone also contained the catalyst of a large non-Catholic presence—Jews and Calvinists, but above all the active and highly organized Lutherans—which sharpened and heightened the sense of Catholic identity among the masses. Even the urban notables revealed themselves particularly conservative toward religion:

---

[14]Those clergy living in a religious community as opposed to the secular clergy, which was composed of archbishops, bishops, canons, and the parish clergy.

[15]A local parlement, located in Artois.

both in their *cahiers de doléances* and in their initially lenient and conciliatory approach to the implementation of the oath. In Alsace, the combination of the linguistic barrier and the immediate presence of so many
"heretics" produced a profound popular suspicion and incomprehension of
the Civil Constitution, and laid the basis, according to Rodolphe Reuss, for
a religious struggle as rude and potentially dangerous as in any region
outside the Vendée. If the religious issue never led to the same kind of civil
war as in the west, it was probably because the National Assembly kept this
border province under much closer surveillance and control. Of the three
eastern provinces, Lorraine was clearly the most heterogeneous. The French-
speaking southern sector was generally more constitutional than the northern "Germanic" sector. This was due, in part, to its separation by language
and by the crest of the Vosges mountains from the Protestants of Alsace
and northern Lorraine. But more importantly, the juring zones revealed the
outlines of the defunct diocese of Toul, where institutional and ideological
peculiarities had rendered the parish clergy exceptionally politicized and
suspicious of the hierarchy. Several cantons of this former diocese would
have among the highest oath rates in the entire northeastern quadrant of
the country.

Southward from the Jura another border zone could be traced between
the left banks of the Saône and the Rhône and the crest of the Alps, a zone
which included Bresse and Bugey in the north—and perhaps Mâconnais
and Lyonnais—and Dauphiné and Provence farther south. Along with
central France, this was the most strongly constitutional sector in the
kingdom. While some Calvinist communities were present, nowhere were
they as numerous or as organized as in Alsace. In fact, most of the
Protestants resided in isolated rural valleys—in Diois, Queyras, the Baronnies,
etc.—and were seldom encountered by the Catholics. Though clerical
recruitment and clerical density were high in some areas, such as Champsaur
or Briançonnais, the overall picture was inconsistent, and in Lower Provence
and Lower Dauphiné there was often a chronic shortage of priests. In the
Mediterranean sectors, a dense implantation of Penitent confraternities[16]
and a vital and independent popular religious tradition may have somewhat limited the clergy's power in the realm of the supernatural. Indeed,
the evidence of sacerdotal recruitment and the clauses in wills would
suggest an unusually dramatic shift in popular attitudes in Provence after
1750, away from a clericalized, "baroque" religion. Already, by late 1790,
anticlericalism and even antireligion were very much in evidence in Marseille.
But the single most characteristic feature of this zone was the extraordinarily powerful and long-lived heritage of curé opposition to the ecclesiastical

---

[16]Organizations to give further opportunities for devotion or religiously oriented activities.
The confraternities of the Penitents were particularly independent from clerical control.

hierarchy. Although Jansenism had not been absent among the clergy of Provence and Lyonnais, the protest originated above all in the local economic structures of the Church, which left 60 to 90 percent of the curés with fixed salaries paid in money. Certain movements of this kind, directed against bishops and "priors," dated back at least to the early seventeenth century. The writings of Henri Reymond, widely distributed and read in Dauphiné and Provence after 1770, helped establish a sentiment of curé independence from the hierarchy well before the passage of the Civil Constitution. Reymond succeeded in encompassing the core of economic grievances in a general proposal for the rejuvenation and purification of the Church, a proposal which soon caught the imagination of both the clergy and the laity.

By contrast, on the opposite bank of the Rhône and through most of the regions of the Massif-Central and Languedoc, the refusal of the oath was widespread and general. Though numerous parish priests received a *portion congrue* here, as in Dauphiné and Provence, the salaries were frequently paid in kind rather than in money, making the curés largely immune to the effects of inflation which so traumatized their colleagues in the Alps. Much of the zone, particularly the upland regions of Rouergue and Auvergne, was characterized by a stronger than average clerical recruitment rate and by a dense ecclesiastical infrastructure that included numerous non-beneficed[17] clergymen and societies of priests. But the unifying factor in regards to the oath was the presence of a large, self-confident Calvinist contingent. Since the time of the Camisards,[18] if not earlier, this presence had served to put into relief the regional Catholic identity, selecting out the most defensive and combative elements of the faith and—partly in opposition to the Huguenot beliefs—placing particular emphasis on the essential role of the clergy in religion. With the implementation of the Civil Constitution, large numbers of Catholics became totally convinced that the National Assembly was controlled by the Protestants and aimed at nothing less than the destruction of Catholicism. By 1791 a veritable siege mentality had taken hold of much of the population, both in the countryside and in many towns like Toulouse, Montauban, and Nîmes. The extreme case was the *pays* of Gévaudan in the department of Lozère. Inhabiting the heart of the Massif-Central, directly confronting the Cévenol Huguenots, virtually the entire population of this region vetoed the oath and offered its absolute loyalty to the local clergy (with the exception, of course, of the handful of constitutionals who might soon find themselves in danger of their lives). The great majority of the refractories apparently remained in their parishes,

---

[17]A benefice was a position in the Church to which particular functions were assigned.

[18]A large-scale revolt of Calvinists in the south of France during the first decade of the eighteenth century.

in and out of hiding, for the duration of the Revolution and the Terror, protected by all but the isolated band of local patriots.

The remainder of the Midi, the Pyrenees, and the southwest, present a far more complex image, with strongly constitutional areas alternating with strongly refractory ones. In this zone too, the Calvinist dynamic might come into play in certain sectors—as in portions of the Pays de Foix —but it was far from being an overriding factor. On either end of the Pyrenees two regions with evident particularist and ultramontane traditions and major linguistic barriers would massively reject the oath: Roussillon and the Basque country. Here, as in the northern frontier provinces, a form of Catholicism imported from Spain—reinforced in the case of Roussillon by a long-powerful Jesuit University—exercised considerable influence. In a few areas, like Cerdagne, that influence could be direct and immediate, with Spanish monks actually crossing the frontier and preaching a veritable crusade against the Civil Constitution among their Catalonian brothers. In the central Pyrenees, by contrast—in regions like Comminges, Bigorre, and Couserans—economic structures in the Church similar to those in the Alps created an ecclesiastical mentality not unlike that found in Dauphiné and Provence. Congruist curés, entirely dependent on fixed moneyed salaries, had been highly politicized throughout most of the eighteenth century. Like the associates of Henri Reymond, the Pyrenean priests accepted the Revolutionary reforms with little conflict or crisis of conscience.

Finally, traveling northward along the Atlantic coast, one came to the great triangle of the "west"—the provinces of Lower Poitou, Anjou, Maine, Brittany, and Normandy. The sweeping refusal of the oath in this zone by laity and clergy alike has been frequently described, though perhaps never fully understood. We have examined in some detail the peculiar nature of ecclesiastical structures and religious culture in the west. The rural clergy, preeminently local and agricultural in its origins, was in a particularly good position to understand and sympathize with popular religious values and to establish a *modus vivendi* between such values and the Catholic Reformation efforts to clericalize religion. A portion of the west was one of the few areas in the kingdom which actually witnessed an increase in clerical recruitment during the last decades of the Old Regime, a recruitment which easily provided candidates for the dense network of rural clerical posts—and which included numerous vicaires, *habitués*,[19] and chaplains along with the curés and rectors. The fact that the western curés were also among the wealthiest of the kingdom could only have added to the clergy's stature in what was surely one of the most highly clericalized

---

[19]Nonbeneficed or semibeneficed clergy who, although based in village parishes, had no clear assignment there.

zones in France. If the clergy had not been untouched by Jansenism earlier in the century, the movement seems to have been rapidly repressed, surviving primarily in a few of the larger towns. This presence of a Jansenist legacy, however, was only one of the elements which sharply differentiated the towns of the west from the rural areas. While entries into the clergy had been stable or even rising in the countryside, they were dropping precipitously in the western cities. By 1789 the urban notables of the region would reveal themselves quite as progressive in their cahier demands concerning the Church as their counterparts in the Parisian Basin. Confronted with problems of implementing the new ecclesiastical policies, these same western notables would appear conspicuously impatient, even harsh and vindictive towards the local clergy, confirming suspicions in the minds of the latter that the Revolution was secretly attacking the Church and the Catholic faith. Yet, as all of the zones described in the present section, the west was by no means a monolith. If the department of Manche was markedly more constitutional than other sections of Lower Normandy, it was perhaps, in part, because of the near absence of important towns throughout the Cotentin Peninsula. If portions of the western Côtes-du-Nord were also notably less refractory, it is possibly because this region had the highest proportion of curés on the *portion congrue* of any section of the west. It also seems likely that certain "structural" problems in the west helped influence popular perspectives on the oath in certain regions. Rivalries and conflicts—of which those engendered by the substantial numbers of western tenant farmers may have been the most serious— gave rise to socio-economic divisions between town and country which closely paralleled, in many respects, the cultural-religious dichotomy.

A CULTURAL REVOLUTION?

It would seem obvious that any attempt to generalize about the long-term impact of the oath in France must likewise take into account regional distinctions. In many sectors of the country—in the Parisian Basin and in the Alpine southeast, for example—the vast majority of the clergy and laity accepted the Civil Constitution and the oath as an altogether natural logical course of events: at times without emotion, at times with real enthusiasm. Numerous priests were convinced that the new provisions would bring about the regeneration and purification of religion, that the Constitution was a gift of God himself, working through the National Assembly. Both laymen and ecclesiastics could be largely content with an arrangement which solidly instated the citizen priest, which regularized and consecrated a social relationship already well developed under the Old Regime. But, elsewhere, the same set of laws might be profoundly upsetting, even traumatic. For large numbers of Frenchmen—and perhaps, especially, for large numbers of French women—near the northern frontier, in the west, in the northeast, in the Massif-Central, and in portions of Languedoc and Aquitaine, the events transpiring in the second winter of the Revolution were probably as disturbing and culturally destabilizing as anything experienced since the Protestant Reformation of the sixteenth century. The endless refrain that the National Assembly was attempting to "change religion" was much more than rhetorical hyperbole. It expressed rather the heartfelt conviction on the part of a great many that the actions of the Revolutionaries had placed the fate of their eternal souls in jeopardy. Issues of such dimensions had in the past and still could take precedence over everything else—even over such earthy problems as taxes and land and social class.

Whatever the specific regional reaction, the oath crisis served to crystallize and bring to the fore local cultural assumptions and patterns of behavior which distinctly predated the Revolution. With the advantages of historical hindsight, it is possible to explore the archeology of many of these mental structures and trace their continuity through 1791 and beyond. And nevertheless—and this is one of the important themes of the present study—it was not necessarily the *same* mental structures which were brought to light by the oath from one region to another. The notable differences in the context of oath reactions in the refractory zones of Languedoc, on the one hand, and of the west, on the other, are particularly revealing in this regard. The Antichrist of the Revolution might take on remarkably different forms from one province to the next: for some clergymen the Civil Constitution was the work of the Huguenots grasping for power; for others it was a plot of anticlericals and philosophers; and for still others it was the hand of the Jansenists which appeared most clearly. Though research in this area is still far from complete, it seems unlikely that any single variable or cluster of variables can "explain" oath reactions in all sectors of the kingdom. No single map of the Old Regime yet encountered matches the geography of the oath—neither the map of Jansenism, nor of Protestantism, nor of clerical recruitment, nor of settlement patterns, nor of popular peasant uprisings, nor of any obvious patterns of economic and social structures. The suggestive thesis of Edward Fox on the two Frances of an internal agricultural nexus versus a mercantile nexus of port cities seems of little value for understanding the oath. Perhaps the closest parallel yet discovered involves the regional rural density of the clergy—as best as it can be estimated for 1790. But here, too, whole sectors of the country, the Alpine southeast in particular, ran sharply counter to the pattern. In sum, nothing from the past seems to have correlated with the oath as well as the oath would correlate with the future patterns of religious practice in the nineteenth and twentieth centuries.

For the crisis of the Civil Constitution and the oath was more than a catalyst and a precipitant. It was a seminal event in its own right. Substantially different regional reactions and trains of logic had come together in forming the oath geography. But, thereafter, the oath itself would rapidly set in motion a complex concatenation of action and reaction and would greatly intensify the polarization of clerical and anticlerical factions throughout the country. It served to unify, to "nationalize," the diverse forces of religious confrontation and thus contributed to the political realignment of French society. Patterns first engraved into the countryside in 1791 would thus be perpetuated into the nineteenth century and, beyond the Industrial Revolution and the economic modernization of the French countryside, well into the twentieth century. The exploration of this later history of the oath and its consequences is outside the scope of the present study. It might easily be the subject of another book. But, whether or not one chooses to describe these events as a "cultural revolution," it does seem clear that the ecclesiastical and religious crisis of 1791 represented for a great many men and women in a great many regions a veritable "événement structurant"; that it played a major role in recasting the gestalt of provincial France. Because of the oath, the mental topography of French society would never again be quite the same.

Hercules and the Radical Image in the French Revolution*

Lynn Hunt

Lynn Hunt may be credited with encouraging much of the new intellectual history of the French Revolution. In addition to François Furet, she has presented the only other general reinterpretation of the Revolution emphasizing ideas (*Politics, Culture, and Class in the French Revolution,* Berkeley, 1984). And clearly she has adopted assumptions other than his that also deserve attention. Unlike Furet, she de-emphasizes origins and concentrates on revolutionary creation. She also reconstructs the events of revolutionary politics as a symbolic system related to the revolutionaries' general political aspirations and hopes. Furet has tended instead to discuss their efforts as designed to press the immediate political advantage of a faction or party. He would emphasize, it would seem, the concrete substance of debates while she would ask what the existence of such a debate communicated about the nature of the Revolution. Put another way, for him the words that triumphed determined the political outcomes; for her they represent in a symbolic way the expression of heartfelt sentiments. Finally, despite her evident interest in ideas, she has not abandoned social history so completely as has Furet. She at least delineates ordinary people during the Revolution though they sometimes appear merely as passive receivers of the ideas of politicians. These aspects that distinguish her work from Furet's have also led Hunt to address other topics and posit many new hypotheses.

The article included in this volume evidences some of Hunt's particular approaches to intellectual history with interesting results. By studying how, after the fall of the monarchy, the revolutionaries used Hercules to replace royal symbols, she focuses on their efforts at creating a fresh new set of images. Discounting historical precedents, she describes their intentions to invest Hercules with new and appropriate meanings. Furthermore, she emphasizes the adoption of Hercules not to better explain political

A portion of this material was originally published in *Representations,* Vol. 1, No. 2, Spring 1983, pp. 95–117, © 1984 by the Regents of the University of California. Used with permission.

competition among elites, but as a symbol of what the revolutionaries in power hoped to indicate about their position. In fact, she finds that they planned Hercules to stand as a natural force, truthful but not intellectual. In this way, the politicians were endeavoring to represent their ideal of the public that would be good but remain safely on the sidelines while its intellectual betters governed. Such arguments and techniques indubitably have infused fresh ideas and genuine excitement into intellectual history.

All political authority requires a "cultural frame" or "master fiction" in which to define itself and put forward its claims. Many commentators insist, in addition, that every cultural frame necessarily has a sense of "center," which has sacred status. The sacred center makes possible a kind of social and political mapping, for it gives the members of a society their sense of place. French political authority under the Old Regime fits this social-anthropological model very well; under the monarchy, the sacred center was represented by the king's body, and the cultural frame of that authority was deeply embedded in long-standing notions of a Catholic, hierarchical order. The cultural frame was so deeply embedded, in fact, that it was considered "traditional": it needed no justification and for the most part received none other than the repeated ceremonial re-enactment of it (in coronations, entry ceremonies, and the like).

When the French Revolution challenged the political authority of the Old Regime, it therefore also inevitably questioned its cultural frame. Revolutionaries enthusiastically embraced the political side of this challenge, but they were less certain about the cultural side. Where would their confrontation lead them? As time passed and as political struggles sharpened, preoccupation with the frame of political authority became increasingly acute. What ensued, in the midst of struggles to fashion a new order, was a "crisis of representation." When the deputies finally voted to abolish royalty and execute the king, they decentered the frame of traditional authority; they exposed the fictionality of the master fiction and in the process created a frightening vacuum or "an-archy" in their social and political space. Where was the new center of society, and who was to represent it? Should there even be a center, much less a sacred one? Could the new democratic Nation be located in any institution or any means of representation? The French Revolution was more, consequently, than just another example of how politics is shaped by culture, for the revolutionaries did not just seek another representation of authority, but rather came to question the very act of representation itself.

The crisis of representation only emerged in gradual fashion as the deputies in Paris confronted the "problem" of royalty in September, 1792.

Everyone agreed that the symbols of the Old Regime had to be effaced, though there was dispute over how public and self-conscious this effacement had to be. At the inaugural meeting of the National Convention on September 21, 1792, one deputy argued that no official declaration of the abolition of royalty was necessary: "I think neither of the king nor of royalty; I concern myself entirely with my mission [to establish a new government] without thinking that such an institution [as royalty] *could ever have existed.*" There was no need to officially declare the abolition of royalty because the reality of the institution was already in the past. In countering this argument, the deputy Grégoire expressed a nearly unanimous opinion; the institutions of the Old Regime might be gone, but the tangible reminders of them had to be rooted out of popular consciousness:

> Certainly, none of us will ever propose to conserve the deadly race of kings in France . . . we must fully reassure the friends of liberty; it is necessary to destroy this word 'king,' which is still a talisman whose magical force can serve to stupefy many men. I demand therefore that by a solemn law you consecrate *the abolition of royalty.*

After a spontaneous demonstration in support of Grégoire's proposal, the Convention went on to approve a new seal for its records: replacing the king as the insignia of the official seal of state was "a woman leaning with one hand on a fasces, holding in the other a lance topped by a liberty cap, with the legend *Archives of the French Republic.*" Soon afterward, this seal (Figure 1) became the seal for all branches of public administration, and the Convention ordered that all public acts be henceforth dated Year 1 of

FIGURE 1   Seal of the Republic, 1792. *(Service photographique des Archives Nationales.)*

the French Republic. Two weeks later, the deputies decreed that the seals of royalty, the scepter, and the crown, all be broken into pieces, transported to the mint, and melted down into republican coins. The markings of the old cultural frame had been transmuted into the material for a new one.

The initial debate about the abolition of royalty barely revealed a tension that was to grow in the months and years that followed. Once royalty and its symbols had been abolished, what was to take their place? Should a sign or insignia be necessary to republican government? In a report given to the Council of Five Hundred more than three years after the initial discussion on seals, the same deputy Grégoire referred to a "strange question" that had been posed: "Is it necessary that there be a seal of the Republic? In the beginning, seals, they tell us, were only employed to compensate for the ignorance or the imperfection of writing." Grégoire says no more about this position since he is most concerned to refute it, but the timing of his speech (January, 1796) indicates that this minority view was most influential during the preceding radical period of the Revolution, the period known as the Terror (summer 1793–summer 1794). There was at least one writer who explicitly denounced the personification of moral principles during the Terror: "The metaphysical principles of Locke and Condillac[1] should become popular, and the people should be accustomed to see in a statue only stone and in an image only canvas and colors." Reason and nature, the foundations of the new regime, needed no representation outside of clear writing and clear speech since they were engraved on the hearts of all men. A people with access to print and public discussion needed no icons.

This extreme rationalist position was in fact rarely taken, and Grégoire's answer of 1796 was much more common. He argued that all civilized people found that "a sign, a type, was necessary to give a character of authenticity" to all public acts. Moreover, he continued, the use of a seal of state was founded on reason, for a seal was more easily recognized than a signature, more permanent, and more difficult to counterfeit. The seal, in other words, made authority public rather than individual; it represented something much more general than a man's signature ever could. True, Grégoire admitted, "the ridiculous hieroglyphs of heraldry are now for us only historical curiosities." The seal of a republic could not be superstitious and obscure like the insignia of aristocracy and royalty. But this did not mean that symbols could be thrown out completely.

> When one reconstructs a government anew, it is necessary to republicanize everything. The legislator who ignores the importance of signs will fail at his

---

[1]John Locke and Etienne Bonnot de Condillac, philosophers who stressed the importance of the material world, are associated with the Enlightenment.

mission; he should not let escape any occasion for grabbing hold of the senses, for awakening republican ideas. Soon the soul is penetrated by the objects reproduced constantly in front of its eyes; and this combination, this collection of principles, of facts, of emblems which retraces without cease for the citizen his rights and his duties, this collection forms, in a manner of speaking, the republican mold which gives him a national character and the demeanor of a free man.

Grégoire offered here his own interpretation of Condillac's psychology; for him, the sign and the symbol, when correctly chosen, could serve the purpose of political propaganda by "grabbing hold of the senses" and penetrating the soul, The seal, then, was not only a representation of public authority but also an instrument of education, an element in "the republican mold."

Yet even Grégoire's spirited defense of a seal was not without its uncertainties. Although most deputies could agree that some kind of symbol was necessary, and not incompatible with democracy, they were not quick to agree on what it should be. Grégoire gave his long report in 1796 because no definitive seal had ever been voted. The decision in September 1792 had been almost haphazard, and the seal proposed was designed initially for the Convention's archives. In 1796, at the time of Grégoire's speech, the seal was still in limbo. Despite Grégoire's efforts, it remained so until the advent of Napoleon.

Yet, if there was no permanent seal of the republic, this was not for want of trying. The seal became an issue whenever the deputies saw themselves turning in some new direction. Debate was most intense at three distinct moments of the Revolution: when the republic was first established in September 1792, during the Terror (the rule of the radicals), and just after the inauguration of a new, more moderate legislative system in late 1795 and early 1796. The debates on seals can be read in two ways: as a record of political conflict over the meaning of the republic and as an especially dramatic arena for working out the role of representation more generally. These two aspects cannot be neatly separated, just as political authority cannot be separated from its cultural frame. Representation, whether political or cultural, whether a question of deputies and policies or signs and symbols, was always, at least implicitly, a political issue. What follows here, then, is an account of how these two aspects of the crisis of representation were intertwined.

In September 1792, when royalty was abolished and the republic declared, the choice of a new insignia seemed almost automatic. The archivist proposed the choice of Liberty, and none of the accounts of the discussion mention any controversy about the type chosen for the new seal. In his study of the "feminine civic allegory" Maurice Agulhon offers several reasons for this virtually reflexive identification: in iconographic tradition, most qualities, and in particular the different principles of government, even monarchy, were represented by female figures; the Phrygian bonnet or liberty cap of the goddess provided a particularly clear contrast with the crown of royal authority (and the female figure reinforced that contrast); Catholicism made the French more receptive to a Marian figure (the sobriquet Marianne was certainly semantically close to Mary, mother of Jesus); and the French Republic could find in the feminine allegory a figure suitably distant from the real life heroes-turned-villians of the revolutionary process. Where Mirabeau, Lafayette, and many others had disappointed their followers and passed from the historical scene, Marianne endured thanks to her abstraction and impersonality.

Agulhon has traced, in addition, the political implications of different ways of representing Marianne. The seal of 1792 showed her standing, young, and determined, though not exactly aggressive. She held the lance of popular revolution, capped by the Phrygian bonnet of liberation. This figuration was in many ways an intermediate one, straddling the middle between the more radical poses of Liberty marching, bare-breasted and fierce of visage, which were current in 1793, and the more conservative poses favored by later governments in the 1790s and in the nineteenth century in which Liberty appeared seated, stolid, tranquil, and often without lance or liberty cap. The same choices between radical and conservative liberty figures would be posed again in 1848 and after 1871, as soon as a republic was proclaimed once more.

After generations of controversy over the republic and as a consequence over its emblem, Marianne, the feminine civic allegory, was not only accepted but widely diffused in France. But during the Revolution her future was by no means guaranteed. The first threat to Marianne came from within the ranks of republicans, who in 1793 and 1794 sought a less moderate image for their increasingly radical republic. In October 1793, after the arrest of the Girondin deputies (who opposed the growing power of the Paris districts and their radical Jacobin leaders) and in the midst of desperate efforts to recast the Republic in a more radical mold, the Convention decreed that the seal and the coins of the Republic should henceforth carry the ark of the constitution and the fasces as their emblem. The seal's new legend, "Le peuple seul est souverain,"[2] underscored the new reliance on popular support. Within a month, however, the Convention changed its mind again. In early November 1793, the artist-deputy David proposed that the Convention order the erection of a colossal statue to represent the French people. Ten days later the Convention voted to make the statue the subject of the seal of state. Thus, the deputies had chosen a giant Hercules as the emblem of the radical Republic.

Although, to my knowledge, no official seal bearing Hercules was ever

---

[2]The people alone is the sovereign.

cast, the intention of the Convention was reaffirmed on at least two other occasions: in February 1794 and again in April 1794. Moreover, the Musée Carnavalet in Paris has several sketches by the official engraver Dupré which match the guidelines laid down by the Convention for the new seal (Figure 2). That David had Hercules in mind as the model for the statue-seal is made clear both by the iconography of Dupré's sketch—the figure holds the distinctive club and his lion skin lies just beside him—and by David's original text: "Que cette image du peuple *debout* tienne dans son autre main cette massue terrible dont les anciens armaient leur Hercule!"[3] A giant, mythic, male figure now dwarfed Marianne.

The political meaning of the Hercules figure is revealed most clearly by the circumstances of its appearance. The first major public use of the figure came on August 10, 1793, during an elaborate festival planned by David. Although the festival was held on the first anniversary of the uprising that brought down the monarchy, it was explicitly designed to celebrate the defeat of federalism, the revolt of the summer of 1793 in support of the arrested deputies known as the Girondins. At this critical moment, David orchestrated a festival which aimed at nothing less than a review of the Revolution's development. It was a morality play with a set of striking, allegorical messages. Four "stations" retraced the major turning-points in the Revolution in preparation for the final ceremony of consecration of the new constitution: a figure of Nature sat on the site of the fall of the Bastille; an arch of triumph was dedicated to the heroines of October 1789; a statue of Liberty memorialized the execution of the king in January 1793; and finally, a colossus representing the French people (Figure 3) used its club to smash the hydra of federalism. The figure in the festival was not referred to officially as Hercules, but the iconography did not escape educated participants. One of the best known Herculean "labors" was the killing of the Hydra, which had been emblematic over the centuries of various sorts of evil, from sophism to vice, from ignorance to the nation's enemy in war. An engraver who visited the site earlier on the day of the festival referred to "la figure colossale d'Hercule, haute de vingt-quatre pieds. . . . Cet Hercule avoit le pied gauche posé sur la gorge de la contre-révolution."[4]

The placement of Hercules relative to Liberty is particularly relevant. The statue of Liberty came just before Hercules in the celebratory procession. By implication Liberty was important but representative only of one particular moment, a moment now passed. At the statue of Liberty, delegates from the departments put the torch to the hateful symbols of monarchy

---

[3]Let the image of the people *standing* hold in its other hand this terrible club which the ancients used to arm their Hercules.

[4]The colossal figure of Hercules, at a height of 24 feet. . . . This Hercules had its left foot placed on the throat of the counterrevolution.

FIGURE 2   Sketch by the engraver Dupré. Musée Carnavalet, Paris. *(Photo: author.)*

and thus reenacted the ritual sacrifice of the monarch to the goddess of the Republic. At the next stop, there was nothing for the delegates to do: Hercules-the French people was the only actor. He gathered the fasces, symbol of unity, in one hand, while he crushed the monster of federalism (half-woman, half-serpent according to observers) with the club in his other hand. The political meaning of the progression was evident: the representatives of the people established liberty when they punished Louis XVI for his crimes, and then the people themselves protected the Republic against the monster of disunity and factionalism. Hercules did not need the help of the deputies, though he planted himself firmly on the mountain, which stood, however inertly, for the righteous deputies within the Convention (including, of course, David). The Republic and its constitution could not be safely enshrined at the last station—the Revolution could not be fully realized—without this intervention by the people. In comparison to Liberty, then, Hercules represented a higher stage in the development of the Revolution, one characterized by the force and unity of the people, rather than by the sagacity of its representatives.

When David proposed the erection of the colossal statue three months after the festival, the political circumstances were different. The federalist crisis had passed, but new issues had arisen to take its place. At the beginning of September, the Convention, surrounded by angry and hungry

FIGURE 3   "The French People Overwhelming the Hydra of Federalism." Musée Carnavalet, Paris. *(Photo: author.)*

sans-culottes,[5] had officially agreed to make terror "the order of the day." A general maximum on prices was declared, and executions by the Revolutionary Tribunal in Paris accelerated. On October 16 the queen was guillotined. Then in November, the most divisive issue of all gathered steam: de-Christianization.[6] During the same session at which David first made his proposal (November 7, 1793), several priests and bishops among the deputies publically abjured their clerical offices; the most noteworthy hesitator was Grégoire. Three days after David's proposal and just a week before the Convention decided to make the colossus the subject of the seal, the notorious Festival of Reason[7] was held in Nôtre-Dame Cathedral, now dubbed the Temple of Reason.

Hercules faced a set of tasks worthy of his name. The most radical deputies and their followers wanted nothing less than a new cultural frame that would repudiate all Christian antecedents. Robespierre, David, and the other Jacobin leaders had to at once respond to this demand (and the demands for a Terror) and try to get firmer control of a movement which threatened to repulse the large part of a population that was still fervently Catholic and wary of the new order. Thus, from the beginning, David's Hercules had to represent radical aspirations while at the same time curbing them.

David's political intentions were evident in the formal speech he gave on November 17, 1793, the day the Convention voted to adopt his statue as the prototype of the seal. The statue was to be a monument to the "glory of the French people," and a remembrance of the people's triumph over despotism and superstition. The "double tyranny of kings and priests" would be overcome symbolically in the construction of the statue's base, which would be made up of the debris from the statues of kings knocked off the porticos of Nôtre-Dame. Thus would the Convention, with its "énergie libératrice," free the present, the future, and even the past from the "shame of a long servitude." The statue would represent the power of the people in the most literal possible fashion; at forty-six feet in height, Hercules would overshadow memories of even the most popular kings, such as Henry IV, whose merely life-size image he would replace on the Pont-Neuf.[8] But behind the statue, motivating it, were David and the Convention.

---

[5]Literally, without breeches. This is a term used to describe the working class, who wore long pants, as opposed to the well-to-do, who dressed in knee pants.

[6]A violent movement that aimed to destroy the established church and that developed most fully during the winter of 1793 and continued into the spring of 1794.

[7]Robespierre organized this festival as a state effort to establish an official, although non-Catholic, religion.

[8]A prominently located bridge in Paris, crossing the Seine River.

The choice of the giant Hercules at once embodied and strained to transcend the ambiguities in the radical view of representation. David explicitly emphasized the opposition between people and monarchy; Hercules was chosen, after all, to make this opposition more evident. But David's speech, and the image itself, implicitly referred as well to the uneasy tension between the people and the Convention, the new sovereign and its representatives. When they chose Hercules for the seal of the Republic, the radicals committed themselves to the view that some sort of representation was necessary. In Hercules they sought the most "transparent" representation possible, a kind of diminishing point of representation. They wanted an image that would convey the sovereign majesty of the people united, and the statue contained no obvious reference to the deputies or to the Convention. Yet even this pared-down representation was constantly subverted by its nature as an image. It was an image-representation of the people provided by the people's representatives, and as such it inherently included the representatives' interpretation of the people. This implicit interpretive element threatened to re-establish in cultural form the very relationship of political authority (authority outside the people) that the radicals were promising to abolish. Thus, even as the image proclaimed the supremacy of the people, it reintroduced the superiority of the people's representatives.

When speaking to the Convention, David sought to underline the simplicity of his conception. "Your Committee [of Public Instruction, for which David spoke] believed that, in the proposed monument, everything, both the materials and the forms, ought to express in a sensitive and forceful manner the great memories of our revolution." The statue itself would be made out of bronze furnished by the victories of the French armies. And, "since it is a kind of national representation, it could not be too beautiful." The enormous size of the figure would impose a "character of force and simplicity," the virtues of the people. In one of his monumental hands, the colossus (now no longer referred to explicitly as Hercules by David) would hold little figures of both Equality and Liberty, pressed close together, which showed, as David claimed, that they depended entirely on the genius and virtue of the people.

In the present of 1793–94, the giant male figure had potent resonances. The distant, feminine statue of Liberty represented a moderate republic now repudiated. The new radical republic had no need of the *"hommes petits et vains"* whom Robespierre denounced as the natural enemies of the Revolution; the Revolution had brought forth a new, heroic man of mythic proportions:

> The French people seem to have advanced two thousand years beyond the rest of humankind; one would be tempted even to regard it, from within its midst, as a different species. Europe kneels before the shadows of the tyrants

we are punishing. . . . Europe cannot conceive that one could live without kings, without nobles; and we, that one could live with them. Europe spills its blood to rivet the chains of humanity; and we spill ours to break them.

Who else but a colossus could break those chains of humanity?

The Herculean metaphor had appeared in radical discourse before David ever thought of using the image in his festival of August 10th. At the end of June, 1793, Fouché described the victory of the people of Paris over the Girondins in this fashion:

> . . . the excess of oppression broke through the restraints on the people's indignation; a terrible cry made itself heard in the midst of this great city; the tocsin and the cannon of alarm awakened their patriotism, announcing that liberty was in danger, that there wasn't a moment to spare; suddenly the forty-eight sections armed themselves and were transformed into an army. This formidable colossus is standing, he marches, he advances, he moves like Hercules, traversing the Republic to exterminate this ferocious crusade that swore death to the people.

Fouché's remarkable statement reveals the compelling force of the Hercules image for the radicals in Paris; this figure was nothing like a Marianne. As Fouché slips back and forth between the people and the colossus, between the past and the present tense, between "them" and "him," we can almost see the startling transformation taking place, as a kind of "terrible" (that is, awe-inspiring and "sublime") monster rises from the depths of the city and its people to wreak its vengeance on the people's enemies. Where is the sacred center now? With democracy it has become a new field of forces: "the people" is everywhere, but when it is assembled, when it comes together in a critical mass, it is transformed into a powerful new energy. "The Terror" was a radical, emergency form of government established to confront a series of life-threatening crises, but we can see in this passage how it was also a very real and disturbing experience for the men who supposedly invented it. The Terror was the people on the march, the exterminating Hercules. Hercules, the people, in the eyes of the radicals who had called it into being, was potentially a Frankenstein's creation.

The development of the terrifying monster association only occurred during the Terror, when the power of the people assembled became more awesome. The Hercules image had before then a long iconographic history which gave the figure a different meaning for educated, bourgeois radicals than it could possibly have had for the popular classes. Hercules was not a "popular" figure; he did not appear, for instance, in the repertory of popular woodcuts or *"imagerie populaire"* which were widely circulated in the kingdom under the Old Regime. Instead, Hercules appeared most commonly as the mythological representation of French kings, the Gallic Hercules or *Hercule gaulois*. This figuration dates from the French Renaissance. In 1549, for example, the triumphal arch designed for Henry

II's entry into Paris was capped by a Gallic Hercules representing Henry's predecessor Francis I. Like many Renaissance versions of Hercules, this one had chains extending from his mouth to his companions' ears, for it was supposedly characteristic of Hercules that he lead by persuasion rather than by force.

By the time of the French Revolution, Hercules had gone through something of an iconographic metamorphosis. Louis XVI, last of the Bourbons, was evidently never associated with Hercules. Instead, the figure had migrated to America. Sometime after 1776, our same engraver Dupré struck a medal for Benjamin Franklin which had the head of a young girl with the device, *Libertas Americana,* on the front, and on the reverse had a young child strangling two serpents. This infant Hercules was being attacked by a leopard, which a goddess holding a shield with a border of fleur-de-lys was about to strike with her lance. Here royal France was protecting the new republican Hercules in America. When a committee was set up on July 4, 1776 to prepare a device for a seal of the United States of America, one of its members, John Adams, proposed Gribelin's engraving of "The Judgment of Hercules" which served as the frontispiece to Shaftesbury's widely read tract on the need for clarity in art (1723). Even in America, the choice of seal was not effortless. The final decision was not made until 1782, after six years of deliberation and false starts. Then the choice of an imperial eagle was, as one art historian claims, "obscure, 'aenigmatical' [in Shaftesbury's sense], and far beyond the comprehension of all but the middle- and upper-class gentlemen who had invented [it]." The eagle was the emblem of Charles V, Holy Roman Emperor, and it had been taken from a German book of emblems and devices.

Hercules appeared on a few prints and engravings in revolutionary France before 1793, but David (perhaps on the urging of Dupré) was almost single-handedly responsible for reviving and transforming him into a powerful new symbol in the revolutionary repertory. Hercules had long since lost his association with rhetoric and persuasion; in the major dictionary of iconology printed in the first years of the Revolution, Hercules appeared only under the entries "Courage" and "Force." The remarks on "Force" indicate, moreover, how allegories had been feminized: "The iconologists represent Force with the figure of a woman covered by a lionskin and armed with the club of Hercules." Thus, David was not so much continuing an iconographic tradition as he was choosing certain elements in it and inverting their meaning. In the eyes of the educated elite, Hercules had stood in French history for the power of individual kings; in the revolutionary present, David turned him into the representation of a collective, popular power. He took one of the favorite signs of monarchy and reproduced, elevated, and monumentalized it into the sign of its opposite.

It is impossible, however, to know exactly what the deputies of the Convention had in mind when they chose Hercules for the seal, since the choice aroused little official comment. They may not have been struck by his iconographic history, especially since that history had been attenuated in the last generations of the Old Regime. But they were almost certainly attracted to the masculinity of the figure, since they had already rejected the female goddess of Liberty. David's Hercules recaptured and rehabilitated a distinctly virile representation of sovereignty (a concept which had connotations of domination and supremacy in any case). The masculinity of Hercules reflected indirectly on the deputies themselves; through his image they too were associated with the kingly power of old. It made them the legitimate successors in the new order. At the same time, Hercules could be taken as a veiled warning to the educated and as a reminder of the ways in which their world had been transformed by the Revolution. The people, the new, formidable giant, had become king. Even the deputies were answerable to it. Yet, what did Hercules mean to the people? The colossus—unnamed as he was officially—was but a mythical giant to the popular classes. The resonance for them was not with the classics or with French history, but with the monsters, heroes, and perhaps even with the saints of popular tales.

The potential interpenetration of elite and popular images of Hercules can be seen in the festival of January 21, 1794, at Grenoble. The festival celebrated the death of the king the year before. On a platform sat a manikin representing Louis Capet[9] (with a crown and the horns of a cuckold!), on his right sat the "so-called" pope, and on his left a figure representing the nobility. When the people gathered in the square cried out for vengeance, two figures representing the "French Hercules" appeared from behind to finish them off with clubs. Then the fallen figures were dragged through the mud and trampled underfoot by the participants. For the elite, the *Hercule françois* replaced the *Hercule gaulois;* he was now a true national figure and not one limited to monarchy. For the popular classes, the *two* Hercules figures became part of a revived carnival scene, which was filled with derision and the inversion of traditional roles. Just as the maypole of tradition had been transformed from a statement of homage to authority into a sign of sedition and peasant power, so too the Hercules of kingly power had been recast as the sign of the people's power.

The cultural context of Hercules was, however, very different. The maypole was a "popular" symbol with deep roots in peasant culture in France, at least southwestern France. Hercules came more directly out of elite culture, even if he could be construed as an image with attraction for the popular classes. The transformation of Hercules, moreover, was not

---

[9]Capet was the family name of the earliest royal family to sit on the throne of France. By referring to Louis XVI in this way, revolutionaries were speaking of him familiarly and ignoring his monarchical claims.

one effected by the popular classes; he was reinvented by the radicals in the Jacobin government of Paris. As a consequence, Hercules can be read as an expression, not only of the radicals' attempt to restructure society along more popular lines, but also of their ambivalence about that power. For Hercules never appears as an intelligent giant. In Fouché's account, he is a mighty force, crying with the pain of betrayal, fierce when aroused; he reacts more like an injured animal than like an agent of his own destiny. David's plan for the statue underscores this aspect in a very curious way: he called for the engraving of several key words on the giant's body. On his brow would be inscribed "light" (a rather weak reference to intelligence); "nature" and "truth" were to appear on his chest; "force" and "courage" on his arms; and "work" on his hands. Hercules brings light and truth to the world in David's vision, not through his intellect or cleverness but through his strength, courage, and "labor."

David's choice of words made the radical view of the people explicit. The giant was a force of nature; his transparency made him nature's medium for truth and light. Apparently without reason, he had no motive for second thoughts, for secrets, or for those most feared combinations, conspiracies against the Revolution. His contribution to the Revolution was not in the realm of ideas, obviously, but rather as soldier and worker; his was the courage and strength without which the radical cause would have been doomed. He was the backbone of that "terror, without which virtue is powerless." And perhaps most important, the giant represented those who worked with their hands, the "sans-culottes," those who wore long trousers rather than the short pants of the leisured classes. Work under the Old Regime had been devalued; working with one's hands made one a member of the "vulgar mechanic classes." The radicals were trying to revalue work as a source of pride and dignity; nothing was more despised by them than the idling rich. Yet, David's Hercules undermined this revaluation while attempting to memorialize it; "work" on his hands became yet another sign of the giant's status as dumb force. Only David's words could make him speak.

David's proposed inscription was only the most striking of many examples of the tension in the people-representative relation. The sheer massiveness of the statue was supposed to convey an unmistakable message: "the people" was monumental and awesome, overwhelming in its force. And the people stood alone. Yet the people's representatives kept creeping back into the picture because they provided the interpretations. When Hercules first appeared in the festival of August 10, 1793, he was labeled the "Colossus of the Invalides," referring to his placement in the festival procession. As the participants gathered in front of the station, the president of the Convention explained just what the people were to see in him: "French people! Here you are looking at yourself in the form of an emblem which is rich in instructive lessons. The giant whose powerful hand reunites and reattaches in one bundle the departments which make up its grandeur and its strength, that giant is you!" Without the interpretation provided by their representatives, the people would not recognize their own image.

The explosive mixture of radical revaluation of the lower classes (Hercules, the classic hero, as sans-culotte), carnivalesque inversion, and ambivalence about the new force were all brought together in a newspaper editorial commenting on David's original speech about the statue. The editor of the *Révolutions de Paris* immediately grasped the import of the image:

> We will see the people standing, carrying the liberty that it conquered and a club to defend its conquest. [Note that liberty now is a female trophy from the war on kings.] No doubt, among the models entered in the competition, we will prefer the one which best projects the character of a sans-culotte with its figure of the people.

He went on to praise David's choice of words for the statue, claiming that the Egyptians wrote on their public monuments because these "were the only basic books of the multitude." The editor could not resist adding his own suggestion: Why not have the same kind of monument in every city and hamlet in France? Why not put a monumental statue at every critical point along the frontier? And since "Homer called the kings of his time *'mangeurs de peuples'* [people-eaters], we will write on these figures of the French sans-culottes, *'Le Peuple Mangeur de Rois'* [The People, Eater of Kings]." Soon after, the paper provided its own printed image of the figure (Figure 4).

Here, the figure has lost his classical allure; he looks just like a rough-and-ready sans-culotte. He is not even monumental; instead, according to the editor, the king is a pygmy, a typical form of carnivalesque inversion. By implication, the sans-culotte will become what he eats, the incarnation of the sovereign nation. This image is more radical than David's because it is more "transparent": it is life-size, non-classical, clear in social content, and explicit in its action. It is neither allegorical nor metaphorical; the sans-culotte *is* the people. Thus the image comes close to the zero-point of representation. It is not at all obscure or "aenigmatical." Nevertheless it, too, required interpretation. The figure acts without thought; indeed, it embodies action rather than reason. And the radical newspaper-man must provide the logos, the reason behind his action. This figure too is "inscribed"; the body of the people has to be written upon before it can take on political meaning. The representatives of the people have to represent the people to themselves; without the reason provided by the deputies, the people can only be a dumb force of nature.

Although David's proposed competition for the statue was put off along with many other projects, some kind of plaster version was apparently constructed. One late nineteenth century historian claimed that a represen-

FIGURE 4   "Le Peuple Mangeur de Rois." Musée Carnavalet, Paris. *(Photo: author.)*

tation of Hercules was in fact set up on the Pont-Neuf, but the description he gives fits the figure of the festival of August 10 (Hercules clubbing the hydra of federalism) and not the Hercules of the statue. Engravings of the Festival of the Supreme Being of June 8, 1794 show a statue of Hercules in a prominent spot next to the mountain erected on the Champ de Mars (Figure 5). This statue does follow the guidelines set out by David for the Pont-Neuf colossus; it is not as big as proposed, but the classical figure holds the two tiny representations of Liberty and Equality in his hand. Is it accidental that the Hercules in this engraving looks very much like Michelangelo's David? Was this a sign of David's own egotism (his name now associated with Hercules and the people) or was this the ironic comment of an anonymous engraver? In any case, the same statue also appeared in the Festival of Victory held at the end of October 1794, three months after the fall of Robespierre and the disgrace of David himself.

Like many of the plaster representations used in the Jacobin festivals, the colossus was destroyed in early 1795. At the end of October 1795, a deputy suggested that the Convention vote for a seal showing a beehive. This proposition was rejected after another deputy remarked that beehives were royalist, if only because they had a queen bee. The proper emblems of a republic, in this deputy's opinion, were the liberty cap and the level

FIGURE 5   The Festival of Supreme Being. Musée Carnavalet, Paris. *(Photo: author.)*

(the symbols of liberty and equality). In other words, after the fall of the radicals, the remaining deputies turned to abstract symbols. Grégoire's report of 1796 shows this influence. He proposed the choice of three designs: a female figure without the distinctive liberty cap; a triangle to represent the union of the two legislative Councils and the Executive Directory[10] (the liberty cap sat on top the triangle); and three interlocking

---

[10]After the fall of Robespierre, his opponents, the Thermidoreans, set up a government called the Directory after its executive branch. There was also a legislature composed of the Council of Five Hundred and the Council of Ancients.

FIGURE 6   Sketch by the engraver Dupré. Musée Carnavalet, Paris. *(Photo: author.)*

circles in the center of a shield whose border would represent the invincible chain of the united departments (with the liberty cap appearing in one of the circles). The seal on the official proceedings of the Council of Five Hundred consisted of an oval with a liberty cap, rays of the sun, a compass and balance. As the American republicans had done before them, the French republicans were moving towards the abstract and enigmatic in symbolic representation. The people were no longer directly represented in imagery; the republic was for the people, but it was neither by nor of them.

Although Hercules did not capture the seal of the Republic, he did not disappear from circulation altogether after the fall of Robespierre and his radical followers. A law passed in August, 1795, divided the coins of the Republic into two types: silver pieces would bear the figure of Hercules "uniting Liberty and Equality" with the legend "Union and Force;" and the lesser bronze pieces would show the figure of Liberty with the legend "République Française." The contrast and tension between the male and female figurations was still there. But Hercules had changed: he had been domesticated. (See Figure 6, which is a sketch by Dupré matching the guidelines of the decree.) Now Hercules is like a big brother to Liberty and Equality; he is no longer a giant, he no longer carries his little sisters in his mammoth hand, and he no longer brandishes the threatening iconographic club of popular power.

Many of the deputies would have liked to eliminate Hercules completely. In July 1798 the Council of Five Hundred proposed that *"une figure allégorique représentant une femme assise"*[11] replace Hercules on silver coins. The legend would read "Liberty, Prosperity." All the radical content would thus be removed; Hercules-the people would give way to a tranquil, inactive Liberty-Prosperity. The higher council, the Council of Ancients, agreed that such a change was "inevitable," because they considered the Hercules figuration "an allegory whose conception and execution were not fortunate." But since the Ancients felt compelled to turn back the rest of the monetary proposal, Hercules continued to circulate a while longer.

After 1799 the memory of Hercules faded in favor first of Bonaparte but then later of Marianne, the figure of Liberty and the Republic. When Marianne reappeared with subsequent republics, so did Hercules, but as a secondary figure: he was revived on French coins in 1848, 1870-78, and even in 1965. But he was never as prominent as he had been during the Terror of 1793-94.

---

[11] *An allegorical figure representing a seated woman.*

Space and Time in
the Festivals of
the French Revolution*

Mona Ozouf

Even before Lynn Hunt's sweeping efforts to fix scholarly attention on the new revolutionary language and its symbolic meaning, Mona Ozouf had already utilized those very techniques to study, in a more concentrated manner, the festivals of the French Revolution. Her book, first published in French in 1976, has recently been released in English as *Festivals and the French Revolution* (Cambridge, 1988). Many would argue that this early study remains the best monographic effort of this genre.

The article published here is based on her book and focuses particularly on the festivals commemorating historical events. Not surprisingly, this essay shares the book's methodological preoccupations and presents a portion of its results. To explain celebrations of historical events, Ozouf never refers to any earlier festivals, suggesting by implication that she views these activities as a new revolutionary creation. Moreover, she analyzes these occasions for their symbolic value by pointing to the psychological role such festivals were intended to play. And she claims that, among other goals, the festivals were to represent the obliteration of social and political barriers and to encourage a universalistic union.

Despite the clear methodological similarities between Hunt and Ozouf, the fit is not exact. To be sure, the case studies presented here both treat the efforts of the revolutionaries as a fresh language that may be understood as an indication of basic values. However, Hunt, in her work, applies this technique quite widely. Ozouf here examines only festivals and clearly states that she seeks to understand these events as symbols because their content requires such an approach. Clearly, her commitment is more limited and her later studies of political theory have tended to accept those ideas on face value without endeavoring to find indications of hidden meanings in them.

Comparative Studies in Society and History 17 (1975), pp. 372–84. Reprinted with the permission of Cambridge University Press.

The study of festivals has only recently caught the attention of historians, who have traditionally shown themselves more concerned with the labours and afflictions of men than with their pleasures and diversions. If from this time onward, festivals become an object of historical enquiry, it will be perhaps because industrial society no longer has festivals—or at least that it has the festival only as pageant in which the passive community of onlookers has been substituted for the active community of celebrants—and because our interest in the festival increases to the extent that we lose it. However, we should also mention the historian's debt to the double stimuli of folklore and of ethnology. From folklorists and ethnologists historians have learned to concern themselves with the armature given to human experience by ritualization, even if anonymous, even if destitute of an explicit system of regulation or of a conscious cohesiveness.

The annexation by historians of this new field or research does not proceed without difficulty. The festival resists historical inquiry in many respects. The activities of the festival do not endure beyond the time given to them; the expectations satisfied within it do not continue in the period that follows. There is no tomorrow: the evidence of an exuberant squandering of time, of energy and of goods reveals the festival's lack of concern with an afterward. Festive time, insularly delimited, opens the parenthesis of uncommon days: separated from daily rhythms, men relinquish the serious use of their time, and their ties with ordinary moral and social values become undone. The festival gives bounds to an autonomous activity: there is, then, between the festival and men's daily life an insurmountable antagonism that Nietzsche has well observed.

Must one for these reasons abstain from undertaking the history of festivals and reciprocally from seeking in them insights into history itself? If festivals often appear as strangers to history, certain of them, those that are commemorative, try, nevertheless, to recapture history (the reader of *Totem and Taboo*[1] might suspect that all festivals are commemorative). And there are, on the other hand, festivals that manifestly join history through their ties with the exceptional circumstances that caused them to arise and from which they retain an air of contingency. This, assuredly, is one of the reasons why the festivals of the French Revolution evoke our interest: an enormous ritual ensemble surges while another—the Catholic ritual—is swallowed up, or appears to be. How could the new ceremonial now bear the trace of the exceptional circumstances that are at once the cause and the subject of its celebration?

---

[1] By Sigmund Freud, published in 1912-13.

The ten years that define the revolutionary period witness, in effect, the flowering of a rich ensemble of festivals. In the first years of the Revolution, these festivals appear one after the other, without a systematic grouping. Each event gives rise to its own festival: in this manner, the national festival of Fédération[2] on July 14, 1790, crowns the movement that, in the preceding winter, 'federated' the municipalities, and the 'gardes bourgeoises'; the funereal festival on July 11, 1791, commemorates the death of Voltaire; the festival on the Champ-de-Mars,[3] April 15, 1792, honours the soldiers of Châteauvieux condemned in 1790 for rebellion and now amnestied. Each of these festivals is the subject of a particular debate and each invents its own ceremony. It was Robespierre, in his famous address of Floreal, Year II,[4] who provided a first attempt at systematization, which was immediately aborted by Thermidor. The 'Thermidorians' were no less interested in making a coherent whole of the festivals; the law of Brumaire, Year IV, organized them in a definite manner, by distributing them with dates throughout the Republican calendar.

Within this overall pattern, there are festivals that attempt to revive Revolutionary history (the festivals of July 14, August 10,[5] Vendémiaire 1st)[6]; others that proceed from a moral or pedagogical inspiration (Festivals of Youth, of Spouses, of Old Age). To these scheduled festivals should be added those that revolutionary events continue to engender: the funereal festivals of Hoche and of Joubert,[7] for example. Celebrated not only in Paris but also in the provinces, in the most distant cantonal municipalities, these festivals left thousands of *procès-verbaux*[8] and gave birth to innumerable press reports: both were used in the nineteenth century by local scholars and mentioned by the historians of the Revolution, but were never made the subject of a systematic study.

However, the revolutionary festivals constitute for the historian a fortunate field of inquiry, first, by virtue of the quantity of archives that they have left (required to write the *procès-verbaux* of the ceremonies, the organizers, in the villages and small towns, were obliged to break the silence that generally surrounds the festivals); then by virtue of the short time in which they develop and which insures their coherence; and finally

---

[2]A festival to celebrate the seizure of the Bastille.

[3]A parade ground adjoining the site where the Eiffel tower now stands.

[4]See the glossary entry *Revolutionary Calendar* for the new form of reckoning time created after the fall of the monarchy.

[5]The day the monarchy was overthrown.

[6]Festival of the Foundation of the Republic.

[7]Revolutionary generals.

[8]Minutes of proceedings.

by virtue of their commemorative ambition. They are explicitly intent on retracing history and thus possibly permitting a better understanding of the history portrayed.

Furthermore, it is necessary to understand how this history is staged in the festival. It is striking that the enormous literature devoted to the festivals commemorating the French Revolution has barely touched upon their specifically ceremonial aspects. Even though we have at our disposal innumerable local monographs describing these events, we still have little idea about what such spectacles offered to the eye and ear. We do not know the itineraries of the processions, nor can we identify the sacred objects that were carried, the temporary edifice which sheltered them or the nature of the ceremonies themselves. One is struck, in particular, by the indifference of these monographs to the scenography of the commemoration and its spatial development.

How is this lack to be explained? Very often, historians of these events have interpreted them as though each ceremony was a response to a specific historical need. They are viewed as a mirror in which the entire Revolution may be discerned. These historians would have us believe that the liveliness of the festivals commemorating the Fédération reflects the stage at which the Revolution was still expansive, still burgeoning with hope. The commemoration of the Supreme Being,[9] on the other hand, would bear witness to the freezing-up of the Revolution. Further, the transformation of the ceremonies glorifying the Directory into universal exhibitions would forecast the advent of the nineteenth century. Viewed in relation to the unfolding of the Revolution's events, these celebrations seem to enjoy but an insignificant autonomy when compared to the Revolution itself. Everything they contain seems to belong to this rapidly changing period alone. That is, they were born in exceptional circumstances and died with them. Furthermore, their content is made to serve the triumph of some particular historical interpretation over its rivals.

Viewed in this light, we can see why political explanations dominate the historiography of these festivals. Aulard[10] was the first to develop this approach, which has been dominant ever since. In his view, the commemorative celebration had one principal function: to serve as an 'expedient' for patriotism. As such, it prospered when patriotism was in distress. When this latter was secure, the expedient disappeared. No sooner were the Austrians defeated than the cult of the Supreme Being began to

---

[9] A deistic and patriotic cult, begun in Paris in June 1794. Robespierre inaugurated this festival to allow religion both to continue and to be channeled toward patriotic ends.

[10] Alphonse Aulard (1849–1928), historian.

fade: Fleurus[11] brought about its demise. The public celebration, therefore, did not manifest any global philosophical project, nor did it suggest
any collective need. Even Jaurès[12] accepted this circumstantial assess-
ment of the celebration: for Jaurès, the Festival of the Supreme Being
is simply a posthumous revenge of Hebertism[13]; behind it, one finds
the decree of Floreal and the decisive political fault that it incarnates.

Mathiez[14] tried to negate this interpretation by considering all the
festivals as a whole and by emphasizing the unbroken chain formed by
the different cults which arose during the Revolution. According to him,
these various cults were inspired by a common determination to replace
the Catholic form of worship with a new one, which could offer its adherents new satisfactions in an era of change. This point of view encouraged
a host of systematic analogies between the old Catholic and the new
civic cults. In its sacred signs, in the display of civic processions, the
patriotic ceremony is presented as a transposition of the Catholic ceremony. It is easy for Mathiez to demonstrate that the nation's altars
correspond to the altars of religion, that civic processions repeat the
itineraries and the rhythms of religious processions. Though very suggestive, Mathiez' thesis suffers from one weakness: namely, that the determination to substitute one cult for another itself depends upon political
motivation. It is a 'remedy'; Mathiez uses this word and has great difficulty distinguishing it from the term 'expedient' used by Aulard. Consequently Mathiez fails to avoid the very flaw in interpretation he himself
denounced.

Why has historiography been so concerned about the intentions of
these commemorations? It is because the events themselves have been
overburdened with rational meanings devised by those who seek to create a
link between goals of a spiritual or political nature and aesthetic intentions.
However, even in those celebrations whose organizers were most intent on
connecting them with a supposedly utilitarian pedagogy, we can easily
discern an overabundance of meanings. This is why I feel we must free
these commemorative festivals from political interpretation. On the one
hand, such interpretation ignores the role of collective need, a need which
is quite apparent in the dusty documents of the National Archives, where
hundreds of nameless ceremonial projects reveal the avidity with which the
men of the Revolution desired these celebrations. On the other hand, and
this is most important, a familiarity with the official accounts of these
events—and the accounts number in the tens of thousands—leads one to

---

[11]Battle of Fleurus, June 24, 1794, in which the French defeated the Austrians.
[12]Jean Jaurès (1859–1914), socialist historian.
[13]Jacques-Réné Hébert (1757–94), radical revolutionary.
[14]Albert Mathiez (1874–1932), historian.

stress the recurrent elements over the unusual ones. Moreover, one tends to cast aside avowed intentions in order to concentrate on the staging and structure of the ceremonial.

It was on the basis of these conclusions about the historiography of the festivals that I was led to examine the use of space in the Parisian processions during the Revolution. Since publishing my article in *Annales*,[15] I have extended my research to include both provincial celebrations and the great national outburst commemorating the Fédération. Although these studies have not fundamentally changed my conception of the space sought by the organizers of these events, they have caused me to reconsider the role of history in civic celebrations.

Any analysis of the elements that determine the nature of sacredness must ask a central question: why this particular place and not another? This principle certainly applies to the ceremonies during the Revolution. Indeed, the entire celebration glorifying the Fédération was itself an attempt to define exactly what is a sacred place. Usually one holds sacred a place where some event has taken place, where an image has appeared, where an object has been discovered. The very nature of sacred observance requires the support of objects. We thus find extremely surprising the minor role of the Bastille in the festival of the Fédération. To be sure, the procession in Paris started out from the Bastille, but the true centre of the event was the Champ de Mars—a deserted spot, barely touched by urbanization. Similarly, in the provinces, plains, heaths and moors were preferred to village squares. On the other hand, nowhere in France do we find dramatic representations of historical events in the festivals of the Fédération. It is true that, in certain villages, where representations, and even the name, of the Bastille were entirely absent from the festivities, a carnival barker might set himself up in the square, offering to show a model of the Bastille and making a handsome profit in the process. Yet the organizers never felt any need for relics or sacred images.

It appears that as early as one year after the event, they found no need to rely upon the visual representation of the Bastille, still less to have recourse to a mimed dramatic production. It was not only because the closeness of the event, present in everybody's memory, made its evocation superfluous, but also because the Festival of Fédération aspired to be the festival of national unanimity; it pretended to a universality that too precise a localization would threaten to destroy. Consequently, they believed that they could maintain the sacred nature of the event without any recourse to objects. What caused the event to become sacred was, in their eyes, the galvanization of the masses and the unanimous

---

[15]*Annales, E.S.C.*, September–October 1971.

determination to be united in one place, which could be chosen arbitrarily; or, to be more exact, which *had* to be arbitrary. It did not seem necessary to have a spring, a mountain or a grotto, or even a place where something had occurred. The anonymous location was more eloquent than a specific one, for it had no history and its arid expanse expressed the very idea of innovation. Accordingly, the nation's sacred altar could rise up anywhere and the event could bring together interchangeable objects. One is tempted to say that the space in which a festival was mounted during the Revolution was a space without any distinguishing features.

Whether or not that is entirely true, we may at least consider the location to have been an open space. The organizers preferred the wild meadow or the plain outside town to the safety of the village square and certainly to the shadow of the church. As a result, municipalities became the scene of countless disagreements with priests who celebrated Mass only in their chapels and at their altars. The choice of a space without limits for the celebration deserves particular notice because of two elements. The first is the system of symbols concerning the open air, which is related to another system, this one involving liberty. Outside, under the vault of heaven, there are no walls which imprison, nor barriers to restrict one's view, and no intermediary between the people and its divinity. An amusing passage taken from the correspondence of Vergniaud[16] expresses very well the passion for open spaces. On January 16, 1790, he writes: 'Dans un village du Périgord, les paysans ont obligé leur curé à mettre une cocarde nationale au Saint Sacrement; ils ont de plus exigé que le curé laissât la porte du Tabernacle ouverte, parce qu'ils voulaient que leur Bon Dieu fut libre.'[17] The second element, the symbols expressing topological liberation, is designed to point to social liberation. Here, for example, is the official account of the return of the federative banner to Angers: 'La municipalité, le département, le district d'Angers, les autres districts et les municipalités voisines ne peuvent contenir leur empressement; ils volent au devant de la bannière; la municipalité ne considère point si c'est hors de son territoire qu'elle s'avance; est-ce que le patriotisme connait aujourd'hui ces lignes de démarcation que la morgue et la petitesse avaient autrefois tracées?' And, immediately following: 'Chacun des officiers municipaux, de département

---

[16]A leader of the Girondins.

[17]In a village in Perigord, the peasants have forced their curé to place the national cockade over the Blessed Sacrament; they have also demanded that the curé leave open the door of the Tabernacle, because they wished their kindly God to be free.

ou de district, tient à son bras une de ces femmes qu'on nomme femmes du peuple et qui peuvent aujourd'hui s'honorer de ce titre qui fut jadis presqu'une insulte.'[18]

This was a space, then, where political and social differences were abolished, a feature that impressed a number of historians of the Fédération. According to Louis Blanc, '1200 lignes de barrières intérieures disparurent, les montagnes semblèrent abaisser leurs cîmes, les fleuves ne furent plus que comme autant de ceintures mouvantes liant des populations trop longtemps séparées.'[19] The use of the word 'liant' rather than one denoting separation emphasizes the relevance of Louis Blanc's observations. Significantly, an analysis of the words most often used in the official accounts reveals the obsessive frequency of two terms, 'connect' and 'expand'. The calling together of delegates to the Festival of the Fédération takes a man out of the intimate, limited space of his village and throws him into the quest for a space without frontiers. It is the hatred of fragmentation, too, which explains the spatial arrangements of the festival. Even in small towns, the Mass is celebrated on all sides of the sacred altar of the nation so that nothing of the spectacle should be lost. The preferred movement of the procession was circular; here geometry seems to carry a spontaneous ethical significance of its own. Furthermore, the most beautiful of dances is round, in which everyone sees everyone else, and in which no participant is more important than any other.

The space is also horizontal. One's line of vision may move at will without ever being broken by natural or man-made obstacles. Similarly, depths are always suspect. In the speeches which punctuate the festivals of the Revolution, the theme of the cavern is always associated with the theme of despotism. Height, too, is condemned because it suggests 'gothic' haughtiness. This rejection of heights extended even to gladly dispensing with elevated monuments. When, in Nancy, a gust of wind struck down the upper part of the nation's sacred altar, many commentators approvingly insisted that such an ornament was superfluous in a national celebration, whose sole crowning limit should be the vault of heaven. An exception

---

[18]The municipality, the department, the district of Angers, the other districts and neighboring municipalities cannot contain their eagerness; they fly in front of the banner; the municipality did not worry if it went beyond its borders; does patriotism today know the demarcations that hautiness and pettiness had formerly traced?

Each of the officers from the municipality, the department, and the district, offers his arm to one of these women—women of the people—a title which today honors and was formerly almost an insult.

[19]Twelve hundred internal barriers disappeared, the mountains seemed to level their summits, the rivers existed only as moving belts linking together populations that for too long were separated.

must be made, however, for the colossal statues with which organizers such as David populated, or would have liked to populate, the towns. One might infer from this that the only acceptable verticality was expressed in human form. These giants seem to bear a force which neither humiliates nor crushes, because they seem to incarnate the very force of the Revolution itself.

Moreover this space allows the simultaneity of action and the unanimity of hearts to manifest themselves. We can measure by many converging signs the powerful hold of the idea of simultaneity on people's mind. This was the time when Hemsterhuis in Holland wrote the Neo-Platonic dialogues that expressed the aesthetic superiority of an art so compact as to be decipherable at a glance. According to him, the soul feels an unconquerable loathing for succession and 'judges most beautiful that which it can encompass in the least possible time'. This was also the time when Brissot declared he preferred a news-sheet to a book, because the latter takes a long time to leave its imprint whereas the former 'quickly enlightens' groups of men 'whose ideas react right away'. 'Right away': this is the obsession of the organizers of the festival; official directions concerning the Fédération prescribe the administering of the Federative oath 'together and at the same moment' to all the inhabitants in all the parts of the Empire; otherwise the sacredness of the oath seems to crumble. One may then understand that the choice of an open space, which allows the indefinite expansion of joy, brings to these men both the means by which to effect simultaneity and the possibility (almost as important for their somewhat distrustful and ever-on-the-alert revolutionary consciousness) of verifying it. This, then, would account for the enthusiasm that greeted the eradication of barriers around Paris and for the host of accompanying symbolic gestures. Around the tollgate buildings, described as 'smoke-filled caverns', the people dance. The women of la Halle come to dig up, beyond the city's barriers, a young tree that they take back to the Louvre, Place du Carrousel, to plant in front of the King's window, in this way symbolically erasing the frontiers between city and countryside.

The desire for simultaneity would also account for the artfulness with which real obstacles to this demand were dodged, if only rhetorically; such was the case, for example, when mountain-dwellers, aware of being for ever walled in by their 'natural ramparts', protested that they nevertheless communicated in the love of country with all their fellow-Frenchmen, and at the very same moment. Occasionally this was achieved by ceremonial means; when bad weather unfortunately obliged the organizers to split the civic lunch that was to have taken place in the open and hold it in several rooms instead, they were very careful when a toast was drunk at the main table to announce it simultaneously at the other tables and in every room 'with such swiftness that everyone drank together for the same object'. It helps us to explain why so many 'Renommées[20] populated these festivals; with their torches, they were allegories of simultaneity, propagating the good news like fire spreading freely in an open space. It is exactly by this conquest of a new space that Fichte, in his 'Considérations', defines the effort of the Revolution: as this luminous flood of light invincibly spreads outward, islets of darkness scatter and fade away, 'abandoned to the winged enemies of light, to bats and owls . . .'

In other words, the ceremonial space of the Revolution was arbitrary, open, horizontal and luminous (luminous because of course there could not be any nocturnal event unless night had first been transformed into day). There are thousands of texts describing the requirements positively or negatively. What one might term an excellent photographic negative of the ideal space for these festivals is contained in a speech given by Barère to the Convention (28 Messidor, Year II) on behalf of the Comité de Salut Public.[21] In this speech, he urged the prohibition of banquets organized by the 'sections'[22] of Paris. These meals seemed to Barère 'a new intrigue fomented by those who were following in the footsteps of Hébert and Chaumette',[23] and he said so explicitly. He denounced 'le modérantisme et l'hébertisme, ces deux écueils entre lesquels nous voyageons révolutionnairement'.[24] To be sure, Barère's intention was essentially political. But his text can also be read as a description of the space in which a revolutionary festival simply cannot be held. It is the space where confusion reigns, where groups are not distributed in any orderly fashion, where this unwieldly mixture ('tous les ménages confondus, tous les sexes mêlés, tous les sentiments réunis')[25] tends to create problems. It is the space which registers shadows, where treachery is plotted under the cover of darkness. It is the space which harbours hiding places. In this sense, despite the fraternal tables which cover it, the Palais-Royal remains a 'forest' of counter-revolutionaries, the cave of gamblers, the den of iniquity. (Note that David's reports on these events are in like manner replete with images through which clandestineness is condemned.) Finally, this space so unfavourable to the celebration of the Revolution is also one of illusion, of disguise, of deceptive representation. 'Il y a deux mois', wrote Barère, 'on avait partout ouvert des temples de la Raison; des jeux scéniques y

---

[20]Allegorical figures, usually statues but occasionally costumed people, that carried torches and that purportedly announced good news simultaneously throughout France.

[21]Committee of Public Safety.

[22]Local jurisdictions that had become very powerful by 1793.

[23]Radical politician, ally of Hébert.

[24]Moderation and the politics of Hébert, these two reefs between which revolutionaries sail.

[25]All the households thrown together, the sexes mixed together, all the sentiments united.

remplaçaient un ancien culte.'[26] Beyond the political allusion, this text is again illuminating: it underlines the rejection of anything that disguises and camouflages. Occasions designed to glorify the Revolution must not be punctuated by decorated lies or 'plastered-over equality'.

For those familiar with the utopias of the eighteenth century, it is clear that the distinguishing traits of the space give it a utopian character. What confirms this correspondence is the pedagogical, even therapy-like, function to which the space was put. The tradition of the entire eighteenth century—as illustrated by the correspondence of Diderot and Falconet—states that to observe well is to be educated, to see is to possess. We can well imagine to what degree this process is intensified when what is observed is the space of the entire nation. For the delegates travelling to the festival of the Fédération, the physical conquest of France's space is at one and the same time a national education, a lesson in citizenship, and a sort of civic cure for the individual. For everything involved in this 'pilgrimage' has positive value: not only the recollection of everything seen, but also the attendant fatigue and exhaustion. The standard-bearers who return home are new men, and those who come into contact with them will be educated in turn.

In another connection, it is clear that we are dealing with a space more dreamed about than lived, for there were many obstacles to the actual realization of the utopian space. A few deserve mention: first, inclement weather might force the celebrants to take refuge in churches. But these churches, even when hastily transformed into temples for the glorification of Reason, retained a spatial arrangement which long ago had become enigmatic. As Morellet suggests, this was so precisely because one cannot take in churches with one simple look; one must progressively uncover the beauties they contain. Furthermore, particularly in small towns, ceremonial customs could easily turn back to the old routines, such as the traditional walk from the church to the town hall. Second, a lack of material means might force the abandonment of plans for the construction of new colossal structures. Also the torpor of men might result in slight attendance at celebrations which, to be authentic, had to be unanimous. But more than all the obstacles just mentioned, we must bear in mind the presence within the confines of the city (where the groups were forced to manoeuvre) of the Revolution's history itself. I have shown for Paris by what means the routes of the processions either avoided the locations significant in this history or changed their importance. I have shown also how programmes for these processions seem to designate the historic places only to avoid them. If, ideally, the Revolution is situated in an

---

[26]Two months ago, Temples of Reason had been opened everywhere; theatrical games had replaced the bygone cult.

utopian place and if, in fact, it tries to flee from or to transform a designated historical space, are we not led to reconsider the problem of the relationship between history and the Revolution's commemorative festivals? We must therefore take up again the problem of the commemoration.

The historiography of the Revolution assumes much too often as obviously true that the purpose of the festival is to commemorate the Revolution so as to remind participants of its glories. It is supported in this, it is true, by the organizers of the ceremonies; from the beginning, they stressed their ambition to embrace history. J.-M. Chénier, for example, wished the festivals to compose 'an annual and commemorative history of the Revolution'. Jean Debry would have liked the festivals to establish 'correspondences between a distant and a present time'. All expected the festival to teach the Revolution to those who had not directly known it. Certainly the event contained an extraordinary recapturing of the past. However, even though it was aided by spectacle, the reverent repetition of the Revolution's situation was much less destined to evoke a recollection than to resuscitate an archetypal situation. As soon as we abandon the limited point of view of political interpretation in order to be more attentive to the production of the ceremonial itself and to its truly ritualistic aspects, this fact becomes really striking.

For example, among all the celebrations glorifying the Revolution, the one concerning 'the just punishment of the last King of the French' was likely to be the most obsessive in treating a concrete historical event. It was certainly political, and one needs but consult the brilliant commentary by L. S. Mercier to be convinced of this. Still, one should consider the thousands of official accounts of this event in order to determine what, beginning in Nivôse, Year III, was actually celebrated.

What does the festival portray of the event? As we have seen, such celebrations in general distrusted mimed representations of history both because of a lack of necessary resources and because of a puritanical aversion for the theatre. It does happen, however, that fake battles, apparitions and miracles were offered to the public. Yet in the case of this particular festival, one is struck by the weakness of the means of visual representation. On January 21, it is true, bonfires in the squares consumed parchments and scepters, but this was a common occurrence at the Revolution's festivals. The processions also carried many busts of Brutus and Franklin. But, lost among these, there were a few figures of royalty, some of them explicitly identified as Louis XVI. Even in these relatively rare cases, the producers studiously avoided making such figures grotesque. To illustrate this point, let me refer to a statue symbolizing Perjury erected in front of the Temple in Bordeaux. Provided a spectator was close up, he could read on the crown of this allegorical image 'Louis XVI'. But official accounts and newspaper stories see only the abstract exemplariness of the statue and above all emphasize the punishment of Perjury. By the same token, in the festivals commemorating the King's punishment, there was no representation of the gallows.

There is not the least echo of the carnival in the festival. It is true that in a carnival insult may be used to unseat a king solidly established on his throne. Then it is good to curse and beat him and to dethrone him for a day. The celebration of the death of this particular King, however, removed a king previously de-throned. The celebration was thus dedicated to repeating an event whose tragic emotion and scandalous force it could not possibly equal. Hence the festival's omissions, which are also noticeable in its speeches. For the reader of such speeches is struck by the consistent absence of two themes: that is, both the specific punishment and the royal personage himself are effaced. The orator's favourite theme is that France has punished in the last of its kings the excesses of his predecessors, no less culpable than he himself had been. This historical indifference allows a distancing from images that would evoke too personal a punishment. There are few references to Louis XVI and fewer still to Capet.[27] At various times the former is referred to as 'the lying king', 'the perfidious king', 'the last crowned tyrant', 'the plaything of an immoral and wicked woman'. An additional epithet shows how clearly the Sacred King of the Capetian royalty is desanctified, reduced to merely temporal power: 'the first of the functionaries', he is termed. One can read these speeches as a neutralization of the inexpressible—and without knowing who has punished whom.

But images and speeches depend upon what is ornamental, which itself would be of no consequence if the ceremonial observance of the celebration did not choose to organize itself around an historical event which is being represented while supposedly celebrated. At the heart of the event, is the solemn declaration of hatred for royalty. From year III to the year VII, the role of this oath continued to grow. An invocation to the Supreme Being preceded it, while imprecations against perjurers lent it support. The festival of the Revolution was a national enterprise in intimidation, whose serious nature each person could appreciate on any given January 21. The punishment inflicted upon a forsworn king was there to illustrate the general lesson, administered by a pedagogy of fear.

Everything works together to make this fear the real basis of the festival: the sacramental formula, written in large letters on the sacred altar of the nation; the steps to be climbed in order to take the oath; the heroic tension the body must imitate, while the arm is held straight up; and the silent coercion of the circle of spectators. There are many indications of

---

[27]The first royal family of France. This reference, often given to the family of Louis XVI, was to make them more like ordinary people by ascribing a surname. In this way, the monarch's name would have the same form as the common person's.

the terror engendered by this ceremony: sudden departure, fainting, mysterious paralysis which strikes participants when they are about to sign.

We could even note the numerous attempts to introduce an alteration in the formula of the oath: the expression 'hatred of the royalty' is at times replaced by 'hatred of tyrants' or by 'hatred of arbitrary power'. Sometimes a long debate is necessary for agreement on the formula of the oath. Sometimes it is decided that one will swear only to 'fight to the death against the royalists'. In other instances, an entire canton refuses to use the expression 'I do swear', which they hastily replace with 'I so declare'. The changes actually made are inconsequential. Nevertheless, to alter an oath is to tamper with the intangible, and the smallest alteration is rightly felt as destroying the oath. We can recognize in such sudden attacks the sincere simulation which constitutes hysteria. But the oath is so terrifying only because fear is precisely the ground in which it takes root. The act of obstinately swearing hatred for royalty and fidelity to the Republic is understood only by reference to the growing fear of a future which would bring back royalty. The purpose of the oath, and of the festival in general, is to affirm an invincible Revolution. The oath acts out the impossibility—to which everyone agrees—either of going back to the past or of there being a future other than one that is merely repetitive. What then is the role of the commemoration? It is to show no concern at all for quickening or fortifying historical consciousness. Repetition of the past serves above all to dull the disturbing shock, to efface the newness of the event. The commemoration is in no way a conscious repetition, in which the past being celebrated would be recognized for what it is, kept at distance and analysed. It has much more the sense given by Freud to verbal repetition: an emotional fixation, acted out repeatedly; a strategy of archaism against anguish; and an exorcism. But in no instance is it history.

In conclusion, let me raise some further questions. First of all, it seems to me that one must admit that returning to the past and conscious recapturing of the past are not necessarily the same thing. Is Dowd's suggestion true that the funeral commemoration at the time of Lazowski's[28] death, with its red flag, tocsin, pike staffs and cannons, really propagated the spirit of insurrection? Is it that, or is it the assurance that there will be no more insurrections? I, for one, incline towards this second hypothesis. (We must bear in mind not only the many texts which accord to these events a conservative finality, but even more give to the internal structure of the commemoration its system of emblems, its ritual.) The commemorative event tolerates change poorly. The history it seeks to revive for its own purpose is reworked, readjusted and divested of movement.

---

[28]An extremely radical Parisian, active during the Terror.

If the organizers of the Revolutionary festivals wanted to hear only this history, it is evident, however, that they did not consider each particular festival as free of history; it is by no means contradictory to recognize in the festival both the rooting in the temporal and the flight toward the extra-temporal. But it is no longer possible to be satisfied with only the first of these traits, as have so many historians, impatient to reduce the enigmatic diversity of the festivals to the simplicity of a political project. We still do not know very well what was seen, said, accomplished in these festivals: the circuits and the detours of their processions, the sacred objects that were paraded, the perishable architecture that sheltered them, the formulae that were uttered there; we know even less how an intention is understood by appearances. Thus the festival requires a collective climate of curious and searching uneasiness, where an historical discipline would anchor and balance an anthropological ambition.

From that we could move quickly to the larger problem concerning the nature of historical consciousness in the Revolution. We consider all too often as self-evident the feeling that the periods of the Revolution are periods in which historical consciousness is fortified and becomes more acute. But this is not certain. For the time which the Revolution seizes as its own is a time capable of regeneration, a time whose commotion seems capable of inspiring a new movement once again. But is the time thus regenerated the time of history or the time of myth?

GLOSSARY

Estates General   A representative assembly of the three estates or orders of the kingdom. The clergy constituted the First Estate, the nobility the Second, and the Commoners the Third. Although the function of the Estates General varied over the centuries, Frenchmen commonly believed that it would be called into session during greatly troubled times to provide advice to the monarch.

Beyond this general definition of the Estates General, little agreement has existed about its precise role or its composition. Without a written constitution, France possessed a very malleable governmental structure, and, in fact, no body was any more subject to different interpretations than the Estates General.

These questions did not stop the opponents of the crown from calling in 1787 for a meeting of the Estates General to be held to approve any new taxes. This appeal had emerged as the principal demand of most politically involved Frenchmen of the day. Indeed, the crown's fiscal problems had led to this state of affairs. Through most of the 1780s, a series of chief ministers— Necker, Calonne, and Lomenie de Brienne—had tried to decrease expenses and raise taxes. Tradition required the approval of the Parlement of Paris (see the glossary entry *parlements*) to register the necessary laws. This body had refused, though, leading Louis XVI and his ministers to try to circumvent it by creating an Assembly of Notables, which would give its approbation. However, the king received no satisfaction from this new institution, and, after continued demands for an Estates General, Louis XVI capitulated, issuing a call for elections on July 5, 1788.

If the opponents of the monarch had a clear desire to have an Estates General, there were few who had already contemplated its structure or the implications for the constitution of politics. Indeed, it had not met since 1614. Then approximately equal numbers from each order had been elected. In addition, each order acted independently and possessed a single vote on matters presented to the entire Estates. People of the eighteenth century believed that such an organization would allow the nobility to dominate, because members of this social group would be also able to control the First Estate (the clergy). Thus, the vote would consistently be two to one in favor of the first two Estates, and the dominance of Old Regime political elites would endure. There were some supporters of the organization of 1614. However, a Patriot party, including most of the politicized commoners and many liberal nobles, wished to double the size of the Third Estate and have each delegate vote as an individual. This would have greatly helped the commoners, for they would constitute one-half of the assembly. Furthermore, the Patriot party expected changes to be instituted that would, in effect, remake France into a constitutional monarchy.

Between the traditional and the Patriot position, the monarchical government equivocated. On the question of votes, the monarch agreed to double the number of delegates from the Third Estate but was silent about the all-important structure of the voting. If vote by order were maintained, the number of deputies made no difference. And the monarchy actually never took a stand, leaving the decision by default to the Estates General.

Elections were very complicated. For example, in the countryside, the Third Estate generally began in the village that sent electors (whose number was assigned in proportion to the population) to larger jurisdictions in which, joined with other delegates, new electors would be sent to yet another meeting. Most often, in the third stage, the electors would nominate deputies. In addition to the elections, each stage was marked by the writing of a list of grievances (*cahiers des doléances*). Theoretically, this compilation of complaints would instruct each member of the Estates General on his duty.

When the Estates General finally met in Versailles, on May 5, 1789, the ambiguities of its structure left open many possibilities. By this time, the king, many parlementarians, most of the Second Estate deputies, and surely a smattering of supporters hoped for a short consultation and hasty dissolution. The king decreed separate verification of credentials, which implied a vote by order, noble dominance of the proceedings, and the maintenance of the status quo. The representatives of the Third Estate, believing themselves the true legislators for the country, refused to abandon their hopes. Again, sympathetic nobles in the Estates, some of whom strangely enough had been elected to the commons, provided assistance. This effort enjoyed social support, especially strong among commoners throughout France who, although they did not necessarily understand all the issues, had placed their faith in their deputies. After a stalemate of several weeks, on June 17, 1789, the Third Estate proclaimed itself the National Assembly, which was, of course, to assert a claim of sovereignty. By also inviting the deputies from the other orders to join the deliberations and by continuing to include the king, the Third was, at this point, still willing to share authority. Because the monarch and his allies could not reverse this unilateral action, the Third had, in its transformation of the Estates into the National Assembly, brought an end to the political system of the Old Regime.

Jansenism   A religious movement that developed within Catholicism in the 1640s. Jansenists concentrated on the sinfulness of man and his society.

With this hostile view of the world, they emphasized withdrawal and embraced the cloister so that they could avoid various temptations. They also focused upon their own personal efforts to achieve salvation and de-emphasized the need for the clergy as a spiritual intercessor.

Although Jansenists wished to set themselves apart from society, they were not to be left alone. French kings believed in their responsibility to enforce religious orthodoxy. In an age in which tolerance was little accepted, states generally required their inhabitants to accept a standard version of the faith. Not only did the monarchy look askance at Jansenists, but so did the Vatican and the French bishops, who felt threatened by Catholics who did not accept the religious hierarchy as a necessary part of religion. Together, these groups opposed Jansenism and set out to extirpate what they perceived as a heresy.

To survive these attacks, which began in the 1650s and lasted for over a century, the Jansenists needed an ally. They shifted their doctrine to accommodate lay participation, possibly to position themselves better to find the necessary assistance from an effective political power. The support that the Jansenists sought would mainly come from the Parlement of Paris (see the glossary entry *parlements* for more on this law court). This body had already established a reputation for opposing papal interference in French affairs. This position also often led these judges to confront the church hierarchy in France, closely linked as it was to Rome. In addition, for most of the last two centuries of the Old Regime, the parlement was locked in a battle with the monarchy. Thus, aiding the Jansenists gave the parlementarians an opportunity to attack their enemies the Papacy, the episcopacy, and the king.

Perhaps the most curious thing about this relationship was its transformation over the course of the eighteenth century. Fewer and fewer French people identified themselves as Jansenists, mainly because, over time, the Catholic church incorporated many of the changes which they had advocated. Nonetheless, Jansenism survived as a political ideology in the Parlement of Paris as the two traditions became interwoven. For example, the parlement became an intense opponent of the religious order of the Jesuits and was instrumental in the Jesuits' expulsion from France. To be certain, elements of the parlementary past encouraged attacking the Jesuits, but for Jansenists no greater evil existed. It certainly seems reasonable to explain this parlementary behavior as greatly influenced by Jansenist sentiments. By the time of the Revolution, parlementary politics had fully accepted the political tenets of Jansenism and integrated them into its own ideology. This interlocking occurred not only because of the compatibility of the two sets of beliefs but also because committed Jansenists insinuated themselves into the parlement and worked to have that body accept their point of view. Thus, Jansenists ensured that Jansenism would continue to speak even as its independent religious existence waned.

parlements   The supreme courts of appeal in the judicial system of the Old Regime. Originally, there was but one parlement, located in Paris, but as the kingdom expanded, new parlements were added as extensions of royal judicial authority. The first provincial parlement was placed in Toulouse in 1437. By 1789 there were eleven others. Nonetheless, the Parlement of Paris was preeminent among them, and its decisions influenced all the rest.

Emanating from the crown, all these parlements exercised throughout the eighteenth century extensive authority that included, but went far beyond, resolving civil and criminal cases. They also administered many institutions and organizations in their jurisdictions.

Their power, though, could be used against, as well as for, the monarch. Because these jurists were venal (owned their offices), kings found it very expensive to shape parlementary decisions by buying out recalcitrant judges and replacing them with more pliant individuals. Furthermore, the parlements exercised one particular function that could give them a great power. Before a royal edict could be promulgated, it had to be registered by these courts, which possessed the right to complain (remonstrate). The parlements proved, in fact, to be no simple keepers of records and often remonstrated. Even under pressure to comply, the parlements developed techniques to thwart monarchical influence. Using many methods for resistance, judges often registered laws only with reservations, and they could even go on strike. Their venality, of course, further protected them.

Against this judicial independence, kings had several weapons. They might exile a parlement to a small town that lacked amenities that these justices would regard as necessary. The king also held the very important power, either personally or through a representative, of requiring the registration of a royal edict in a formal session called a *lit de justice.* One should not overestimate, however, the value of this last weapon because, once the king or his minion had departed, parlements might simply reverse the action they had just taken.

Although historians can agree on the formal powers of these justices, there is much conflict about the actual balance of power between kings and parlements in the eighteenth century. Until recently, most scholars saw the judges as increasingly aggressive, with their powers cresting on the eve of the Revolution. New scholarship has suggested that they were always somewhat reticent and, after being disbanded from 1771 to 1774, they were virtually silent until 1787 when opportunities once again beckoned.

Further disagreement has centered around the motives for parlementary resistance. In the eighteenth century, public opinion regarded these bodies as the defenders of personal liberty against the despotic monarchy. Most twentieth-century scholars had, until recently, rejected this verdict, claiming that the parlementarians used libertarian language only as a cover for their desire for power and wealth. Historians argued that the judges simply were protecting their privileges against a reform-minded government that threatened the rights deriving from their office and their noble station. These courts led the entire nobility against monarchical efforts to use merit instead of birth as the system for making awards. Some scholars now disagree with this judgment and believe the claims of the parlement to have been sincere. To reinforce the notion that the parlement acted on principle, historians point to many internal disagreements among the nobles to show that in no way were the parlements simply the ringleaders of a selfish defense of a particular class. In this version, the parlement thus emerges as a conservator of individual freedom.

revolutionary calendar   A method of dating set up by the Jacobin government in October 1793 to give France a time system reflective of the new political realities. The Jacobins retrospectively set the first day of the first year as September 21, 1792, the day the French national government abolished the monarchy. Each year thus began in September, and the calendar endured into the Napoleonic era before it was abandoned.

Vendémiaire	1–30	*the month of vintage*	= 22nd September	– 21st October
Brumaire	1–30	*the month of fog*	= 22nd October	– 20th November
Frimaire	1–30	*the month of frost*	= 21st November	– 20th December
Nivôse	1–30	*the month of snow*	= 21st December	– 19th January
Pluviôse	1–30	*the month of rain*	= 20th January	– 18th February
Ventôse	1–30	*the month of wind*	= 19th February	– 20th March
Germinal	1–30	*the month of budding*	= 21st March	– 19th April
Floréal	1–30	*the month of flowers*	= 20th April	– 19th May
Prairial	1–30	*the month of meadows*	= 20th May	– 18th June
Messidor	1–30	*the month of harvest*	= 19th June	– 18th July
Thermidor	1–30	*the month of heat*	= 19th July	– 17th August
Fructidor	1–30	*the month of fruit*	= 18th August	– 16th September

17th–21st September inclusive: *sans culottides*

Books of Interest
Available in English

Birn, Raymond. *Pierre Rousseau and the Philosophes of Bouillon.* Geneva, 1964.

Censer, Jack R. *Prelude to Power: The Parisian Radical Press, 1789–1791.* Baltimore, 1976.

Censer, Jack R., and Jeremy D. Popkin, eds. *Press and Politics in Pre-Revolutionary France.* Berkeley, 1987.

Chartier, Roger. *The Cultural Uses of Print in Early Modern France.* Trans. Lydia G. Cochrane. Princeton, 1987.

Darnton, Robert. *The Great Cat Massacre and Other Episodes in French Cultural History.* New York, 1984.

Gelbart, Nina. *Feminine and Opposition Journalism in Old Regime France: "Le Journal des Dames."* Berkeley, 1987.

Jacob, Margaret C. *The Radical Enlightenment: Pantheists, Freemasons and Republicans.* London, 1981.

Kates, Gary. *The "Cercle Social," the Girondins, and the French Revolution.* Princeton, 1985.

Levy, Darline Gay. *The Ideas and Careers of Simon-Nicolas-Henri Linguet: A Study in Eighteenth-Century French Politics.* Urbana, Ill., 1980.

Ménétra, Jacques-Louis. *Journal of My Life.* Ed. Daniel Roche. Trans. Arthur Goldhammer. New York, 1986.

Popkin, Jeremy. *The Right-Wing Press in France, 1792–1800.* Chapel Hill, 1980.

Roche, Daniel. *The People of Paris: An Essay in Popular Culture in the 18th Century.* Trans. Marie Evans. Berkeley, 1987.

Sewell, William H., Jr. *Work and Revolution in France: The Language of Labor from the Old Regime to 1848.* Cambridge, 1980.

About the Author

Jack R. Censer is Associate Professor of History at George Mason University in Fairfax, Virginia. He received his B.A. from Duke University and his M.A. and Ph.D. from The Johns Hopkins University. His specialties are French history and the history of the press. He has also taught at the College of Charleston.

Recently he has held fellowships from the Max Planck Institute, the National Endowment for the Humanities, the American Council of Learned Societies, and the American Philosophical Society. His publications include the books *Prelude to Power: The Parisian Radical Press, 1789–1791* (1976), *Press and Politics in Pre-Revolutionary France* (1987), which he co-edited with Jeremy Popkin, and numerous articles.